HOW DO I TAX THEE?

A FIELD GUIDE
TO THE GREAT
AMERICAN RIP-OFF

KRISTIN TATE

ALL
POINTS
BOOKS

www.allpointsbooks.com

Library of Congress Cataloging-in-Publication Data

Names: Tate, Kristin, author.
Title: How do I tax thee? : a field guide to the great American rip-off / Kristin B. Tate.
Description: First edition. | New York : St. Martin's Press, [2018] | Includes
    bibliographical references.
Identifiers: LCCN 2017059121| ISBN 9781250169662 (hardcover) |
    ISBN 9781250169679 (ebook)
Subjects: LCSH: Taxation—United States. | United States—Politics and government.
Classification: LCC HJ2381 .T257 2018 | DDC 336.200973—dc23
LC record available at https://lccn.loc.gov/2017059121

Our books may be purchased in bulk for promotional, educational, or business use. Please
contact your local bookseller or the Macmillan Corporate and Premium Sales Department at
1-800-221-7945, extension 5442, or by email at MacmillanSpecialMarkets@macmillan.com.

First Edition: March 2018

10 9 8 7 6 5 4 3 2 1

To my brother, Austin.

CONTENTS

INTRODUCTION

THE TAXMAN OWNS YOU

You don't *pay* the taxes—they *take* the taxes.

—Chris Rock

Remember how it felt to tear open your very first paycheck?

Such pride! Such excitement! Such . . . *Damn! I have to pay what now in taxes?!*

If you've made it to the wage-earning age, you knew this day was coming. Taxes have become so ingrained in our national psyche that we never even think about them. We blindly accept them as an un-avoidable fact of life—a cost that's completely out of our control, or at least is the necessary trade-off for living in a civilized society.

Our parents thought this way, too, and so did their parents. And just like a lot of *other* unwelcome hand-me-downs (lookin' at you, $20 trillion national debt), it's never occurred to most of us to question the fairness and quality of the multilayered system we live under, because we weren't privy to the decisions that led us to this point in the first place. And now we're getting slapped with a big fat price tag, while Baby Boomers retire to Florida and play pinochle.

No one ever taught us to ask questions like, "Are our tax policies still appropriate and fair?" or, "Where's all that money actually go-ing?" or, "Am I comfortable with how the government is spending my tax dollars?" When a policy seems out of your control, it's easier to abdicate personal responsibility and accept the circumstances for what they are.

And that, my dear reader, is a problem.

But here's the thing: The taxes that come directly out of your paycheck—federal, state, Social Security, and Medicare—are only the ones you *know* about. The ugly truth is, you're getting gouged all day, every day, by taxes hidden and applied to every aspect of your life. Through the manifold taxes that are applied to necessary expenses like rent, transportation, and utility bills, to leisure activities like taking your date to the movies, and to seemingly free things you do like walking the dog or recycling an empty kombucha bottle—federal, state, and city governments are covertly taxing your countless activities and effectively siphoning money out of your bank account. When we fill out our W-2s, we acknowledge that we're contributing a portion of our salary to the government. But hidden taxes? We don't even know about them most of the time. And if you don't know about them, you can't object to them, which is precisely why they're hidden in the first place.

The average millennial brings home $35,500 a year, pretax. In New York City that translates to a take-home salary of about $27,500 after state and city income taxes. Imagine trying to make it in the Big Apple, where the average rent for a one-bedroom apartment is $2,700 per month, on a $27,500 a year salary. And *on top of all that,* every time you buy something from a store, use any form of transportation, eat at a restaurant, go out for drinks with friends, or pay your cell phone, gas, cable, or trash bill, you pay additional taxes—often unwittingly—in the form of sales taxes, service charges, miscellaneous fees, and price tags that are inflated to pay for the cost of government regulations. No wonder you have 17 jobs.

Don't believe me? Pull out your latest cell phone bill and look at all the itemized charges. Extra line items on your bill, in addition to what you're paying for the actual cell phone service, are often camouflaged by vague, important-sounding language that makes the charges appear essential—like "documentation fee," "service charge," or "equalization fee." These charges are essentially taxes. They are costs levied on you by the government, directly or indirectly, that increase government revenue and finance government activities.

We're not angry about those charges and fees (read: "taxes") because we usually don't know or notice when we're being charged (read: "taxed"). And when we do know that such fees are being assessed, we delude ourselves by believing that the fees really should be paid in the first place. Who wouldn't be opposed to an *equalization* fee, you ask? Wait until you find out what's really happening with the money you pay. Most of us want to believe that when we pay hidden taxes to the government, the money is used well; but these ideas are also delusions, in need of a close revisiting.

Every year, Americans pay at least $657.5 billion in hidden taxes. Total personal income taxes represent *less than half* of our total tax burden.

Here's how it works: We elect government officials. And what do We The People claim to detest more than anything else? *Taxes!* So candidates often run on the promise of reducing (or at least not raising) our taxes, ever. But cities and counties and states have budgets to balance, and oftentimes problems arise that require additional funding. Your elected official knows he can't raise your taxes, or you'll remember it next November and vote him out of office. So instead of putting a new tax to a vote, he invents a fee and attaches it to something *we already have to spend our money on anyway,* such as our cell phone or internet bill.

Maybe you're thinking you're somehow exempt from this hidden tax situation. You've scored a fancy job with a big-shot salary and killer benefits. Or maybe you're capitalizing on the gig economy, livin' that laptop lifestyle. It doesn't matter—the taxman comes for us all, and he does NOT play nice. Millennials in particular stand to get especially taken advantage of by this system. We're at the beginning of our adulthood, meaning most of our lifetime earnings are still ahead of us. We're saddled with higher debts than any generation before us, and we're about to bear an even heavier burden when it comes to caring for our elders. In fact, by 2033, we'll be supporting more people over 64 than under 18. At the same time, we are in a unique position to do something about all this. We represent more than one-quarter of the total U.S. population; we make up the largest share of the voting-age population. If we wanted to, we could sway a presidential election by voting for one candidate or the other (or by just staying home and binge-watching *Stranger Things*).

This book is for everyone who pays taxes, regardless of political affiliation, age, or income bracket. *Taxation is not a partisan issue, at least not within the scope of this book.* No matter which party is in control, or who's writing the federal, state, and city budgets—governments at every level continue to operate with minimal transparency and abysmal efficiency. Regardless of where your political affiliation lies, we can all agree on the basic right to know where and how our money is being spent. We can agree on the basic responsibilities of a government by the people and for the people, and we can all be honest and admit that even the people we voted for don't always operate with our best interests at heart.

In the spirit of full transparency (that's what this book is all about, after all), I'll tell you where *I* stand in all this: I like having things like a working fire department and structurally sound bridges. But I *do* believe the government has gone overboard with its regulations and impositions, and I think I should be allowed to decide for myself what kind of siding I'd like on my starter house, or to opt out of a particular safety recommendation if it's not within my budget and no one bears the consequences except me.

This isn't about the rightness or wrongness of where the money is going; it's about the fact that *we don't know* where the money is going in the first place. You might be fine with how the government has decided to spend your tax dollars, and that's great. But you can't be fine with it if you don't know how the money is being used.

In this book, I'll peel back the veil and show you where the hidden taxes are lurking and how the resulting revenue is spent. Each chapter will take a detailed look at a different product, service, industry, habit, or necessary life purchase and reveal how federal, state, and municipal governments gouge us at every turn. And if you think the defense to these policies is obvious—that the taxes are used to make your country, state, and city a better place—keep reading. You'll find out here that the taxes you're paying often don't go to the causes they claim to serve, and are put to use in ways that are by no means sure to make the world, your state, or your city a better place.

The chapters roughly follow the chronological order of adult life, starting with the basics—transportation, food, cell phones, and wine (obviously). Then we move into advanced adulting—home ownership, kids, medical expenses—before settling down with our knitting to wait for the Grim Reaper (who also charges a tax). And just when you're ready to deport yourself to Canada (no dice; they have taxes there, too!) we'll look at some potential alternatives and action steps.

Look, I know our generation has a bad rap—we're entitled, lazy, obsessed with our phones, and we suck at working. But while we're certainly not the only generation that's blind to this matrix of hidden taxes and fees, we do have a unique and pressing responsibility to get informed and stay informed, and to push back against hidden and reckless uses of our money. Not only do we stand to lose more of our hard-earned income than any generation before us, but we're the only generation with the numbers and resources to powerfully affect change.

Ready? Let me show you how deep this rabbit hole goes.

PART

ONE

THE BASICS

ONE

TRANSPORTATION

THE FLEECING STARTS ON YOUR WAY TO WORK

> Collecting more taxes than is absolutely
> necessary is legalized robbery.
>
> —*Calvin Coolidge*

Do you like horror stories? I want to tell you my Tax Monster origin story. It was years ago and I was on my way to my first job—an entry-level position fetching coffee and writing scripts for mean producers at a cable news network in New York. My wide smiling face spelled the words "naive country girl; fresh out of college." I itched to make it in the Big Apple. I didn't know how to spot the Tax Monster yet. Hell, I barely knew how to feed myself, other than downing my usual Lucky Charms each morning. All I knew was that I was finally a "Working Girl" in New York (the Melanie Griffith kind, don't get smart) and ready to take on the world . . . That is, until a ghoulish creep began lurking behind every corner I turned, with his hand out.

No, this was not one of New York City's ubiquitous panhandlers; this was a faceless monster who kept reaching into my pocket to take $1 here, $2 there, and 50 cents everywhere else. I didn't realize it, but I had just been introduced to the elusive Tax Monster. Whether you know it or not, you have encountered this ever-present pain in the ass on your way to work, too.

But I wasn't going to let one fire-breathing brute ruin my first day of work—I knew I was one of the fortunate millennials who had actually landed a full-time job out of college. My salary seemed to be enough that I *probably* wouldn't have to spend the next year begging for kombucha in Washington Square with all the NYU grads who majored in French.

MEET YOUR TRANSPORTATION TAX
DOLLARS—NOT HARD AT WORK

The second I stepped into the subway station, my olfactory senses were bombarded by the lovely fragrances of stale urine, old lady perfume, and patchouli stank hanging low in the humid summer air. Ah, the New York City Subway—catch the feeling!

As I leapt over a rat dining on a slice of pizza, I thought, *No one can ruin this day for me!* Shortly after tempting the Devil, there he was again.

I clutched my wallet as I moved toward a turnstile. But the Tax Monster was in pursuit. Especially here on New York City's MTA (Metro Transit Authority), which loses more than $6 billion per year.[1] How is this thing still in business? *Great question.*

Just as I was about to swipe my MetroCard, I noticed the MTA had raised the price for a ride (*yet again, apparently*) and my card was out of funds—*Dammit!* So much for arriving on time to my first day at work. I walked over to put more money on my MTA card while my train left the station without me. I checked my wallet and all I had was five bucks—now only good for one measly ride on the subway where a one-way trip costs $3.

Couldn't I have picked a better way to get to work?

Not really! The Tax Monster lurks behind every form of transportation these days. Elected officials around the country routinely pass public transportation fare hikes because they drive huge amounts of revenue to city coffers—meanwhile, these same politicians don't have to tell their constituents that they voted for a "tax" increase. This is just a "fare" increase . . . Even though a fare increase *is* a tax increase, particularly for those who are dependent on the subway to get to work.

Most transportation-related taxes, fees, and fares, in New York as elsewhere, never fix our nation's crumbling infrastructure. Instead, the money usually goes toward paying bloated employee salaries in the transportation system or toward municipality "general funds" where the money can be spent on almost anything—transportation related or not.[2] General funds consist of any revenues collected by the state or city that are not dedicated *by law* to a specific purpose, creating massive slush funds for bureaucrats to spend however they please.

As I hopped the next subway, the thought of a $3 ride struck me as a rip-off. But most major metropolitan cities today charge similar ticket rates: a one-way subway ride costs $2.75 in Boston, $2.25 in Chicago,[3] and up to $6 in Washington, D.C.,[4] probably the most dangerous subway system in America.[5] Many city dwellers like me just pay these expensive fares without thinking about it, but if you happen to travel by bus, train, or subway into work every day—aren't you curious why the cost of your ticket keeps going up? It's not because these transportation authorities are reinvesting in great technologies for the future (wouldn't that be a novel concept!). It's in significant part because taxpayers and riders have to subsidize the mistakes and inefficiencies of city departments and managers who have little accountability, as well as wildly above-market salaries, benefits, and pensions for transportation workers.

Take MTA salaries for starters. Average MTA workers (the vast majority of whom are bus and train operators, station agents, and cleaners) make a base salary of $90,000 before overtime. Cushy MTA employee salaries, benefits, and retirement packages cost New York City $10 billion annually—$2 billion more than the city rakes in from MetroCard sales each year.[6]

Some MTA workers earn better salaries than CEOs of private companies. More than 8,000 of them earn over $100,000 per year; more than 50 earn over $200,000![7] And for what? Those trains are highly automated today. They nearly drive themselves. Most of us can wrap our heads around C-level executives making a six-figure salary, but I'm having a hard time wrapping my noggin around the fact that many MTA repairmen rake in well over $200,000 per year.[8]

How on earth does this happen? The base pay for these repairmen is about $70,000 per year, but the majority end up earning nearly $150,000 more than that due to vast amounts of overtime pay. MTA workers alone racked up $1 billion in overtime pay in 2015![9]

Don't get me wrong. There's no problem with honest overtime work and compensation. The problem is that overtime at the MTA is not what it seems—it has morphed into a scam, and one that is also seen at transportation authorities in many other cities.

Here's how it works. Thanks to union rules, overtime pay at time-and-a-half (at least) is paid to MTA employees who work more than eight hours per shift. On some holidays like the Fourth of July, MTA employees take home overtime at five times the normal rate.[10] Workers are well aware of these rules and they collaboratively take advantage of them to schedule their workweeks so they accumulate as many overtime hours as possible. (Why wouldn't they?!) So a subway operator who would normally operate five days per week for eight hours per day instead may operate three days per week for 13 to 14 hours per day. Routine abuse of this system leads to a significant salary bump over the course of a year.

High rates of unplanned absences make it even easier for drivers and conductors to cash out on overtime; MTA employees enjoy 21 annual vacation days (including their birthdays), 15 sick days, and a handful of "mental health" days. Meanwhile many workers take advantage of the Family Medical Leave Act, which allows drivers to take up to 60 more unplanned sick days a year.

One Long Island MTA repairman named Dominick Masiello pocketed over $250,000 in one year. Another genius named Dennis Reardon, a train conductor for the MTA, also cashed out big-time due to massive overtime accrued; Reardon tripled his salary, turning a base of $75,389 into a whopping $240,251! Yet another conductor named Benjamin Jankowski tripled his salary with $155,000 in perks and overtime.[11]

If you live in a big city and think this is somebody else's problem, think again. Most of that money is coming from your ever-increasing subway and bus ticket costs. And since the MTA spends more than it collects from fares, the city literally inserts "MTA surcharges" into New York residents' utility bills and cab fares. To underline this point: You are not only paying for the MTA's inefficiencies when you pay for fare hikes and your city and state income taxes; *you're paying for the MTA's inefficiencies when you pay your electricity bill.* We'll discuss this in more detail later.

The mere idea of such overtime schemes happening for a long time in any private sector company is ludicrous. You may think Masiello, Reardon, and Jankowski are anomalies—but stories like theirs are common in big city transportation departments. The problem, after all, is ultimately not with Masiello, Reardon, and Jankowski themselves, who were making money for their families within the boundaries of the rules. God bless them for that at least. The problem is management and city oversight that is so inefficient, and so apparently ambivalent about tax-paying citizens, it regularly allows employees to make three times their base salary and deflects the cost of their mismanagement to you.

This overtime racket is not unique to New York. In San Francisco the average base pay for a MUNI bus and cable car operator is roughly $60,000 . . . But that's before a guaranteed bevy of overtime pay. Nearly 100 MUNI operators bring home more than $100,000 a year! In 2016, a bus driver earned $78,722 in overtime and brought home a total of $146,498 in pay.[12] This is insane, but obviously the people in San Fran hardly pay attention to this issue, so the scheme continues.

Who knew driving buses, cable cars, and trains would be so lucrative? Put down the Rice-A-Roni; driving a MUNI bus is the ultimate San Francisco treat!

THE MTA'S BAILOUT PLAN STARS YOU!

Back to NYC's MTA nightmare. Rather than fixing their obvious budget, staffing, management, operation, pension, and overtime problems, NYC's elected officials recently chose to ignore these underlying issues. In 2015, the MTA faced yet another operating deficit just as ride-sharing services like Uber and Lyft were picking up steam in New York. Rather than working to reduce administrative bloat in the MTA, elected officials and state and city bureaucrats chose to address the deficit by . . . *drumroll please* . . . raising subway and bus fares, and slapping a 50-cent surcharge on all yellow cab rides.

They called it the "MTA bailout plan," and not only did it raise ticket prices, it also imposed a new 34-cent tax on every business for every $100 that businesses pay out to their employees.[13] The tax applies to businesses in New York City as well as in surrounding counties. Yep, local politicians are trying to save the MTA by hammering businesses with payroll taxes, treating private businesses like "collection agencies for the state."[14] If you believe you're not being affected by policies like this, think again. Companies pass the expense of such payroll taxes on to consumers. Take Con Edison, for example, which provides electricity to the vast majority of New Yorkers. Con Edison recoups the cost of the MTA tax by adding a 22-cent surcharge to its customers' electricity bills.[15]

But it's more than just payroll taxes; the MTA gets money from several other hidden taxes on utility and phone companies. They include three levies—an MTA surcharge, sales tax, and excise tax—that add an average of 68 cents to New Yorkers' cell phone bills. Total taxes increase monthly NYC phone bills by as much as 37%. Meanwhile, electric bills in the city are about 30% more expensive due to similar "surcharges and fees."

Hey, New Yorkers, what did you get from this backroom deal? Your buses and subways still break down, and your trains are still crowded at rush hour. Nothing has changed, except that YOU get to pay more for your ride! And if you don't like it, too bad. New York politicians truly could not care less, so you'd better get a bicycle or a good pair of pumps.

The Tax Monster doesn't just live in New York. Ask Boston residents about their subway system, the clown show that is the Massachusetts Bay Transit Authority (MBTA). Furious protestors lined up in droves last year to complain when MBTA fares rose (yet again) by 9.3%. Of course, the MBTA transit agency board unanimously approved the price increase despite all the angry riders who swarmed their meeting and briefly drowned out the vote. Bean Towners have good reason to shout—the MBTA ticket prices keep going up and up with no end in sight. In 2014, the MBTA increased train and bus fares between 5 and 7%.[16] Before that, a 2012 hike raised prices by an average of 23% system-wide.[17]

Just like New York, the city of Boston uses the collected revenue from price hikes to subsidize eye-popping employee salaries. One MBTA worker, Mark Flaherty, earned over $327,000 in 2015.[18] Despite having a base salary of $84,800 (which is still pretty damn high for a public employee), Flaherty collected well over that amount due to overtime pay. Think about what you could do with $327K! Would you buy a lake house? Or a Lamborghini? All you have to do is become a Boston bus driver! That same year, 59 other MBTA employees collected at least $100,000 above their base salary because of overtime.

Why is overtime pay so high? Again, my problem is not with Mr. Flaherty, who is probably a hard-working guy who just knows how to use the rules to his advantage. Lax management, little oversight to control costly operating procedures . . . and sometimes straight-up illegitimate conduct. A recent audit revealed that in 2015 the MBTA paid $32 million in overtime pay to employees who worked fewer than 40 hours a week. Union rules let workers collect overtime when they work over eight hours a day, so working three 10-hour days and collecting overtime allows employees to collect more than they would by working five 8-hour days.

Wouldn't you love to make a six-figure salary while working fewer than 40 hours a week? Audits have also revealed numerous cases of individuals approving their own overtime pay. Yet nothing is done about these issues, thanks to strong unions and management that hasn't been doing its job. And thanks to the fact that city government can raise fares to pay for its failings while facing barely a peep from the population that pays for these increases.

SUBWAY JANITORS: THE NEW DREAM JOB?

Want to make over $200,000 a year? No problem. Go work for the San Fran subway system as a janitor. I can't make this stuff up, folks. Liang Zhao Zhang may be America's luckiest janitor. He cleans the subway stations in downtown San Francisco. Zhang grossed $235,000 in 2015, four times more than his base pay; he did this by racking up lots of overtime hours.[19] Each hour of overtime pays much more than a regular hour of work, so it's a great way to exploit the system. When you add up the ridiculously awesome benefits, Zhang cost San Francisco taxpayers more than $270,000 a year!

Hey, let's be fair. Maybe the dude just worked his ass off?

Uh, this isn't the first time Zhang made six figures. He has received $682,000 in pay and benefits over the past three years. How does this happen?! Once again, don't blame Zhang. It's due to gross incompetence at the management level.

In the private sector, ineffective department managers would be canned. But this is the government, where accountability is all too often in short supply. As these agencies continue to bleed money, they just raise the price of your bus, train, or subway tickets. Most people have become so desensitized to this hidden tax cluster-pluck, they just shrug their shoulders and accept the higher price. Hey, it's inflation, right? Prices for other stuff goes up, too.

Try using this logic on your boss and see if you get that next raise you've been angling for. Spoiler alert: It won't go well.

Don't accept the tired old excuse that it's inflation's fault. It's not. It's the fault of corruption and an inefficient use of taxpayer money. It's the fault of the local government agencies that operate these huge public transportation departments, which are apparently deemed "too big to fail" and get a taxpayer bailout every year to survive.

If NYC's MTA were a private company, it would have filed bankruptcy, cleaned house, and reorganized its operation years ago. Instead, as the MTA continues to lose billions of dollars annually, New York City and the state of New York keep propping the MTA up year after year by increasing taxpayer subsidies (in other words *making us pay for their losses*)—resulting in one of the worst run, most expensive, least productive transit systems in the world.

Will Elon Musk please finish the hyperloop already so we can be done with government-run public transportation forever?

THE TAXOLOGY OF TAXI RIDES

Maybe now you'll decide not to take the crowded subway or bus. Hopping in a taxi seems like a natural solution . . . but you've probably noticed how damn expensive cab rides are these days. Would it shock you to learn that the Tax Monster is boosting taxi fares in more ways than one?

New York City has been home to a large-scale taxi service since 1898, and it didn't take long for city bureaucrats to start regulating the industry. In the 1920s city workers considered creating an MTA-style, publicly run taxi system as a solution to unlicensed drivers and rickety cabs causing problems. The mayor at the time, Jimmy Walker, looked into the "solution," with both ears and hands fully open.

Walker used his newly created "Board of Taxicab Control" to solicit bribes from the largest taxi company in the city, J. A. Sisto, which angled to become a monopoly under city auspices. The taxi board reduced competition from smaller cab companies by limiting the number of new drivers allowed in the boroughs and implementing tight licensing restrictions. In return, Sisto gave the mayor $26,000 worth of bonds (almost a half-million bucks today). Walker was busted for taking the bribes in 1932, and he was forced out of office and his taxi board was dissolved.

But with Walker gone, officials continued to control cabs. Today, there is an entire city agency, the Taxi and Limousine Commission— affectionately known as the TLC—devoted to taxi regulation.

NYC began issuing medallions, metal plates that identify a taxi driver's registration with the city, in 1937. Without a city-issued medallion, it's illegal to drive a cab. The first medallions only cost $10, but the artificially limited supply of medallions increased their price beyond recognition. By 1947, one medallion already cost $2,500 (which is equal to roughly $26,000 today) and by 2014 the price shot up to $280,000. Today, a medallion costs half a million dollars! And that price is DOWN from 2014, when the city charged $1 million for each metal plate.

The city understands that the medallion market is a major meal ticket—selling them drives prices sky high, and the money goes straight into the city's coffers. In 2014, medallion auctions brought in $338 million![20] This steady stream of cash, along with NYC tax dollars, funds the cushy salaries and pensions of the TLC's 600 employees. Next time you pay a bloated taxi fare in the Big Apple, you can take comfort in knowing that you're subsidizing the six-figure salaries of bureaucrats at the TLC.[21] Meera Joshi, the TLC's chief operating officer, rakes in well over $200,000 per year.[22]

And it's not just insane salaries being funded by medallion sales. This consistent cash flow has allowed city bureaucrats to go on regular administrative shopping sprees, spending money like drunken sailors. The TLC's "administrative" expenses increased from $46 million in 2014 to $69 million in 2016[23]—that's a 50% spending hike! Two thirds of that money goes to personnel costs and almost $16 million goes to "supplies and contracted services." More than $1.1 million alone goes toward new computers each year—that's over $1,800 per employee. Wouldn't it be nice if *you* could use someone else's money to buy yourself a new MacBook every year?

Cabbies themselves are also getting screwed by the TLC's regulations and taxes. In addition to the $500,000 medallion price tag, drivers must pay $1,400 in taxi fees to New York City every two years plus an annual $1,000 "Commercial Motor Vehicle Tax."[24]

What do exorbitant medallion prices do to your cab fare? The TLC has historically had to raise cab fares so that drivers can pay for the medallions they purchased and still make a living. Meanwhile, although taxi fares in New York City have slightly appreciated in the last 20 years, they have not appreciated enough to keep many drivers out of foreclosure by the banks they borrowed from to purchase the medallions in the first place.

But it's more than just the medallions inflating what you pay for taxi rides. Every time you step foot into a cab, you're on the hook for a base fee of $3.30, 80 cents of which are taxes—that includes a 50-cent MTA surcharge and a 30-cent improvement surcharge to pay for wheelchair accessibility.

The MTA surcharge has been around since 2009, and was intended as a "temporary" measure . . . But there's no sign that the city will be removing it anytime soon. The surcharge was part of a $2.3 billion state bailout for NYC's failing public transportation systems that also included a 5% car rental tax, a business payroll tax that charges employers 34 cents for every $100 of payroll, a $16 hike to renew driver's licenses, and a $50 hike to renew regular car registrations. The package was a proverbial turd sandwich, increasing your average fares overnight with *nothing to show for it.* The subway is still slow and dirty, although I'm sure the pizza rats really appreciate the effort.

As if all that wasn't enough, New York governor Andrew Cuomo is proposing yet another surcharge for taxis operating in parts of Manhattan.[25] Under his new plan, all cars entering busy parts of the borough would pay a $2.75 toll (trucks would pay even more) and several bridges that are currently un-tolled would gain one. Cuomo claims the $1.5 billion annual tax package would both reduce traffic and create another MTA and bridge-repair slush fund. I guess it's a step up from Mayor Michael Bloomberg's original $8 per car proposal.

Meanwhile, cab drivers are calling for Cuomo to bail them out, as they face stiff competition from ride-sharing apps like Uber and Lyft. In a 2017 letter to Governor Cuomo, 6,000 members of the Taxi Medallion Owner Driver Association called for Uber and Lyft to be taxed.[26] Massachusetts now has a "temporary" Uber tax that literally transfers money to the taxi industry. NYC may follow suit, issuing a bailout for the taxi drivers negatively affected by the MTA bailout. Crony capitalism at its finest.

Since New York's 2009 MTA surcharge passed around the time ride sharing boomed in popularity, it added nails to an already outdated system's coffin. And yes, ride sharing really is putting the old taxi system in its grave. Medallion demand is falling faster than ever. Between 2015 and 2016, taxis' share of the NYC market fell from 84% to 65% with Uber and Lyft taking up the slack. It's easy to see why: For an average 10-minute trip over five miles, you can expect to shell out $18 for a taxi and $16 for Uber. And 7% adds up after a while.

Of course, the powers that be want Uber and Lyft destroyed. There's a serious push to have the ride-sharing apps pay the 50-cent MTA tax to pay their "fair share" toward a public transit system its users are trying to avoid. I'll expose how the Tax Monster is working overtime to ruin the sharing economy in a bit . . .

In the meantime, I'll keep my Uber app at the ready. I want to be able to hail a Checker without being stuck between the chess game of the taxi lobby. Sometimes I'm amazed by the lengths that some agencies and special interests will go to make life in an already-expensive city even more expensive. I'll give the drivers and big government some credit—they all seem to understand that the more competition and market forces come in, the lower prices go. Bad for them, good for us.

YOU COUNTRY FOLKS ARE GETTING SCREWED, TOO!

If you live in a small town you're probably laughing at the travails of us silly city folks. You may even think you're beating the system by avoiding all the hidden transportation taxes that come with riding on a big city transportation system. Nice try, but the Tax Monster has his own set of transportation taxes for you!

I should know—before I moved to New York, I grew up in rural New Hampshire, where if you wanted something in life, you had to work for it. When I was old enough to work, I got a job at the first place that would hire me: a hospital kitchen. My primary duties involved removing food and vomit from used plates, then loading the dishwasher. It wasn't the most glamorous of jobs but I was only 16 years old and grateful to have a paying gig. The only problem was I had a 35-minute commute from my house.

During my drive to work, I was being powered by fossil fuels; our federal and state governments love to hammer our fuel consumption by taxing our gas pumps to death.

See, country kids, you can't get away from the Tax Monster *that easily.* To paraphrase *The Godfather: Part III,* "Just when you think you're out, [the Tax Monster] pulls you back in."

The gas tax is no new thing; it's older than our grandparents. The feds first started taxing gasoline consumption at 1 cent per gallon in 1932 (equal to 16 cents today). Fast-forward to today, and the feds collect approximately $600 per person in "fuel and energy excise taxes." Federal taxes increase your price of gas by 37%.[27]

We love to complain about big, mean oil companies—*those cigar-smoking Exxon executives are ripping us off with their high oil prices!* Well check this out: Oil companies make about 7 cents profit on every gallon of gas they sell us. But the government takes more than 48 cents per gallon.[28] The feds are profiting seven times more from your purchase of gas than "Big Oil" is!

And it's not just the feds skimming off our gasoline bills. No way, this is a sweet racket everyone wants a piece of—so naturally all 50 state governments already have their own versions of a gas tax. Yes, all 50.

Strangely, this state gas tax craze began way back in 1919, before the feds had enacted their own. Oregon was the first state to drop a gas tax on its citizens, at 1 cent per gallon. By the end of the 1920s, every other U.S. state had already followed suit. By 1939, every friggin' state had an average 3.8 cent gas tax per gallon!

Every day, state legislators around the nation are debating whether to increase their gas tax yet again, which may affect your life very soon.

The good news for all you truck-loving, gas-guzzling Americans is the federal gas tax is at 18.4 cents per gallon, and has not been hiked since 1993. Why? First, it's a hard sell on Capitol Hill politically—no serious politician has ever run for office promising to raise the federal gas tax. Our unapologetic politicians also point out that the federal gas tax is set at a "fixed rate," meaning it's not indexed to inflation, which (by the way) increased by a total of 64.6% from 1993 until 2015.

While raising the federal gas tax is a toxic campaign issue for D.C. politicians, state lawmakers are salivating over gas taxes. In 2017, California, Indiana, and Tennessee signed laws to raise fuel taxes. The states with the highest gas tax in the nation are Pennsylvania (58.2 cents per gallon), Washington (49.4 cents per gallon), and Hawaii (44.39 cents per gallon). If you live in those states and do a lot of driving, you're screwed. Only God knows how many public sector workers' retirements you are paying for with all those tax dollars!

Conversely—can we take a moment to appreciate the awesome rebel state of Alaska, which has the lowest state gas tax rate in the country at 12.25 cents per gallon? Way to stay free up there in Kodiak Country! They haven't slain the Tax Monster yet, but at least they've kept him relatively small.

Gas taxes used to fall under something called the "benefit principle," which meant revenue that is taken from drivers would go toward the public projects that benefit them—which makes sense. Except for one problem. Gas taxes almost always end up in *Ye' Old General Fund—which is pretty much a government slush fund* that bureaucrats can spend however they please.

In 2013, all gas taxes, tolls, and motor vehicle license fees that were allocated for infrastructure covered just 41% of all state and local road spending.[29] And that percentage keeps falling since many state gas tax rates are not indexed for inflation. So what should we do about all these crumbling roads? Here's a novel concept—why not just automatically raise gas taxes every year? That's just what 19 states (like Maryland, Pennsylvania, Rhode Island, Utah, and Virginia) suddenly did in 2016 so their gas tax rates could go up along with inflation. Politicians love this plan, because now they can automatically raise your taxes every year, but they never have to vote on it. That way, they don't have to tell their constituents that they voted to raise taxes. It's a big win for big-spending bureaucrats, and a big kick in the pants for their constituents. Now 54% of the U.S. population lives in a state where the gas tax rate goes up every year.[30]

Whether you believe your gas tax dollars will go toward a worthy infrastructure project or into the general fund—the bottom line is no matter where you drive in the United States, as of 2017 state and local taxes and fees added 31 cents to the cost of a gallon of gasoline. When you add that to our 18-cent federal gas tax, every American is getting taxed 49 cents per gallon for gas.[31] So basically, *we are all getting taxed half a dollar for every gallon we buy.*

Want to know if the Tax Monster is coming to a gas pump near you? All you need to do is find out if your state has a current budget deficit—if it does, then look out, buddy! Every state must balance their budget and gas taxes are an easy way to rake in extra funds. So if you find your state is in a financial pickle due to things like bloated state worker pensions and out-of-control spending, who do you think is going to inevitably put the cape on and save the day here? You are!

If you want to see how close your state is to raising gas taxes, find out if your state is one of the 31 states that reported budget shortfalls in 2017. New York, Texas, Connecticut, Delaware, Massachusetts, Pennsylvania, Virginia, Illinois, Indiana, Kansas, Mississippi, and Alaska (to name a few) are expected to face some kind of revenue imbalance in the upcoming legislative session. Uh-oh. You, too, Alaska? Looks like the Alaska Tax Monster may be coming out of hibernation.

THE GOLDEN STATE IS MADE OF FOOL'S GOLD

Can you name a transportation service that involves hundreds of dollars in unexplainable fees? How about paying for your *annual license fees and car registration?* How does this scam work? Kinda like all the others we have discussed in this chapter, *except this time with cars!*

It all goes back to the fact that 31 states are currently claiming budget poverty. Clearly, generating enough dough for Ye Old General Fund is a big state problem. Where can these broke-ass states forage around for some sure-fire extra dough? I can see it now, after hours of brainstorming, suddenly some state official gets a bright idea . . . *We have a budget shortfall and vehicle owners are a giant captive audience— hmm, let's raise money by jacking up their registration fees!*

How many people would even notice a price hike when the DMV bombards us with so much stress and frustration that we'll often pay whatever it takes just to be done with it? I know whenever I walk out of my DMV I'm always in an angry daze, wondering what the heck just happened to the past few hours of my life.

The vehicle registration tax is a straight money grab—the state arbitrarily increases the price of car registration and claims the extra funds collected will go toward that magical catchall category of "improving infrastructure"—which is almost always a total lie. Where does all that money really go? To pay for the state's budget shortfall, of course. No matter where you live, it's a safe bet that all that money you pay every year for car and license registration doesn't make its way into any road maintenance projects in your area.

My friend Juliette recently moved to California from Arizona and got to experience the Cali DMV firsthand. It was horrible; much worse than the average DMV nightmare you typically get (you know:

the insanely long lines, the bad license photos, and overall crappy service of employees who look down on you with disdain). No, Juliette encountered a hidden little transportation tax at the DMV I had never even heard of.

California has a sneaky little car registration tax called a "Use Tax" on "tangible personal property." Show up at the DMV to register a new car (purchased out of state in the last year), and the Golden State will charge you a "use tax," which is just another vehicle registration fee like the one you already paid in your previous state.[32] What the hell? Why does this law exist? To hammer customers, that's why! And, apparently to discourage California residents from fleeing the state to purchase *tangible* personal property.

Juliette also had to pay the registration fee ($43), a vehicle licensing fee ($84), a new registration origination service fee ($19), then she had to pay the cops with a California Highway Patrol fee ($23), as well as a whole slew of other inexplicable fees ranging in cost from $1 to $6. Add the magical "use fee," and her total fees due came to $689.

Welcome to California! Now give us your wallet!

I won't spend any more time hammering the DMV, since we've been trained since birth to loathe the Department of Motor Vehicles—but I will say, at least when the Tax Monster steals from us in other transportation-related areas, we are overpaying for some product or service that we actually use. What does the DMV give us? It's just a bunch of stickers on your car.

What fun is that?

TWO

FOOD

TIME TO PANIC: IT'S TOO EXPENSIVE TO BUY ORGANIC!

> Just taught my kids about taxes by eating
> 38 percent of their ice cream.
>
> —*Bill Murray*

Has anyone ever told you that your eating habits kind of suck?

Go ahead, you can admit it—you're not the only one who's being shamed by our elders. Perhaps you've been so busy stuffing your face that maybe you didn't hear all the old trolls punking our generation's food fetishes. Believe it or not, the biggest complaint I hear from Boomers and Xers is actually not related to our generation's chronic obesity, it's that *we tend to waste our money on food* in so many foolish ways.

Well . . . I hate to admit it, but our so-called "wise" elders may be right: The biggest food hang-up for young Americans is actually not the quantity of food we ingest (which, granted, is a big problem, thanks to our national obsession with *consuming mass quantities* like that weird Conehead family used to do on *Saturday Night Live*); it's how much money we spend on what we eat. And you can thank the government, at least partially, for the increasingly high cost of food. Sure, there's no national "food tax," but almost everything you eat is subject to state sales tax and often to additional meal taxes. What you ultimately shell out depends on which state you live in (more on that later in the chapter). And then there are burdensome regulations imposed on the agriculture industry, restaurants, and grocery stores that also increase what you pay to eat.

I'm not here to give one of Michelle Obama's "Let's Move!" public service announcements; I'm here to expose all the hidden "free radical" tax toxins we all suck down daily. We're eating hidden taxes in our meals every day y'all. To borrow a line from the anti-Trump #Resistance—we need to get straight WOKE on this subject because if we don't, we may end up so broke, beaten, and morbidly obese we will have to start wearing government-mandated lap bands.

AT LEAST YOU DON'T HAVE TO BUY
COOKING OIL FROM ONE PHARAOH

Hidden tax spiders have been crawling into unsuspecting mouths since the beginning of time. Depending on your heritage, the odds are very good that your long lost ancestors were getting royally screwed on their mead, gruel, blood sausage, and hogshead cheese purchases long before your great-grandmomma was a twinkle in your great-great-grandfather's eye.

If your family migrated to the United States from Egypt, your ancestors were probably getting ripped off by the resident pharaoh, who had his own food tax going. Ancient Egyptians were forced to buy heavily taxed cooking oil from the pharaoh's monopoly and were prohibited from reusing previously purchased oil.[1] I always wondered where Marlon Brando got the idea to start up the Genco Pura Olive

Oil Company in *The Godfather*—now we know he lifted it from the pharaoh.

Besides cooking oil, our old seasoning standby, salt, has been (and continues to be) a very popular food item to drop a hidden tax on. Why? Every human needs salt in their diet to survive—so, of course, the powers that be are going to find a way to tax that necessity. If you're of European descent and could go back in time to see how your ancestors were taxed on just their salt purchases, you'd get total itchy gag reflex déjà vu. I certainly did when I realized the exact same scam that worked on my dead ancestors still works today. Yes, our old cousins, the uptight, dentist-shunning Brits, placed a tax on salt hundreds of years ago. Even my favorite Euro snot bags, the French, instituted a salt tax called "le gabelle" in the mid-14th century, which did not work out so well for them—it actually angered so many French citizens, it was one of the contributing factors to the French Revolution.[2] That and the whole "let them eat cake thing," which I'm sure was taxed, too. The "salt bae" tax, as I now call it, got so freaking popular, it eventually got worldwide attention when Gandhi staged a series of nonviolent protests against it in India.

Wow, maybe Gandhi was onto something?

Maybe we need a food tax revolution in the United States?

I'll shave my head like Natalie Portman in *V for Vendetta,* if you will . . .

HOW DOES THIS ILLUMINATI-LEVEL
FOOD TAX RACKET EVEN WORK?

Why is food so expensive here in the good ole U.S. of A. these days? It's not just inflation, folks. Everything is more expensive now, because every food product we consume has already been (to use a Mafioso term) "stepped on" (i.e., taxed) repeatedly by everyone who has touched the product, from farm to table.

Before dinner ever lands on your plate, the price of your food has already gone up while the quality has gone down. And I haven't even mentioned all the disgusting hidden taxes, fees, and surcharges you get hit with when you pay your normal bills that go toward things like the overregulation of the food industry, GMO labeling, food workers' minimum wage, the plastic bag ban, and farmer subsidies.

To quote my kooky Aunt Harriet after she's had a hard day at the office, "Calgon, take me away!" I wasn't around for whatever the origins of that joke are, but it sounds apt for this moment. Even Harriet's old bones would agree that all of these hidden taxes are sending a lot of middle-class Americans to the poorhouse.

Aunt Harriet doesn't care about our plight because she's old, but *you should.* Whether you cook at home (a rarity these days) or are one of the many millennials who eat out all the time, we all keep paying more. But *eating out is way, way worse.*

Many cities levy "meal taxes," which are incurred at restaurants in addition to your state's sales tax on food; they're applied to any meal eaten at a restaurant or taken "to go" (my bugaboo). These meal taxes usually range from between 0.05 and 5.5%. Virginia Beach, Virginia, has the highest meal tax in the nation, 5.5%. Denver, Minneapolis, and Omaha also have high rates: 4%, 3%, and 2.5% respectively.[3] The Tax Foundation compiled the largest U.S. cities with meal taxes. When combined with normal sales taxes, you can pay upward of 10% in taxes when you dine out.[4] Listed on the next page are the nation's largest cities that have a specific meal tax, which is levied *in addition* to the states' normal sales taxes.

What is the point of meal taxes, you ask? Do they go to fight childhood obesity, or something? *Come on.* The revenue generated almost always goes right into your city, county, or state's "general fund," which means they are collected for no real reason other than to rake in more funds for city pensions and bloated government projects.

Population Rank	City	State	Sales Tax	Additional Meals Tax	Combined Tax on Meals
1	Chicago	IL	9.50%	1.25%	10.75%
2	Jacksonville	FL	7.00%	2.00%	9.00%
3	Indianapolis	IN	7.00%	2.00%	9.00%
4	Charlotte	NC	8.00%	1.00%	9.00%
5	Boston	MA	6.25%	0.75%	7.00%
6	Seattle	WA	9.50%	0.50%	10.00%
7	Washington	DC	6.00%	4.00%	10.00%
8	Denver	CO	4.10%	4.00%	8.10%
9	Milwaukee	WI	5.60%	0.05%	5.65%
10	Kansas City	MO	7.85%	1.23%	9.08%
11	Virginia Beach	VA	5.00%	5.50%	10.50%
12	Omaha	NE	7.00%	2.50%	9.50%
13	Raleigh	NC	6.75%	1.00%	7.75%
14	Miami	FL	7.00%	2.00%	9.00%
15	Minneapolis	MN	7.78%	3.00%	10.78%

EAT AT HOME LIKE THE AMISH? NICE, BUT YOU'RE STILL SCREWED

Okay, so maybe you're out there beating your chest, and saying, "I'm a fancy pants who likes to cook every meal at home, what do you have to say about that?"

Well I say, congratulations, you are clearly a better human being than I am! But you may not be out of the woods, depending on the state or city where you live. Tax meccas (like pretty much every blue state, with California being king) are definitely taxing your ass when you cook at home—but what about the good ole red states? None of those pistol-packing Bubbas would be dropping sneaky little hidden taxes on our plain old nonorganic groceries, would they? The world is a strange place . . . *of course they do.*

West Virginia (unlike its borderline hippie cousin Virginia) is a good wholesome rural state, full of coal miners, John Denver fans, and so forth. But if you eat all your meals at home in West Virginia, you may need to start living like the Amish to pay for it. West Virginia recently reinstituted a 3% sales tax on all groceries in their state.[5] This grocery tax is no small potatoes—the estimated annual haul on this tax is a whopping $78 million. No wonder they "reinstated it" after phasing it out in 2013. Guess who needs to line their general operations fund again? You guessed it, the state of West Virginia! I hate to pick on your state, citizens of West Virginia—you can take comfort in knowing you're not alone. A general grocery tax is actually spreading all over the red states.

Alabamans have an even bigger beef with their state legislators over hidden food taxes than the coal miners do. Alabamans have to pay an ungodly 10% tax on all their groceries. Alabama is one of only three states (joining South Dakota and Mississippi) that fully tax groceries.[6] People who pay the tax seem to really hate this law, and for good reason.

Think about it: More than 90% of Alabama's population lives in rural areas (I bet they eat most of their meals at home). So a 10% tax on all food could really bring in some revenue. Yet, for all its unpopularity, funny how Alabama's politicians haven't tried to repeal the tax—gee, I wonder why? It's a cash cow! Naturally, state legislators say all the revenue generated from the food tax goes to fund the Education Fund of Alabama, so they don't want to stop the tax. It brings in an astounding $364.4 million a year, which is nearly 6% of the entire Education Fund. *Three-hundred and sixty-four million dollars?*

Alabama has been taxing groceries since their legislature created the sales tax in 1939! According to the Legislative Fiscal Office, there are 89 separate exemptions to Alabama's sales tax, ranging from prescription drugs to chicken antibiotics. But groceries for humans sold in a supermarket? It remains subject to the full tax.

"We've got a lot of tax breaks out there—agricultural breaks, breaks for luxury purchases, cars, and boats. But people who can't afford a car or a boat have to pay a full 10% tax on basic food like rice and beans?" said Kimble Forrister, executive director of Alabama Arise, which has campaigned against the grocery tax for decades.

Arkansas, Hawaii, Idaho, Illinois, Kansas, Mississippi, Missouri, Oklahoma, South Dakota, Tennessee, Utah, and Virginia are also home to grocery taxes.

For a lot of poor or middle-class folks in these states, being forced to pay these taxes takes a toll. It's not just that their groceries cost more money; it can make it harder for poverty-stricken families to even buy enough food to live on. Do we really need to tax a little old lady in Alabama 10% of her monthly beans and rice allowance? That's pretty low, Tax Monster. Go get your pound of flesh somewhere else. Like California.

But it's not just grocery taxes making supermarket food more expensive. City, county, and state officials often insert hidden food taxes in the form of a slight uptick in sales tax. No one will notice them, right? Guh. I do! I won't delve too deeply into these, since we have bigger fish to fry—but after perusing these little gems, you've gotta know America is way more sane than all those other countries, right?

Er, I'll let you be the judge of that . . .

- **Maine** | Employs a special tax on those darn blueberries, a super valuable state resource. Also, if you dig a good Maine clambake, prepare to pay more. Mahogany quahog clams are taxed at a rate of $1.20 per bushel. Nice, I'm out Maine.
- **Colorado** | Drops a 2.9% tax on nonessential food-related items like napkins, bibs, utensils, lids, and straws. Oddly, the law deems the actual coffee cup essential, but the lid nonessential. Tell that to the second-degree burns in my mouth.
- **Indiana** | Marshmallow cream is tax exempt, but marshmallows are considered candy and therefore taxed at a higher rate? You must really hate s'mores, Indiana.

- **Mississippi** | Has a 3% "salt bae" tax on all salt produced from land or water in Mississippi. The old salt tax trick again, eh? I guess it never gets old.

- **New York** | Big Apple bagel addicts get to eat an 8-cent "bagel-cutting tax" on any bagel that comes sliced or is served to be eaten immediately. New York, you cut me up, in a bad way. I'll bring my own Bowie knife next time.

- **California** | Fresh fruit bought through a vending machine is subject to a 33% tax. $4 apples from a machine? Talk to the hand, Cali.

- **New Jersey, Iowa, Pennsylvania** | No matter how close to Halloween it is, these states categorize pumpkins as food so they are sales tax exempt, unless the pumpkin is "painted, varnished or cut and sold as decorations," then sales tax applies. Thanks for that. You ruined Halloween for me forever.

- **Florida** | The good news is most Florida food is not subject to the 6% state sales tax, or the local sales tax . . . except for fast food. Knocking my habits again, Florida?

- **Georgia** | Their 4% sales tax does not apply to groceries. Yippie—wait, I can't cook—but your local city governments may still apply it? (Baaaah!)

- **Tennessee** | Tennessee's sales tax on "food and food ingredients" was recently reduced from 7 to 5% (awesome), but it does not apply to candy, alcohol, or prepared food, my three favorite food groups. (Boo!)

Many of these hidden food taxes are simply "special" state, county, or city sales taxes that are applied to specific food or food-related products.

Why do our legislators love the sales tax so much?

Gradual sales tax increases seem to be the easiest hidden taxes to sneak into law.

A lot of states and counties routinely pull this stunt but if you want to know where these rackets almost always start, all you have to do is just show up at your next city council meeting and look your local city councilmen (and councilwomen) in the eyes. Maybe squint at them like Dirty Harry a bit, because if you're paying a hidden food tax, or several dozen, those (let's just say it) preternaturally ugly people in front of you are the ones doing the screwing.

Get them! Just kidding. Do NOT attack your local city council!

Now boo or hiss them? Maybe.

Vote the bad ones out of office? Definitely.

If you think I'm being silly, you seriously should show up at one of their meetings to let them know you're watching them. Because nearly all of these hidden food taxes come from money-starved municipalities that concoct these grand schemes to make some extra cash. I'm not some hardened political sage (yet)—but I think it's safe to say that any time an elected official tells you they're doing something "for your own good," if you're not immediately suspicious, then you are most likely missing the subtext, big-time . . .

A GLIMMER OF HOPE ON THE KANSAS PLAINS?

If you're looking for a bright side to this national tax food fiasco, there isn't one—but at least one Kansas lawmaker is trying to fight the good fight. Alas, he is not exactly lighting the world on fire with his amazing results yet, but I want to shine a light on this dude to encourage crusaders like him to never give up. If you happen to be reading this in Wichita, Kansas, why don't you take a minute and call your local State House representative and say a word of thanks?

He is Rep. John Whitmer (Wichita). He is one of the only elected officials trying to stomp out the hidden tax spiders crawling around our nation's dinner tables. Someone in Kansas give this guy a hand.

Whitmer recently introduced an amendment to the Kansas State House of Representatives that would reduce the state's sales tax on food by a whole percentage point (from 6.5% to 5.5%). Naturally, since the world is a corrupt cesspool that is slowly destroying all of my altruistic tendencies, his proposal was shot down by the rest of the Kansas House in a landslide, 85–32.[7]

Why so little support for his amended bill?

All Representative Whitmer was trying to do was bring the sales tax back down to a "normal" level of 5.5%, which it was as recently as 2015. You may be wondering—*Why was the food sales tax raised in the first place?* I bet you can guess. In 2015, the state of Kansas approved the raising of the state sales tax to 6.5% for that old chestnut of an excuse: to generate operating revenue[8]—which usually means to line people's pockets and fund pensions. Even though his amendment got rolled, Representative Whitmer had a plan to make up for all of the lost sales tax revenue that involved deleting exemptions on lottery tickets, bingo cards, and other sales.

Hey Representative Whitmer, if you are reading this—let me buy you an over-taxed Hungarian energy drink to keep your spirits up. "I tried," Whitmer said, "Sales tax on food is regressive." I'm sending a case of delicious, highly taxed gummy bears to his office, ASAP.

THE REST OF THE WORLD IS
JUST AS INSANE AS WE ARE

First, let's take momentary solace in the fact we're not the only crazy country who drops hidden food taxes on our people. Corruption happens everywhere. Take a look at France's even more stuck-up neighbor, Belgium, for a perfect example of what I mean.

If you were invited to a BBQ in Belgium in the last decade (I know I have been), you may have noticed that in 2007, the government of Wallonia, which is a region of Belgium with a population of 3.5 million, put a damper on what must have been nonstop BBQ parties popping off in their hood by adding a 20-euro tax for the privilege of cooking on your own grill.[9]

Now people are getting taxed for grilling in their own yards?

This may sound nuts to every American, but I'm sure some nature-loving town in California will follow their lead soon. Because the local brain trust in Wallonia believes outdoor grills release up to 100 grams of greenhouse gases into the atmosphere, they're "doing their part to fight global warming" by forcing their citizens to pay for the right to grill. *Pay for the right to grill?* Just typing that sentence made me feel un-American, almost as un-American as tasting French fries with mayonnaise (another Belgian pastime).

Now, if you think the Belgians don't enforce this law, you would be wrong. The Wallonia Police take this law very seriously; they even have a police helicopter (full of hungry officers, no doubt) with thermal imaging cameras to hunt down rogue grillers. Being a dog lover, I really hope the cops at least deploy a pack of ravenous police dogs to crash the hot dog parties that haven't paid the Belgian Tax Monster.

All I can say to all you Wallonia lawmakers is—did Al Gore put you up to this? Silly Belgians, you make great chocolate but your views on grilling meat are totally absurd.

If you want another European example of this moronic phenomenon, just hop a train from Belgium to Hungary. The Hungarian government wanted to make food healthier for citizens so it created something called a "chipsovy tax"[10]—which sounds like a delicious "savory chip," right? Alas, it is not delicious. It taxes Hungarian junk food addicts on pretty much every snackable delight worth binge eating. This Draconian law has been on the books since 2011 and adds a tax on a whole range of prepackaged snacks like chips, crackers, cookies, packaged cakes, as well as energy drinks. Energy drinks, too?

Aren't those like one of the five basic food groups now? Guess not in Hungary.

Maybe you think it's just our Euro brethren who are still unleashing the food Tax Monster on citizens? *If it were only so . . .* I might consider relocating to a country that did not give the Tax Monster a green card—but I can't find one.

Want another weird example of what I mean?

Let's hop a slow boat to China—I mean, what could the hidden food Tax Monster possibly prey on in healthy-as-hell, veggie-loving, miso-pounding, communist China? Why, chopsticks of course. The Chinese authorities recently introduced a special 5% tax on disposable bamboo chopsticks.[11]

GMO LABELING: YOU IGNORANT LITTLE HIPPIE, YOU

The biggest and, yes, lamest excuses that governments around the globe tell their citizens to justify food-related taxes is that they're *for your own good.* If I hear that one more goddamned time, I'm gonna slap a congressman, or at least some unsuspecting congressional page, right in his lying face. Ask any bureaucrat, democrat, or even an autocrat about it, and you will hear the same company line: *Well little lady, you may be surprised to learn that most of these hidden taxes you're complaining about actually go to ensuring your food is safe.* Blah, blah, thanks for the mansplanation, but I'm not buying it.

Yes, that's a perfectly acceptable excuse *in theory.* I'll definitely pay more to make sure my food is not radioactive—but bureaucrats (bless their heartless little souls), *being who they are,* tend to go a little crazy, and just overregulate the hell out of everything.

A new report proves my point. It estimates if the total cost of federal regulation flowed down to U.S. households, the average American family would *pay* $14,809 annually in a hidden regulatory tax.[12] That's *in addition to all the income taxes, state taxes, Social Security, sales taxes, property taxes, and even estate taxes,* through which the government literally taxes you for being a freaking dead person. This amounts to 21% of the average income of $69,629.

Let's focus on one specific example of overregulation on the food industry, which we can all understand over a piece of overpriced avocado toast: It's called GMO labeling.

GMO stands for Genetically Modified Organism. When farmers or scientists modify a plant's DNA, you get a GMO (lookin' at you, huge red strawberries). In July 2016, under President Obama, Congress passed a GMO-labeling bill; within a few years, when the new law is fully rolled out, consumers will be able to find out whether any food in the supermarket contains GMO ingredients.[13]

The thought of eating genetically modified organisms is scary for people who don't know much about the science involved. Politicians know this, and they use it to their advantage. These do-gooders tell voters they're "looking out for us" by making GMO labeling mandatory. But in reality, there is no evidence that GMOs, which are currently in about 80% of our food,[14] are inferior or unsafe—even the Food and Drug Administration has said that GMO foods aren't any different than regular ones.[15] But that didn't stop Obama from signing the 2016 labeling bill.

The end result? Food companies are forced to spend money on labeling, and then pass those costs on to the consumer. And none of us are any safer for it.

In 2016, Vermont passed its own bill to make GMO labeling mandatory. Any company that didn't comply faced a $1,000 penalty per day for every unlabeled item.[16] That's a significant fine, especially for small producers who have more limited budgets than the big guys. The bill was ultimately superseded by Obama's federal law, but during the short time that Vermont's rule was in place companies responded by raising prices, swapping out ingredients, and opting out of selling in the state altogether.

Campbell's was the first company to go public with their plans, stating that they would label all products across the United States because labeling for just one state was "incredibly costly" and not workable. Labeling isn't just some simple text on a can; it involves reviewing supply chains, checking all the recipes, looking at sourcing options, and considering a whole bunch of logistics. In the end, these increased costs are passed down to consumers at the grocery store.

Several companies replaced ingredients out of fear that labels would be a sort of scarlet letter and scare off customers. One small company, Vermont Fresh Pasta, switched from using canola oil to olive oil. This increased costs by 10%, without any noticeable increase in sales. When Ben & Jerry's, another Vermont-based company, removed GMOs from their ingredients their new products averaged 11% higher in price.[17]

And then there were other small to midsized companies—like Herr Foods Inc., based in Philadelphia—that considered pulling out of Vermont altogether thanks to the GMO bill. "Just the logistics, the expenses are horrendous," Herr's senior vice president of sales said.

We saw the horrendous effects of mandatory GMO labeling in Vermont. Why would we expect different results from Obama's federal bill?

Sadly, mandatory GMO labeling isn't the only regulation increasing the amount we pay for food. There are more. There are always more. Especially when it comes to the government's efforts to push us toward organic products. Full disclosure here, I'm not one of those vehemently anti-organic Brosephs. But like the GMO debate, much of the organic/non-organic debate is based on fear mongering instead of science.

For example, did you know there's no reason to buy organic fruits or veggies if they have hard outer skins? No toxic pesticide can penetrate the hard outer skin of a coconut, plantain, onion, or even our snooty pal, the avocado.[18] But do you think the organic avocado, coconut, onion, and plantain-growing community has packed up shop, just because they are making completely useless products? Of course not, people still buy organic avocados for their avocado toast all the time.

The organic footprint is currently about 4% of the marketplace by dollar amount, but the industry has spent liberally to influence legislators and government agencies. The industry is kept afloat, in part, by massive subsidies by a variety of USDA agencies and programs (searching "organic agriculture" on USDA.gov yields 257,000 results). Federal spending on organic agriculture under the USDA Farm Acts increased from $20 million annually in 2002, to nearly $170 million in 2014.[19] I guess the bloated subsidies make sense, given that Obama's secretary of Agriculture, Kathleen Merrigan, had a resume that included decades of radical pro-organic ideology.

Reminder: These are YOUR tax dollars, folks. We're routinely forced to pay for regulations and subsidies that make it more costly for certain producers to do business; those costs are then passed down to us. But it's unclear what we get in return for all of this.

According to many activists, there still aren't enough regulations and/or subsidies on the food industry. Celebrity chef Tom Colicchio is currently pushing Congress to include even more government subsidies for organic fruit and vegetable growers, as well as higher wages for farmworkers.[20] His agenda sounds good, but it would create just another big-government mandate that's "being done for our own good."

Colicchio wants to outlaw farmers from using technologies like GMO engineering, which will raise the price of food even more, since farmers will no longer be allowed to use pesticides to increase the yields of their crops.

Tom, buddy, if you are out there—I'm sure you're a great chef, but this half-baked idea contradicts your goal of making food more affordable for everyone. *Empirically speaking, organic food is more expensive!* There are reasons why American farmers refuse to grow organic crops (only about 1% of U.S. farmland is currently dedicated to organic crops). It's more labor-intensive, time-consuming, and produces lower yields.

And contrary to the "think global, act local" theoretical appeal of buying organic fare—guess what? Most of that organic fare you shovel down your quinoa holes *does not* come from your local organic urban farm. In fact, the vast majority of every organic product you eat is imported from Mexico, Eastern Europe, and South America.

Here's one final reason we shouldn't go 100% organic: All the overblown media reports that say non-organic food will kill us really do brainwash people, even the heads of poor families. Can the organic craze actually *prevent* lower-income people from buying fruits and vegetables? Several studies have shown that lower-income households may avoid purchasing fruits or vegetables if they can't afford organic.[21] Why? Because they've been led to believe regular produce is full of harmful pesticides!

Um, in case you didn't know, *organic farms use pesticides, too,* just non-synthetic ones, but Colicchio and his organic warriors lobbying Congress act like we could flip some glorious switch, and suddenly live in some organic utopia where hundreds of well-tanned hipster farmers with man buns gently talk tiny bugs off of our fruit with their kind words. That actually sounds kinda hot, but it's not reality!

You gotta wake up from your fantasy, Colicchio. Or move to Brooklyn and let the rest of us normal humans eat our non-organic gummy bears in peace.

BLOATED BLUEBERRIES IN MAINE

I could end it right there, but I'm rolling on another gummy bear sugar high now, so here's one more example of a state government throwing taxpayer dollars at a problem that involves our favorite overpriced antioxidant deliverer—the beloved hipster of all fruits, the blueberry—and the state of Maine.

Maine is all about growing blueberries. It's what they do, they've been doing it since the 1800s, they're pretty good at it, but they currently are in the middle of a wild blueberry crisis. They have a glut of blueberries yet all of their government agencies are still using subsidies and grants to encourage Maine farmers to keep growing the crop. Too bad no one is buying them. Blueberry prices have plummeted in the past year—Maine's 100 million pounds of blueberries used to sell for $1 a pound, back in 2011, but now? They only sell for 25–27 cents per pound. Yikes.

Anyone know where that Violet chick from *Willie Wonka & the Chocolate Factory* retired to? Unless she cannibalized herself after Willie turned her into a blueberry, she may be able to help Maine's politicians reduce their backlog. They may need it. Maine is not backing down just because of something like a massively tanking market.

Instead of suspending their subsidy program to farmers and seeing how the blueberry market shakes out this year, Maine governor Paul LePage is doing the exact opposite. He's injecting the market full of even more steroids to hope it grows further, essentially praying that he can solve a problem (exacerbated by government spending) by even more spending.

You're quite the riverboat gambler, Governor LePage.

LePage has approved spending $2.5 million more of taxpayers' money on "agricultural marketing" to promote Maine agricultural products by advertising the nutritional benefits of wild blueberries and promoting the berries at trade shows.[22] His hope is that the new marketing will lead to expansion into new and exciting food markets in which wild blueberries could be desirable, like uh, Asian cuisine.

Blueberries in Chinese food? You call that a plan? C'mon Maine.

It pains me to say this—since I'm a country girl at heart who loves farmers—but I think the governor of Maine should stay on the sidelines and let the market play out naturally. If he does, one thing is for certain—we, the consumers, will thank him in the long run for not screwing us with the bill for his bizarre experiments in blueberry marketing. That is, unless Kung Pao Blueberry becomes a thing.

You never know.

I'm looking at you, California.

THREE

RENTING

RENTING? WELCOME TO THE 4TH CIRCLE OF HELL

> Okay, Marge, if anyone asks: You require 24-hour
> nursing care, Lisa's a clergyman, Maggie is seven
> people, and Bart was wounded in Vietnam.
>
> —*Homer Simpson (while filing his taxes)*

When you're about to graduate college, everyone's all, "Are you ready for the real world?" and, "Where will you be working?" and, "Where are you going to live?" And you're all, "Huh?! I'm graduating now! Isn't life easy from here on out? Why are you terrorizing me with all these questions?"

But . . . *oh, crap. Where AM I going to live?* Daddy turned your sweet childhood bedroom into his man cave, where he can sit quietly, smoke his pipe, and get away from Mommy.

Renting an apartment is one of the first steps toward fully autonomous adulthood. At first, it seems too good to be true: You found your first place and it's a horrible dive but you don't care. You don't mind waking up each morning to the sound of scurrying rodents; that's the sound of independence and freedom from your parents!

But sadly, not from the government. Yes, now you can go to bed at 4 a.m. without a lecture from your dad, you can cook dinner naked with impunity, and you can pop your zits onto the bathroom mirror without angering your loved ones. But even as you're doing your best to make your own way, the government is constantly inflicting costs on your life—and your new apartment.

In this chapter we're going to look at a number of ways the government imposes unreasonable costs on you not just through taxes and fees but, indirectly, also as a result of policies it implements that would seem, at first glance, to cost you no money at all. But as you'll see, these policies do cost you money and in many cases send your money, in one way or another, back to the coffers of your city, state, or federal government.

THE ROACHES WERE HERE FIRST!

Right out of college I lived in New York City, where the rental situation is like something from Bizarro World.

Some states, like New York, are actively "pro-tenant." These states have laws that make it difficult for landlords and property managers to evict tenants. *Pro-tenant!* Sounds good, right? *I'm a tenant, so pro-tenant laws are surely good for me!* While these laws make it less likely that you'll be tossed out on the street if you're late mailing the rent, these "pro-tenant" laws ultimately *raise* your rent and *damage* your living experience.

Rules like these make it harder for landlords to discern who might actually pay rent, as opposed to, say, trashing the place and skipping town. Many states' data regarding nonpayments and eviction are placed into a "tenant blacklist," which gives landlords a way to weed out risky tenants. But in 2012, New York State stopped collecting this data, calling it a "tenants' rights" issue.[1] Wait, whose rights—those who didn't pay their rent?

The result of this policy is that landlords face a higher risk that more tenants will fail to pay rent. Landlords protect against this risk by increasing your rent—the rent of the responsible tenant—as a means to assure they won't face a shortfall in rent income at the end of the year. And so you as a result pay the higher fee in the end. Thanks for the pro-tenant rent increase, New York.

At first glance, this may not look to you like a government tax. But when your rent goes up, you are paying for a government policy that you were never consulted on. Sure, theoretically if you don't like the policy you can work to vote out the city councilmen and mayors who put it in place, but who is watching government policy closely enough to track the never-ending stream of costs like these that are imposed on the average New Yorker?

The Big Apple still wants to take it a step further; the city is considering banning property owners from requesting prospective tenants' credit scores and information about their debts.[2] Last year a city councilman took it yet *another step further* by introducing legislation that would guarantee a taxpayer-funded attorney for all tenants facing eviction.[3] Just think of the many strings attached to this (because he sure didn't). Now, each landlord must consider the increased time and money that's at risk, *every time* he or she rents out a unit. If a bad tenant gets booted for selling dope in the halls, YOU—the Goody Two-shoes who consistently pays his bills on time—will now be on the hook for both the higher rent to compensate for your landlord's vacancy *and* your share of the cost of the city's attorneys defending deadbeat tenants (your tax dollars hard at work).

Don't get me wrong, tenants need protections. Some landlords are diabolical, and everyone forgets to mail a payment on time once in a while. But why make renting more expensive for responsible tenants in the name of protecting criminals, deadbeats, and drug addicts?

Sooo . . . if rules protecting bad tenants actually *increase* my rent, then who is protecting *me?* Perhaps the provisions intended to help would-be renters from being cast as "bad tenants" only help people that actually *are* bad tenants.

And then there are property taxes and fees, which are passed directly on to renters. In New York City, property taxes on apartment buildings are far higher than property taxes on single-family homes. Landlords get stuck with a 4% average annual property tax rate for large apartment buildings *in addition* to the hefty property taxes paid by all building owners in the state.[4] People who shell out big bucks to buy apartment buildings naturally expect a reasonable return on their investment. These high apartment building taxes will also get passed on to the tenants, most of whom can't afford to buy a home in the city.

By the way, the long reach of government interference in your rent bill doesn't stop with your lease. Turn on a light switch or up the thermostat, and you quickly become a victim of more bad government policy. I've got some hilarious and infuriating doozies to share with you about your utility bills a little later, so stay tuned.

THE "SECTION 8" HOUSING SCAM:
THE FREE LUNCH YOU ARE PAYING FOR

Government-subsidized housing was intended to offer stable, secure, and centrally planned neighborhoods after World War II. Many of these buildings became dangerous hellholes, riddled with drugs and crime. The violence is so out of control in many of these government-run buildings that some cops are scared to intervene in public-housing conflicts.[5]

Even when they are designed by Republicans to be more moderate versions of social engineering, such plans backfire. Take the "compassionate conservative" approach to government housing assistance espoused by Tricky Dick Nixon. Nixon wanted to shift many of the urban poor from the violent, decaying public housing to available housing in almost any neighborhood. Section 8 of the National Housing Act allows the government to pay recipients' rent in the apartments of the tenant's choice. This $20 billion[6] federally funded program is ubiquitous in all 50 states.

But—spoiler alert—this well-intentioned government program had unintended consequences. Section 8 played a role in creating a permanent underclass in America. Here's how it works: Once a family starts making more than a minimum earning threshold, they lose much or all of their Section 8 subsidies—same goes if they marry a spouse that makes "too much" money. In New York City, this perversely incentivizes recipients to remain indigent so they can continue receiving benefits.

Section 8 and other affordable housing mandates may be better than building more projects, but programs like these also contribute to the raising of your rent even when you have nothing to do with them personally. Developers and building management companies are required to designate some number of apartments for low-cost rent; owners of these buildings then make up the shortfall by increasing the rent on apartments offered to tenants who pay the rent without government assistance. Additionally making your rent more expensive is that landlords are perversely incentivized to accept Section 8 tenants over self-paying tenants. Why? First, because Section 8 tenants are never late with their rent—the government is paying it for them. Second, because landlords can raise the rent on Section 8 tenants knowing that the government is likely to pay the premium without question.

The New York City Housing Authority (NYCHA) is in charge of Section 8 city housing. NYCHA receives its funding from federal subsidies and employs 13,000 bureaucrats[7]—all with good-paying jobs and hefty pensions. Naturally, there is zero incentive for the employees at the Authority to transition people into private apartments or home ownership. If tenants begin leaving Section 8 housing in significant numbers, the money going to the NYCHA dries up. If that were to happen, all those cushy jobs and pensions would no longer be ensured. And make no mistake, NYCHA is not a well-run, efficient organization—management is so poor that the agency is in a perpetual "budget crisis."[8]

The federal Department of Housing and Urban Development (HUD) has a budget of nearly $50 billion[9] and provides funding for public housing programs like Section 8. The result of this government monstrosity is huge market distortions, which end up enriching wealthy landlords and hurting working people like you.

So in summary, let's review what subsidized housing creates:

- Higher overall rent? *Check.*
- Huge costs passed on to taxpayer? *Check.*
- Government disincentives to get off of welfare? *Check.*
- Allowing slumlords to inflate rents as a means to game the system? *Check.*

Remember, all of this may not be a direct tax, but you are paying for these policies and programs through the aftershocks they have on the market where you are the big sucker. If the programs were working well and the offices that administrated them were effective, that would be one story—we'd have less to complain about if we saw that the salaries of administrators were reasonable, the budgets balanced, and the number of people on housing assistance were going down each year. But the trends in all three areas are going in the opposite direction, and it's on your dime.

Rent control is another well-intended government program that ends up hurting working stiffs like you. Instead of lowering overall rents, these programs create a bizarre scenario where many rich tenants have their rent subsidized by *you,* the poor, hardworking, ramen noodle–eating shmuck.

Rent control sticks with residents—regardless of their income—for as long as they stay put or until they voluntarily move or die. If a landlord wants to remove a tenant from a "rent-controlled" apartment, good luck! New York's attorney general wants to make that a felony.[10]

I know a guy I will call Nick, who has a high-tech job and lives in a Manhattan rent-controlled apartment. Nick moved into his apartment 15 years ago when he was making $20,000 a year. His rent was $500 per month. Today he makes $127,000 a year, but still lives in that same Madison Avenue pad for a mere $750 per month. Meanwhile, people like you and me have to work our tails off to afford flea-infested apartments the size of coffins. Rents in parts of New York and California with rent control are astronomically high. The average monthly rent payment for a New York City apartment is more than $3,000, with the average rent-controlled apartment costing less than half of that.[11] In short, the newly arrived college grad who works two jobs is subsidizing the martini-sipping Upper West Sider who sanctimoniously lectures you about how you should be eating free-range chicken.

GOVERNMENT IN YOUR BEDROOM—
AND ALL YOUR ROOMS!

Another government program, another bureaucracy, another acronym, another mess: Enter the Community Development Block Grant (CDBG) program from HUD. Many states use these federally funded grants to provide affordable housing to poor people. But the House of Representatives' Financial Services Committee found that much of this funding intended to house the poor instead is spent on "public beautification."[12] (Yes, the Financial Services Committee is yet another big bureaucracy designed to analyze another bureaucracy. Hah! Don't you love it?) In 2013, the committee found that almost

$800 million was diverted from low-income housing programs and spent on planting flowers in parks, building elegant fountains, and erecting stylish streetlights. Now understand, no one is against urban beautification—but should hardworking taxpayers be forced to foot this $800 million bill under the guise of "providing housing for the needy"? Gah!

When there's this much money up for grabs, there are bound to be questionable deals. The *Mountain Eagle* newspaper revealed that in rural Schoharie, New York, Steven Aaron—a real estate developer with connections to Governor Andrew Cuomo (who ran HUD during the Clinton administration)—was awarded $11 million in CDBG funding to build affordable housing for flood victims in 2013. Cuomo had received over $280,000 in campaign contributions from firms and corporations connected to Aaron.[13] Four years after receiving the grant, Aaron's housing project is *still* not completed. Meanwhile, numerous contractors who have worked on the buildings claim they haven't been paid yet.

To be fair, the CDBG money won't be paid out until the project is completed.[14] But eventually, millions of taxpayer dollars will be funneled into Aaron's pocket despite his project being several years behind schedule and his connections to Cuomo. Who are the big losers here? Not Cuomo—he received hundreds of thousands of dollars for his campaign. And certainly not Aaron; his company is set to receive millions in grant money. The losers are the flood victims, many of whom remain homeless, and of course you—the taxpayer.

Wasteful spending has become the norm when it comes to HUD-funded projects. The city of Honolulu wasted millions in HUD money from 2012 to 2015. An audit revealed that $16 million was spent on property acquisitions that were unnecessary or violated federal guidelines governing the use of the funding.[15] The Hawaiian bureaucrats knew if they didn't spend the entire HUD budget by the end of the year, the funding would be cut the following year. So they spent all of their government money foolishly and furiously, like drunken sailors. Here's a breakdown of where that $16 million went:

- $10 million to purchase a housing apartment complex—which was more than $4.2 million over the property's assessed value
- $3 million to buy another apartment building without documenting why it was necessary to do so
- $1.6 million to purchase fire trucks. This has nothing to do with housing, but that didn't matter; remember, every cent had to be spent by the end of the fiscal year. So yeah, fire trucks! (Hell, everyone likes fire trucks.)
- $1.45 million for a "questionable contract," despite a conflict of interest

These Honolulu city workers had no problem purchasing buildings at inflated prices. Why should they? It's not their money. The federal government gives them millions of dollars like it's confetti. If the feds won't hold them accountable for good business practices, why should they hold themselves accountable? Had this happened in the private sector, heads would have rolled. But luckily for them, they work for the government and have access to that endless pot of taxpayer money. *Your* money.

In Trenton, New Jersey, city bureaucrat Sam Hutchinson used federal HUD grant money to shamelessly hire his office an administrative assistant.[16] The assistant's $38,479 salary and benefits were being funded through grants meant to provide housing to low-income people. It wasn't until over a year later that the Trenton City Council discovered the misuse of funds. Did Hutchinson get fired? (Hah! You're adorable.) He didn't even get a measly reprimand. He just begrudgingly assigned his assistant to a different cost center. Again, what's the big deal? It ain't his money—it's only *yours*.

There are countless stories like these in government housing bureaucracies throughout the country.

In addition to HUD's waste and fraud problems, the agency has
set up numerous restrictions that create perverse incentives for developers and landlords. Tenants' rights organizations and state laws
often prevent landlords from renovating their apartments. If tenants
can't ever be asked to leave their apartments, it's impossible to re-
hab old buildings. Some building owners are taxed to the hilt *and*
receive below-market rents—so they simply cannot renovate their
buildings.[17]

Successful landlords are rarely stupid people. If you tax them
heavily and force them to keep their rents low, why would they make
improvements to the building? They won't. Which is why you've got
those insane cockroach orgies in your crappy apartment seven nights
a week.

BAD POLICIES COST YOU

In the 1930s, the federal government collected payroll taxes in a very
different way. Instead of deducting taxes from each paycheck, taxpayers had to send in a lump sum once per year. The American people
despised paying taxes, and they dreaded tax day. Imagine having to
pull out your checkbook and write out an enormous check for thousands of dollars to the IRS once each year.

Today, naïve Americans look forward to tax day, grinning ear
to ear like moronic simpletons, waiting gleefully for their "refund
checks" to arrive in the mail. Many people think of their refund as a
midyear bonus. Of course, these dummies fail to realize that they've
just given the government an interest-free loan—their refund is just
their own money that the government withheld from them. A great
economic wake-up call for these taxpayers would be to force them to
write out a check to the IRS once a year for the full tax liability, just

like the good old days. My, my, how quickly we would all come to despise "tax day" again.

Similarly, government policies, housing regulations, and zoning restrictions significantly increase the cost of housing for most Americans. Itemizing these costs, and forcing tenants to pay for them annually in one lump sum, would shatter illusions around state and federal protections.

Overregulation on new construction in New York City adds a staggering $200,000 to the construction costs of the average apartment building.[18] Local and state politicians like to lecture us about how regulations prevent the rich from exploiting the "little guy." Instead, they create a crooked monopoly that allows the government to siphon off of everyone—builders, landlords, renters—like a mighty bloodsucking tick.

Take preservation laws. Most states have some version of a "Historical Preservation Office" (HPO)—California state law regarding historic preservation is 92 pages long! Put on your reading glasses, grab a glass (or bottle) of wine, and cuddle up.

Let's say you're a developer, and you have plans to erect a beautiful apartment building. You've bought the land, paid for the architectural plans, filled out the thousands of pages of regulation paperwork, paid for the construction crew, and now you're ready to break ground. The bulldozer belches out a plume of black smoke and jerks forward, pushing that very first mound of dirt and rocks. Wait—what's that? It looks like a piece of pottery. Uh-oh. You'd better smash it and hide the remains, or else the state HPO will get involved. Maybe it's just a piece of junk from the thrift store next door—but there's a small chance it's from an ancient Indian tribe. The only way to find out is to alert the HPO; they'll create a commission to study that little shard of pottery, bring lots of scientists on-site, and begin a new architectural dig on your land. Oh, and send the construction crew home, because this investigation is likely to take several months. It's probably just a little piece of pottery from next door, but no matter—the sanctimonious investigation is on. And if it *is* from an Indian tribe? Your expensive project has just ended. Yes, you've spent millions preparing for this building, but . . . you know, the Indians . . .

Excessive regulation hurts tenants around the country. In Portland, Oregon, for example, construction regulations have long prevented the building of new apartments. This has created a housing shortage resulting in skyrocketing housing prices. Instead of decreasing red tape to encourage more building, the bureaucrats, in their infinite wisdom, are now pushing for caps on rent prices.[19] Ceilings on rents create the unintended consequences of reducing construction of new apartment housing for those who need it the most. Why would a wealthy builder erect a large apartment building if the city tells him his rents will be capped? It's a vicious cycle created by government bureaucrats, which ends up hurting everyone—the builders who can't construct new housing and the renters who can't find affordable apartments.

The increased costs and man-hours required to meet the tidal wave of regulations go straight into a never-ending and ever-growing bureaucracy. It creates a government slow to act and always gluttonous for its own survival and growth. It's the *freaking Blob*.

Do you really think the bureaucrats in your city care what you pay for rent? Nah. What they ultimately care about are their jobs, their pensions, and their benefits.

The NYC Housing Authority, which I mentioned earlier, is abandoning much of their stated mission in favor of self-preservation mode. While their stated goal is to create affordable housing for the poor, more recently they've been leasing land for high-end condos.[20] If a developer can cough up $25 million up front, the thugs at the Housing Authority will allow developers to demolish city parks and playgrounds to build housing for the *rich*. For all of the talk of "it's for the *chiiiiiildren*" and "it's for the less fortunate," when the bureaucrats' backs are up against the wall, they're willing to kick everyone—rich, poor, builders, landlords, tenants—to the curb to protect their own agencies, jobs, and pensions.

If a housing agency's mission is to lower the price of housing, but instead the agency raises it, should the agency still exist?

FOUR

UTILITIES

HELP! THE TAXES ARE COMING
FROM INSIDE THE HOUSE!

Taxation without representation is tyranny.

—*James Otis Jr.*

Got any hot plans for next weekend? Aw, come on—are you really going to stay in, make paella, and "Netflix and chill" with your main squeeze *all weekend?* That actually sounds fun (I love paella). But don't think you'll avoid the Tax Monster by staying home—the creep already has his long tentacles firmly entrenched throughout your house. Every time you turn on a light, watch TV, use your stove, take out the trash, or use the internet, you are feeding the beast. Insidious utility taxes and fees are constantly draining your savings. They give the feds, as well as state and city governments, a stealthy way to fill their coffers.

Not to throw a wet blanket on your relaxing weekend, but I want to show you something. Go get your most recent electric bill.

Now as you look at your bill, you may think, *What's the big deal? I don't see a million hidden taxes and fees here.* But just because you can't see them, doesn't mean they aren't there. Power companies have become really good at hiding them. Sure, some taxes are itemized on your electric bill—like sales taxes and gross receipts taxes. But there are lots of other hidden taxes that you're paying in addition. In fact, 25% to 30% of your electric bill consists of taxes![1]

WHY ARE WE PAYING OUR ENERGY COMPANY'S PROPERTY TAXES?

Let's say you live in New York City, where the average resident pays more than $85 each month in hidden taxes and fees related to living expenses including electricity, gas, phone, TV, cable, and transportation.[2] Big Apple residents are forced to use the regional monopoly energy company Con Edison for electric, gas, and steam. "Con Ed" is the city's biggest property tax payer in the state of New York. Do you think Con Ed pays its own $1.1 billion annual property tax bill to the state of New York?

Not if they can get us to pay for it instead.

Con Ed and many other utility companies pass their annual property tax charges directly on to their customers.[3] Taxes and surcharges make up 27% of every Con Ed electric bill, and 27.9% of every cooking-gas bill. Here's a breakdown of the levies and surcharges in a typical monthly Con Ed electric bill:[4]

Typical monthly charge: $59.11
- Property taxes: $12.78
- Sales tax: $5.02
- Income tax: 19 cents
- Gross receipts tax: $3.60
- Other business taxes: 3 cents
- Sales and use tax on company purchases: 2 cents
- MTA payroll tax: 22 cents

Total taxes added: $21.86

You're paying around $260 annually in taxes on your electric bill (we haven't even gotten to the other utilities yet). A few hundred bucks per year might not hurt so much if you have a great job, but for lower-income folks, that really stings.

Now I understand that Con Ed is a company, and they have to remain profitable to stay in business. So yes, of course they're going to pass the cost of their taxes on to you. But here's the problem— they're a monopoly. They don't have to compete with other power companies for your business. So when New York politicians decide to raise Con Ed's property taxes, Con Ed management shrugs their shoulders and says, "Okay. It's no big deal." They are just going to pass on the tax hike to you! And there's nothing you can do about it—you can't get your power from anywhere else.

New Yorkers have been complaining about high taxes in Con Ed bills for decades, yet nothing is ever done to lower them. Last year, residents were given the gift of additional fees on their electric bills due to an unlegislated state tax hike.[5] At Governor Andrew Cuomo's order, the New York Public Service Commission (PSC) now requires electric bills to subsidize two new things: money-losing nuclear power plants in upstate New York and "renewable" energy sources (mainly solar). In 2016, the New York legislature set an ambitious goal to have 50% of the state's power come from renewable energy by 2030. But renewable energy is costly and inefficient. Otherwise, every home in America would have solar panels and windmills.

Despite more than a decade of federal and state subsidies, re-newable energy still can't provide enough power to justify the cost. Market and weather conditions make them uncompetitive, even with huge government subsidies (i.e., taxpayer money). The PSC never provided an estimated cost for this oh-so-noble green energy initia-tive, but a study by the Empire Center for Public Policy estimated that just the first five years of taxpayer subsidies will cost $3.4 billion. Ouch. That's a lot of inefficient and expensive "clean energy." But that doesn't matter. When you're a monopoly run by the government, efficiency is a quaint anachronism.

Cuomo says that if he and his bureaucrat buddies can make New York's reliance on renewables reach 50%, New York will become a "leader of the global effort to combat climate change." Yet even if the ambitious goal is met (which it most likely won't be), the reduction in annual emissions will only amount to less than a quarter of 1% of the carbon dioxide annually emitted by China.

Your tax dollars at work, New Yorkers!

You may assume this electricity bill tax scheme only happens in the Empire State, but this is going on all over the country. In San Diego, roughly $60 million is funneled to the city each year via hidden electric and gas taxes.[6] Local governments see utility bills as a great way to collect big tax dollars from you, because everyone pays for and uses utilities. The taxes are often itemized on the bill using misleading or nebulous terms, like "consumption charge," "system benefits charge," or even just "other charges."

I called my electric company to ask what the "system benefit charges" were that I was paying for. I was on the phone with a sweet lady for 10 minutes and I still don't know exactly what these charges are. It has something to do with "energy efficiency programs" of some sort. All I know is that I'm paying for it every month, and it is listed between the equally confusing "stranded cost recovery charge" and the "distribution charge."

And this doesn't just happen in big cities—rural America is getting hit hard, too. Take a look at what's happening in Delaware, where nine towns—Clayton, Dover, Lewes, Middletown, Milford, Newark, New Castle, Seaford, and Smyrna—have municipal-owned electric services; this means that local officials have complete control to set rates at their own discretion, without oversight.[7] These all-powerful bureaucrats charge residents more for electricity than what they pay for it, ensuring a steady stream of revenue into municipal coffers. The additional taxes and fees on local electric bills subsidize 40% of "general fund needs" in Newark and 37% in Middletown—meaning the revenue can be spent on just about anything. That's great if you work for the town of Newark, where many city employees got 7% raises last year. Did you get a 7% wage increase last year?

Here's a breakdown on the average revenue collected from eight of the nine Delaware towns annually:[8]

Town	Monthly residential bill	Electric agency transfers to General Fund
Newark	$153.18	$10,000,000
Seaford	$152.40	$2,730,000
Middletown	$144.00	$8,350,000
Smyrna	$143.00	$2,300,000
Milford	$141.48	$2,500,000
Lewes	$137.99	$570,000
Dover	$127.98	$10,000,000
New Castle	$125.70	$530,000

THE BIGGEST UTILITY TAX SCAMMER IN THE NATION: RICHMOND, VIRGINIA

If you live in Richmond, your utility bills may be the biggest rip-off in the nation. The city rakes in tens of millions every year from bogus utility "tax" charges that show up on residents' water, gas, and electricity bills.

Here's how the scheme works: At their own discretion, and with no oversight, Richmond officials can jack up the cost of city-owned utilities with numerous charges that appear on customers' bills as taxes. These officials argue that similar tax fees are regularly passed down to customers by private utility companies. Of course, they ignore the fact that government entities, like Richmond's municipal utilities, are tax-exempt—so the city of Richmond just *makes up* charges so they can spend more money on any pet project they want. Residents who use the city's utilities are burdened with some of the highest rates in the nation.[9]

You may be semi-comforted to know that the Richmond stunt is not the norm in most other U.S. cities; city-owned utilities almost always offer lower utility bills to citizens than private providers do. A private company usually has to pass along the cost of federal and state taxes to its customers to make a profit—but a tax-exempt government entity does not have to pay taxes like a business.

But if you happen to live in Richmond?

Sorry buddy, your elected cronies love spending your money on their own salaries, benefits, and pet projects. The city of Richmond has an army of well-paid city employees making six-figure salaries with generous benefits. Many of their county managers and school bureaucrats make over a quarter million dollars per year. Marcus Newsome, one of the city's many school superintendents, made nearly $300,000 last year. Wouldn't it be great to be part of a monopoly that can levy taxes to pay for your big raise every year? It adds new meaning to the name RICHmond.

Richmond officials have been sticking customers with these charges for more than 60 years. Technically, these arbitrary taxes are allowed under rules that were added to city law via Richmond's charter by their city council back in the 1950s. In true form, government officials wrote the rule in typical legal gibberish to confuse citizens, so they don't understand how they're being screwed. Section 13.06 of the city law reads, ". . . taxes not actually accruing but which would have accrued had the utility not been municipally owned shall be paid annually into the general fund." The term "not actually accruing" is a way of saying that the taxes aren't actually owed; but Richmond officials simply decided to add the tax anyway, to collect more revenue for the general fund.

These utility charges are an enormous burden to taxpayers. In 2017 alone, Richmond's public utility taxes raked in $28 million for the city!

Richmond's law requires revenue from all city-owned utilities be put into the city's general fund. Not surprisingly, Richmond boasts having the most expensive per capita city bureaucracy in the state. The corruption in Richmond has become flagrant; the city's gross incompetence and penchant for quid pro quo deals for political cronies have earned Richmond the label "cesspool of corruption." And that nickname was bestowed by a former mayor. Nice.

Back when the city's tax scheme was enacted, few of its citizens could afford to own property or a business, both of which would be subject to city taxes. So when Richmond bureaucrats wanted to raise taxes, they realized taxing water and gas would be an easy way to rake in tons of dough for the city coffers.

So Richmond adopted the law, and WAH-LAH! The poor people of Richmond are still getting screwed by the Tax Monster 60 years later.

HERE'S THE KICKER: MANY UTILITY COMPANIES PAY NO FEDERAL TAXES

So now you know your electric and gas companies are ripping you off with hidden taxes that increase your bill by 25 to 30%. Adding insult to injury is the fact that your utility company may be paying *no federal taxes* themselves. Of the 30 biggest U.S. companies that pay no taxes, 12 of them are major energy companies![10]

And trust me, it's not because these companies are losing money. On the contrary—these are very profitable companies for their shareholders. Take a look at the following chart of these corporations, along with their 2008–2010 profits, and the amounts the government gave them in tax subsidies (in millions):

Utility	08–10 Profit	08–10 Tax Subsidy	08–10 Rate
Pepco Holdings	$882	$−508	−57.6%
PG&E Corp.	$4,855	$−1,027	−21.2%
CenterPoint Energy	$1,931	$−284	−14.7%
Atmos Energy	$897	$−104	−11.6%
Integrys Energy Group	$818	$−92	−11.3%
AEP	$5,899	$−545	−9.2%
Wisconsin Energy	$1,725	$−85	−4.9%
Duke Energy	$5,475	$−216	−3.9%
Consolidated Edison	$4,263	$−127	−3.0%
CMS Energy	$1,292	$−29	−2.2%
NextEra Energy	$6,403	$−139	−2.2%
DTE Energy	$2,551	$−17	−0.7%

Many utility companies pay no income taxes. How is this possible? The 12 utilities listed above received $3.17 billion in government tax rebates (or "negative taxes"). Between 2008 and 2010, the utility industry as a whole paid a measly 3.7% corporate income tax rate.

Utility companies take advantage of an array of tax loopholes and strategies that let them avoid paying what they owe. The most lucrative loophole is "accelerated depreciation," which allows companies to deduct the cost of equipment from their taxes at a rate faster than those investments depreciate in value. These companies additionally deduct performance-based pay—including stock options—from their federal income taxes. This means that bonuses to executives, who already make exorbitant salaries, turn into government subsidies. So if a CEO makes a $5 million bonus, or is awarded millions more as stock, the company writes it off.

By the way, the CEO of Pepco Holdings made $4.9 million in 2015.[11] The CEO of PG&E took home $11.6 million that same year.[12] (Heck, maybe they earned this money; they were smart enough to find genius bookkeepers to get them all those billions in government money.)

Gas and electric utilities enjoyed one of the highest rates of tax subsidies from 2008 to 2010, with an industry-wide tax subsidy bill of $31.2 billion![13] In 2015, 23 utility companies paid no federal taxes and received $11.5 billion in tax benefits from depreciation.[14] So we're essentially getting taxed twice on energy: once when we pay our monthly utility bills and again when our income taxes fund utility company subsidies. While we keep paying higher and higher taxes on our bills, the CEOs of these utility companies are raking in millions and their companies are getting 100% tax breaks from Uncle Sam.

Utility companies have powerful lobbyists for them. The same companies that we are subsidizing pay K-Street lobbyists millions to keep the government subsidies coming. You can go to the website OpenSecrets.org to see how much these utility companies spend on lobbyists. In 2016 electric utility companies spent $120 million on lobbyists. That same year, Southern Company alone shelled out over $13 million on lobbying. It must be worth it; they've been paying their lobbyists these big bucks for decades.

So shut up and pay that bill from the electric company. Along with their property taxes. And that CEO's salary. And those lobbyists' salaries. Or they'll unplug you and leave you in the dark!

THE TAX MONSTER IS A DUMPSTER DIVER TOO? PEE-YEW!

The Tax Monster feasts on your trash, too. You're getting stuck with all kinds of taxes when you pay your trash bill.

Let's check in with our old frenemy, California, to get a closer look at how the hidden trash tax racket works. In 2013, the Southern California city Anaheim awarded an exclusive trash collection contract to a company called Republic Services for $35 million annually. Interestingly, before being awarded this contract, Republic

Services offered the city of Anaheim a "franchise fee" of $2.5 million and agreed to "pay back" the city $1.25 million every year going forward. What a bizarre agreement! What are these payments anyway? Anaheim city officials like to call them "host fees."[15] I prefer to call them downpayments on a monopoly.

Many cities grant "exclusive franchise rights" to only one trash hauler. In exchange for the sole right to collect garbage within its boundaries, a city gets an additional piece of the pie by demanding more money from the trash haulers. Most municipalities ask for 5 to 10% of a hauler's gross or net receipts as a franchise fee, but it can be a lot more than that. Take Anaheim's neighbor, Santa Ana—it gets 18% of the hauler's annual revenue in an annual kickback![16] Dozens of other California cities like Orange, Tustin, Huntington Beach, Irvine, Laguna Beach, and Westminster have also gotten in on the action, awarding exclusive garbage collection contracts in exchange for franchise fees.

Now you may be asking: *What are trash haulers hoping to get out of paying these franchise fees?* They aren't doing it for their health; they are doing it to keep their exclusive contracts with these cities.

And do you think the garbage companies are the ones paying the franchise fees themselves? Of course not—you are! Once a company locks down an exclusive contract, it can ratchet up what you pay for garbage collection since it no longer has to compete with other trash companies; you're stuck with them, regardless of what they charge. Then the exclusive trash hauler makes more money *and* covers the franchise fee costs.

Instead of having these waste companies kick back this money every year, why doesn't the city just reduce the contract price by that amount each year? *Because these government bureaucrats love that extra cash, and they have no intention of returning it back to you!* They want more of your money, but they're not honest enough to pick your pocket themselves. They'd rather hire these garbage collection companies to levy the tax for them. It's truly like the 1970s mob families have taken over the local governments.

Exclusive trash contracts awarded by city governments in California have generated $285.7 million for trash haulers in 2013. Those haulers in turn paid back more than $29.2 million to cities in franchise fees and other kickbacks.[17] Which means the bureaucrats and politicians are bringing 10% of the annual revenue back to city coffers (which pays for their salaries and generous benefits).

Thankfully, not all of us live in California. The good news is that some American cities actually require that all garbage licensing fees must be paid by the haulers—and not by residents or businesses who pay their trash bills. Yippee? Well maybe not so much. There are many other cities that "don't play that." Most of these cities just make their residents and businesses pay for the rising cost of trash collection (in the form of hidden franchise fee taxes).

One way or the other, these greedy and clever bureaucrats are going to find a way to get as much of your money as possible, while blaming someone else. It's enough to make *The Simpsons'* beloved (but evil) Charles Montgomery Burns blush.

FIVE

CABLE

WHAT *GAME OF THRONES* REALLY COSTS YOU

> The only difference between a tax man and a
> taxidermist is that the taxidermist leaves the skin.
>
> —*Mark Twain*

Now that I've completely bummed you out, who wants to go over our cable bills to see who else is screwing us?! Sounds like fun, right?

If you actually sit down and examine your cable bill, you'll find a baffling list of hidden taxes, fees, and surcharges, all created to feed the Tax Monster's insatiable appetite. Here's my latest monthly Comcast cable bill . . .

Taxes, Surcharges, and Fees (6):
- State and local sales tax: $15.64
- PEG fees: $1.34
- FCC regulatory fees: 19 cents
- Franchise fees: $6.49
- 911 Equalization fees: 6 cents
- 911 Fee(s): 50 cents

Total Taxes: $24.12

My total bill is $230, which means that the $24.12 in taxes make up more than 10% of what I'm paying.

Where does that 10% go?

Certainly not toward better service. Several federal, state, and local telecommunications taxes inflate the cost of your multimedia experience. Technology and innovation drive down prices each year, but municipalities' loyalties to bloated bureaucracies keep driving them back up.

In New York City, the number of cable and landline taxes are astonishing—beyond the sales taxes on my bills, I'm also charged a State Gross Receipts Tax, School District Taxes, a State Excise Tax, an MTA tax, a NYC Excise Tax, Franchise Fees, a City Gross Receipts Tax, and more . . . We can see some of the charges and how they affect your recent *Game of Thrones* binge by looking at my bill and several other common charges.

THE FCC: FRAUDULENT, CROOKED, CRIMINALS

The Federal Communications Commission (FCC) levies a 17.9% tax on cable and telecom companies' interstate and international activities. Of course, this tax is then passed down to consumers.[1]

On my Comcast bill, the cost of complying with a myriad of regulations is listed as "FCC Regulatory Fee," but some bills don't itemize FCC taxes whatsoever. The collected revenue goes to the FCC's Universal Service Fund (USF—yay, another bureaucracy and another acronym!), and is then redistributed to companies in order to provide cable and phone service to people who cannot afford standard rates— the UFC disburses about $8 billion a year. Between 2000 and 2014 the FCC's tax rate on cable companies nearly tripled . . . but the revenue less than doubled. This is because changes to wireless tech and companies' bundling services to avoid taxes resulted in the sharp decline in contributions. The solution? Keep hiking the tax rate! This means that shmucks like you and me have to keep shelling out higher taxes every year to provide free service to more poor people every year.

Forty-four states have their own USF as well. The total costs of these state programs increased to nearly $1.5 billion by 2014. Both the state and federal fees are passed right along into your bill.

The USF claims a number of oh-so-saintly duties, like subsidizing low-income Americans' access to the internet. But (shocker) it is one of the most waste-filled and fraudulent programs in the federal government! (That's a remarkable accomplishment all its own.) In 2010, for example, the FCC became aware that $6.5 million was fraudulently obtained by one telecommunications company owner, Albert Hee . . . yet the agency did nothing about this blatant fraud until four years later. During those four years of inaction, more than $100 million in taxpayer dollars meant to help poor people obtain cable service were funneled into Hee's own pocket. Using these taxpayer funds, Hee treated himself to a life of luxury including $90,000 in massages and $17,000 to stay at a lavish Hawaiian hotel.[2]

Other regulatory fees cover the FCC's massive $388 million annual budget . . . and when the agency isn't regulating what you can hear on the radio or television, it finds other ways to waste your money. In 2009, the FCC spent $350,000 sponsoring NASCAR driver David Gilliland to promote digital television.[3] Do we really need to spend more than a third of a million dollars to stamp an FCC policy objective on a racecar? Perhaps not surprisingly, Gilliland's race car got into an accident at the O'Reilly Auto Parts 500 in Phoenix in 2008—and lit on fire.

A major effort to connect Atlanta schools to high-speed internet in 2013 instead wasted millions: Ajit Pai, the current FCC chair, said the major push resulted in $2 million wasted on brand-new smart phones for school administrators.[4] Meanwhile, 75% of students at the school had less than one hour of internet access a day. Your tax dollars at work, folks!

CITY BUREAUCRATS WANT YOUR MONEY, TOO!

We've talked about the feds' misadventures in basic cable. But what about some of the other more local taxes? Sales and "communications" taxes are often the largest share of direct taxes on your bill, which include state, county, and local taxes. In New York City the rate is 8.875% and some parts of Long Island pay up to 11.625%! That's a hefty chunk of your cable bill. A Public, Educational, and Government (or PEG) Capital Fee is sent to localities to fund public access television programs, often through a 1% levy. Did you ever see those Public Access shows where gay porn scenes were mixed with half-naked guys "discussing important topics"? Or how about the ones that featured a man's face, shot upside-down, with facial features scribbled on his chin and a wig around his neck? Yeah, that was on Public Access television.[5] And if you live in New York, you paid for it.

A "regulatory recovery fee" is a nebulous term that Time Warner uses to pass on assorted and indirect "federal regulatory" costs. This can vary per bill and location. Companies also have a separate, additional line for "state regulations." Because, you know, we can never have too many regulations . . .

A closer inspection of your bill will reveal even more doozies. Most municipalities charge a Franchise Fee that cable companies pass right back to you. New York City's is 5%. This Franchise Fee has been around since the Cable Communications Act of 1984. States, counties, and cities claim it's not a tax itself and it's used for the privilege of using public right of ways . . . but many municipalities also levy a separate right of way tax. Companies have to pay for the privilege of traveling over public property and putting cable and phone lines near already existing infrastructure. Efficiency is not the goal here. Nor is honesty. This revenue goes straight into the city's general fund, so those bureaucrats can spend it on whatever they want. Like on their own salaries.

Next up on my Comcast bill: 911 fees. Who would be against funding 911 emergency services? Turns out that such efforts are less virtuous than originally designed. An "Enhanced 911 fee" pays for emergency communication needs in all 50 states. Like most government plans, the fee seems innocent enough: States raise money for the tech needed to track cell phones and other devices in emergencies. The FCC mandated a national version in 1999 and states followed suit with their own funds and taxes. After years of collecting the Enhanced 911 fees, most of the upgrades making this tracking possible around the nation are complete. We all know that adding new taxes is easy, but old taxes never die. State governments like the reliable, seemingly noncontroversial revenue stream. So . . . they simply keep the 911 fees in place.

Every state levies such an imposition. Wisconsin just renamed their 911 fee the "Police and Fire Protection Fee." You don't hate firemen, do you? Of course not. So pull out your wallet! But actually, none of that money directly goes to fire or police protection. Instead, it goes straight into the state's general fund.[6] The rates differ by state; Missouri wins the prize for highest rate at 15%.

Some places also have "E-911 Equalization Fees," which fund access to emergency services for parts of the state or region that don't have funds for such services—often rural areas. If you live in the city, you're paying for service out in the sticks. Okay, maybe that's fair. But don't obfuscate what it is. Call it the "911 Subsidy for Rural Areas Tax."

As if my Comcast bill didn't list enough taxes . . . it still doesn't tell the whole story. Consumers in some locations face even more taxes! Illinois residents pay a number of "supplemental telecom taxes." Chicago is considering a 28% (!) increase of its monthly per-phone line surtax to pay for bloated union pensions.[7] You know . . . because it's not fair to make union employees work past the age of 50.

Smaller Illinois cities have expressed regret and surprise that increasing their telecom taxes has resulted in lower long-term revenues.

They're learning the basic principle of Economics 101—if you keep raising taxes on something, people will buy/use less of it. (This is why states keep raising cigarette taxes—to try to reduce cigarette consumption.) In this case, Illinois residents got fed up with paying these ever-higher telecom taxes and just dropped their cable service altogether.

These taxes take a bite out of your discretionary income. Perhaps the most offensive part of this whole thing is that the government, at every level, thinks you're too dumb to realize the taxes and fees are there. It certainly plays a role in an industry losing over 900,000 subscribers per quarter.[8]

Hidden taxes have been in our cable bills for decades. Congress's 1984 Cable Communications Policy Act allowed local governments to levy franchise taxes and the 1992 Cable Act allowed tighter regulation of the industry.[9] In 1991 the Supreme Court determined 7–2 that states and cities could also impose taxes on satellite and cable service, following an Arkansas law extending sales tax to cable. (You'll never guess who was governor of Arkansas at that time.) Over time, governments at each level realized just how much money could be squeezed through Americans' love of the ol' boob tube. In addition, the maze of regulations and the costs of complying with them crushed many small startup telecom companies' abilities to take on the big guys. After all, the small companies don't have the same lobbying budgets that the big players have.

Your bill shows the results.

A TINY RAY OF HOPE?

Is there any hope that cable taxes will ever go down? There has been modest success in some states. In 2015, Florida cut its cell and satellite taxes from a staggeringly high 22.38% to 21.12%.[10] (Yes, it's still staggeringly high.) The state's tax cut saved the average consumer about 20 bucks a year. Hey, I'll take a couple of burgers over paying more of these offensive taxes.

The FCC's oversight of the telecom industry often does more harm than good, by stifling growth of new companies and preventing competition with the big players. Remember AT&T's (American Telephone & Telegraph) monopoly until the early 1980s? USF disbursements act as subsidies to the big companies while smaller competition gets crushed. Local regulations make construction and breaking into the market even harder. On top of all that, states allow local service monopolies.[11] Allowing a single business to be an effective regional monopoly is one of the main reasons cable companies can get away with murder. Many places, especially rural areas, face a dearth of consumer options. (Why do I have to pay $15 a month for all these crappy channels like MSNBC and BET, when all I wanted was Fox News?)

The FCC's arcane rules stifle competition. The FCC is often staffed with former telecom bigwigs. There's little room for new competition when the agency is controlled by the companies it regulates. The list of industry chiefs in charge of the agency is long and growing. The last FCC Chair, Tom Wheeler, is a former industry lobbyist and former head of the Cellular Telecommunications Industry Association, or CTIA. The new Broadband Deployment Advisory Committee is similarly staffed—16 of the 30 members work for the big guys.[12] One former FCC Commissioner, Meredith Baker, went from the agency to vice president of NBC Universal (owned by Comcast) then to CEO of CTIA. Acronyms aside, the incestuous relationship between the industry and its overseers ends in predictable results. And higher bills for you.

When the revolving door isn't turning, the FCC is making bank. One of the FCC's major roles is to regulate radio, TV, and wireless transmissions. The method of controlling broadcast wavelengths is . . . *surprise!* . . . a cash cow. The FCC controls and auctions off different waves and bands to big companies for billions of dollars. In one rare case where the agency decided *not* to artificially constrain invisible radio signals . . . the technology development exploded. So much so that by 2017 Microsoft started using these signals for widespread broadband access in rural areas.[13] Where the FCC didn't interfere, the free market innovated and worked! No auction fees went to the Treasury and the resulting product is now likely to be far cheaper than any subsidized version. The FCC is like that nosy, overbearing mother who just doesn't believe that you don't need her help.

Cut the apron strings, America!

SIX

DEBAUCHERY

TOO FADED TO NOTICE YOU'RE GETTING SCREWED?

> They can't collect legal taxes from illegal money.
>
> —*Al Capone*

Are you a *sinner?*

Do you do *bad things?*

If you haven't browsed your hometown's tax code lately (and I'm sure none of you have, because they are boring as hell), you may be shocked to learn what falls into the category of "sin" these days—not in the eyes of a wrathful God, mind you, but in the eyes of your local punitive government.

In 2017, thousands of upstanding citizens were being cast as sinners by the government, forced to pay *sin taxes* to engage in totally legal activities, which (if you ask me) is a stunning twist in our so-called free democratic culture.

Before the 21st century—for hundreds of years in the eyes of the U.S. legal system, and for thousands of years in the eyes of the "dude upstairs" (if you believe in that sort of thing)—the term "sinning" was a big, scary verb that wrought terror in the hearts of mortals. When someone called you a sinner back in the 20th century, it usually meant you just got busted doing something that was "R-rated movie" bad, things like coveting thy neighbor's spouse, lying to the police, cheating on your taxes, or mowing down innocent civilians on a tri-state killing spree. Now that's what I call some real Old Testament–style sinning.

But that's not how we define it anymore.

Today, the concept of sin has been downgraded to preschool level— from felony to misdemeanor, from R-rated horror show to G-rated Willy Wonka kiddie show. Are you breathing a little easier? I wasn't asking you to confess to being a real bona fide sinner back there—that would be the old *Natural Born Killers* way of looking at sin. No, for this exercise, I want you to take the concept of sin down several notches in your mind and think about it the way many progressives do today, on a much broader scale—kind of like how children view "being bad."

Remember when everything fun was considered bad? That's the mind-set you need to get into if you want to understand why we're being treated like a nation of sinful children by the Nanny State, in which the government has become our Mommy AND Daddy.

NESTLE CRUNCH BARS: THE NEW GATEWAY DRUG

Let's use my cute five-year-old cousin Aiden as an example. Last week, I caught little Aiden sinning. Oh, it was bad. He was sneakily wolfing down a giant soda and *family-sized* Nestle Crunch bar at the movies. When I saw evidence of little Aiden's "sinning ways" I asked him if he had eaten the candy bar we were all supposed to share, and he shook his head, "no." Unconvinced, I played judge, jury, and executioner.

I said, "Oh yeah? Let me smell your breath . . ."

All I had to do was raise an eyebrow, and Aiden started singing like a canary. He opened his mouth and out spewed the evidence in the form of a stream of half-eaten candy bar, all over my new jeans.

Aiden exploded in tears, which ruined the ending of *Guardians of the Galaxy Vol. 2* for everyone around us. Afternoon semi-ruined. New jeans definitely ruined.

One of the Nanny State's biggest targets is little Aiden's burgeoning soda and candy bar addiction. In the eyes of do-gooder bureaucrats, Aiden needs help. After all, he did eat a candy bar, not only that, a family-sized candy bar, all by himself, and washed it down with a large Mr. Pibb. Aiden must be on the road to becoming a future diabetic, drug addict, or even maybe a serial killer.

Someone *must pay for this.*

In cities like San Francisco, Philadelphia, Berkeley, Boulder, or Oakland—someone must literally pay for this. According to the laws of those cities, Aiden is a sinner who must pay a fee for doing something as innocent as eating a candy bar or drinking a sugary beverage. *How dare we . . . do things that are completely legal?* Wait. What?

Don't we have better things to do at city council meetings? When did local governments lose their minds and start trolling for some toddler coin?

The answers to those two questions, in order, are *no* and *just a few years ago,* when certain progressive pockets of our country took it upon themselves to take sin taxes to a whole new level of absurd. They didn't stop with the usual sin tax suspects like alcohol, cigarettes, and gambling. No, they had the balls to tax the other "white stuff" we all love to inhale—sugar—and started enacting laws against sweetened products of all kinds to save us from ourselves.

You can thank the city of Berkeley, California, for conceiving this one. Of course, San Francisco's tripped-out next-door neighbor was the first city in the United States to pass a targeted tax on soda. As of January 2015, the distributors of soda, sports drinks, energy drinks, and sweetened iced teas have been forced to pay a 1% *per ounce* tax in Berkeley. Meaning a 16-ounce soda bottle would get taxed at 16%. In case you were wondering: No, the funds collected don't go to fighting obesity, educating children about healthy eating, or subsidizing gym memberships for fat people. The money goes right into the general fund of the city of Berkeley.

And how, exactly, does the city spend this money? According to Berkeley's 2016 budget, "employee salary and budgets make up 74% of the City's General Fund."[1] Simply put: The sugar tax is being used to pay the salaries of overpaid government workers; I say "overpaid," because on average public employees in California make TWICE as much as private sector workers.[2] They also get cushy benefits often not enjoyed in the private sector: 14 paid holidays, 12 "personal days," and 20 or more vacation days as they acquire seniority.

Ultimately, 47% of Berkeley's soda tax was passed through to higher sweetened beverage prices and 69% was passed through to higher soda prices. Given that poor people drink more soda than other segments of the population,[3] it's an unfair burden on them. The Tax Foundation found that a 10% soda tax could burden high income families by $24.29, while poor families would be harmed nearly twice that amount at $47.38.[4]

A few years after Berkeley instated its soda tax, something unexpected happened . . . The straight-arrow, Benjamin Franklin–loving patriot of a city, Philadelphia, followed Berkeley's lead and enacted a sugary drink tax of its own. Philly passed a 1.5 cent per ounce tax on soda and other sweetened and diet beverages, effective January 2017; the tax increases the cost of a 16-ounce bottle of Coke by 24 cents. It didn't take long for soda and other sweetened beverages to skyrocket in price—cheaper store brand soda shot up in price nearly 100% in many cases.[5] Sports drinks like Propel got hit hard, too. With the new tax added, a 12-pack of Propel ends up costing more than a 12-pack of cheap beer.[6]

As consumers feel the burn, Philadelphia's local economy has also already taken a hit. Soon after the ban was put in place, PepsiCo saw a 43% drop in sales and announced it would be laying off 100

Philly-area employees (out of 423) as a result. Canada Dry, also seeing a dip in sales, fired at least 25 workers. And it's not just big beverage companies feeling the pinch—it's local retailers, too. The owner of Brown's Super Stores said he plans to lay off at least 300 workers at his company's Philly locations as a direct result of the tax.[7]

Businesses affected by the tax also get stuck dealing with more paperwork. Retailers have been instructed to keep all of their bills, invoices, and records to prove compliance with the new rules. As I write this, the city is in the process of hiring extra tax collectors to make sure that everything is paid up. "The Soda Police," as I like to call them.

The tax is costing jobs, raising prices, and hurting local business . . . But it's not even bringing in the stable source of revenue that the city claimed it would. During April 2017, the city brought in $6.5 million in revenue from the four-month-old tax.[8] That marked a 7% drop-off from March and is more than $1 million less than officials had anticipated. Despite the downward trend, city officials (who seem to be the only ones happy about the tax) say the funds are badly needed. The mayor has promised to spend about half of the funds on expanded pre-K. Sounds like a noble effort at first, but spending tens of millions of dollars to expand pre-K in a city where public schools are already failing to educate children (even according to the most optimistic reports[9]) probably isn't the smartest idea. The other half of the tax revenue will be spent on other things, including city parks and benefits for city employees. By the third year the soda tax is in place, 30% of its revenue will go toward the city general fund—meaning it can be spent on just about anything.

But here's another question worth pondering: Did Philly's soda tax actually have the intended health effect? Are residents drinking less soda, and as a result, less likely to be obese? Proponents of the tax will point to declining soda sales in Philadelphia-based grocery stores and claim that it's been a big success. But consumers who purchase less soda are likely to do so in favor of other high-calorie drinks. Cornell University released a study indicating that many soda drinkers end up switching to beer.[10] Another study found that even if a 58-cent soda tax were imposed (which is roughly equal to the state and federal cigarette taxes, combined), it would only decrease the average U.S. Body Mass Index by 0.16 points.[11] That's equal to less than a pound for a six-foot-tall person. These findings make sense, since soda only makes up about 7% of total calories consumed;[12] taxing such a small percentage of calories isn't enough to have a significant impact on our nation's obesity epidemic.

There's also evidence that Philadelphia's tax has resulted in people simply going outside city limits—where the tax isn't in place—to get their soda fix. Philly is a relatively car-friendly city so it's not difficult for many residents to hop in their vehicle and drive 10 minutes to a grocery store outside city limits. There, they can load up their cars with multiple liters of Dr Pepper, drive on home with it, and they'll probably drink more than they would have otherwise since they have tons of soda sitting in their houses. So far, the data seems to suggest that at least some people are doing this: Just one month after the tax was installed, there was a 20% uptick in suburban soda sales.[13]

Even though there's no proof (at least not yet) that Philly's soda tax is working, the sweetest taboo is becoming a nationwide trend that seemingly no one wanted in the first place.

Boulder, Colorado, three new Bay Area cities (San Francisco, Oakland, and Albany), as well as all of Cook County, Illinois, have all passed taxes on sugar-sweetened beverages.[14] Several other cities, like Baltimore, are poised to do the same. These communities joined other sweet-drink-hating countries like Mexico, France, Hungary, Ireland, and the United Kingdom, who all have sugary beverage taxes on the books. Why the global hate for sugar?

Did Satan come down and curse our sugar bowls with his vengeful claw?

IT'S NOT SATAN'S FAULT,
IT'S MICHAEL BLOOMBERG'S

It's not the Devil's fault. You can actually send your Thank-You letters to "Nanny State warriors" like Michael Bloomberg (the former mayor of New York City). Bloomberg is famous for running New York City more like a day care than the fifth largest city in the world. In 2014, a New York Court of Appeals shot down his proposed ban on the sale of sodas and other sugary drinks over 16 ounces. But during his 12 years as mayor, Bloomberg was able to ram through plenty of other regulations and bans, in the name of saving us all from ourselves. Many of these rules increased burdensome costs and administrative work for local businesses; if you've been paying any attention, you know that these costs are often passed down to the consumer. Here are just a few of Nanny Bloomberg's bans: No trans fats in restaurants (2006); No non-fuel efficient carbs (2007); No chain restaurant menus without calorie counts (2008); No Styrofoam packaging in single-service food items (2013).

Since leaving office, Bloomberg has tried to shove pacifiers in the mouths of citizens *around the nation.* In 2016, he spent $18 million pushing soda tax measures in Oakland and San Francisco.[15] Following heavily funded campaigns in favor of the tax, the ballot measures ultimately passed in both cities. Thankfully citizens in Santa Fe, New Mexico, were smart enough to vote down Bloomberg's attempt to impose a Draconian soda tax law on their city. Bloomberg had injected nearly $1 million into the effort to get Santa Fe to pass what would have been one of the most expensive sin taxes on soda in the country, coming in at *2 cents per ounce,* which would nearly double the price of a two-liter bottle of soda.[16]

I'm sure New York billionaires don't know or care what food costs, but to regular folks, you can't just double the price of something people love without getting some consumer blowback.

Now, you may be wondering: If the Santa Fe sugary beverage tax had managed to pass, where would the tax revenue have actually gone? Santa Fe voters were told the city would use it to pay for pre-K schooling, which sounds great, but we've heard these promises before from other cities like Oakland, which is already backing out on its promise to use its sin tax revenue to fight the Big Soda Lobby.[17] Oakland had a shortfall in their 2017 city budget, so guess what? Forget helping fat kids cure their sugar addiction—its raiding the soda tax coffer to cover its ass in other areas. The mayor is now saying that the soda tax money will be spent on budget items including libraries, fixing potholes, and subsidized housing (basically, normal day-to-day business of any city's operations). The money is routed through the general fund so that the city can spend it however it chooses. And that's exactly what it's doing.

What happened to the altruistic integrity of local politicians?

I'll let you ponder that one while I point out what Nanny-State warriors like Bloomberg don't seem to get: (a) Sin taxes rarely work, (b) they always hurt the poorest consumers the most, and, (c) the money these taxes generate never goes toward saving citizens from their own vices. Politicians use them as a way to con voters into giving up more money—and then, like magic, the money mysteriously disappears into the local government's "general funds" coffer to be squandered away.

So, why are sin taxes still so popular, again? Did our entire nation all watch *The Handmaid's Tale* and lose our ever-loving minds?

AMERICANS: FAT, DRUNK, AND STUPID
FROM THE BEGINNING

No, sorry—it's not Hollywood's fault *this time*.

This new wave of "legal behavior policing" was going on long before *The Handmaid's Tale* came into public consciousness. Taxes on tobacco and alcohol date back to the Revolutionary War. British sugar taxes like the "Sugar Act" of 1764 helped start the American Revolution by raising the price of our favorite import, while also disrupting our other favorite pastime, drinking rum like pirates. Alcohol was so hard to come by in the colonies in 1764, it almost became its own currency.[18]

So when you think about it—our forefathers built this country just so we could guzzle rum and eat raw sugar by the mouthful. That may be a slight generalization, but it's clear that we crazy Americans have been out-of-control drunken sugar fiends since the beginning.

But even after we "fought for our right to party" like the Beastie Boys always said we should, and became our own nation . . . sin taxes remained part of American policy. In 1790, Alexander Hamilton proposed a tax on whiskey to refund debts from the Revolutionary War.[19] The whiskey tax was eventually rescinded after it spawned a rebellion, but just four years later Hamilton introduced another excise (this guy was basically the Bloomberg of the 18th century)—this time on tobacco products. Even though Hamilton's tobacco tax failed, because it had an insignificant impact on the federal budget, it wasn't long before another tobacco tax was put in place.

President Abe Lincoln signed the Revenue Act of 1862, which levied taxes on many sin items including liquor, tobacco, playing cards, gunpowder, feathers, pianos, yachts, carriages, billiard tables, and jewelry. The act was supposed to help fund the Civil War, but by 1863, tax evasion and organized crime had become so widespread that Congress authorized the hiring of detectives to investigate alcohol tax evaders. This marked the first coordinated effort between tax collection and law enforcement.

Today, alcohol is still taxed like crazy, but only on the state level.[20] Tobacco, on the other hand, continues to be federally taxed to this day ($1.01 per 20-pack of cigarettes). Of course, states are eager to get in on cigarette taxes, too, because they're an easy way to rake in revenue while simultaneously beating the "healthy living" drum. Cigarettes are taxed the highest in New York (why am I not surprised?), at $4.35 per pack. Even my home state of New Hampshire, the "Live Free or Die State" that prides itself on having no sales tax, levies a $1.78 per pack cigarette tax. On average, sin taxes make up about 55% of the price of a cigarette pack.[21]

Meanwhile, there's little evidence that these taxes are actually effective at reducing smoking. The highest-in-the-nation cigarette tax in New York has failed to drive down smoking rates[22]—instead, the higher costs only unfairly punish the poor.

It also appears that newly legal marijuana industries in states like Colorado and Washington will also be subject to sin taxes—which leads me back to the modern sin tax revolution going on today. Is it really just a continuation of the "Sugar Act" of 1764? All you have to do is replace smug British oppressors who thought we were a nation of drunks with smug elected officials who think we're a nation of irresponsible pigs—and you can see the correlation.

And then there's gambling. What happens when you want to throw away your money—I mean, actually and actively lose it at a casino? Government at every level would like a word with you. Beyond the hundreds of pages of regulations on the industry, gambling taxes are some of the heaviest sin taxes in the civilized world.

Of course, the way that the IRS does it is convoluted and time-consuming. Click your pen, print out a Form W-2G, and look at the varying levels of taxes.[23] You'll be taxed on winnings of $1,200 and above for bingo and slot machines, $1,500 and up for a keno game, $5,000 and higher for poker, and $600 or more on a horse race (if the win pays at least 300 times the wager amount). Confused yet?

So if you win, you get taxed. But what if you don't play at all? You still wind up playing. Gambling losses are tax deductible, meaning that the rest of us game-of-chance impaired have to foot the bill.

Altogether, no matter what you do—win, lose, or don't play at all—you always lose.

Does this ring a bell with anyone other than me? Are we trapped in a never-ending circle of righteous lawmakers that dates back to the Revolutionary War?

And if so, who the hell is going to do anything about it?

The Beastie Boys?

WTF IS ILLINOIS DOING?
NOT EVEN KEEBLER ELVES KNOW

Maybe you think I'm exaggerating, and my little candy bar–loving cousin Aiden has nothing to worry about. I'm not. All you need to do is Google "crazy sin taxes" to read about the shenanigans local governmental politics have been pulling lately, which (to my nose) all have a stench slightly reminiscent of the "Sugar Act" of 1764. Look around and see for yourself how behavior policing is morphing into dozens of ridiculous tariff monsters, right before our eyes.

Take what happened in 2009, when the state of Illinois decided to tax candy at a rate five times higher than other food.[24] But what is candy, exactly? Can you define it? Can anyone?

Apparently not! The state of Illinois ordained that *if anything had flour in it, or required refrigeration, it was not considered candy.* This brilliant deduction was, of course, confusing to pretty much everyone. Illinois classified yogurt-covered raisins as candy, but yogurt-covered pretzels as food. Baby Ruth bars were considered candy, while Twix bars were considered food. Milky Way Midnight bars were considered candy, but original Milky Way bars were considered food.

What in the name of a flaming Wonka bar is going on here?

The answer is simple: It's the work of the misguided Nanny State, like Fran Drescher on Adderall.

THE WACKED-OUT THINKING BEHIND THE "CRACK TAX"

The sinful examples I've given you so far are one level of absurd—but sometimes our elected officials lose their minds completely and start dreaming up sin taxes that may sound good in some Utopian dreamscape, but are impossible to enforce—like in 2005 when the state of Tennessee tried to institute a sin tax on illegal drugs. They called it the "crack tax."[25] It applied to illegal substances of all kinds, including cocaine, marijuana, crack, and even moonshine.

This whole crack tax idea sounds great in a perfect world—but exactly how do they plan on enforcing it? Oh, yeah, *that*.

Here is the really insane part: Drug dealers were required to voluntarily pay the "crack tax" *anonymously* at the state revenue office, where they would receive a stamp to prove their payment but would *not* be arrested for being a drug dealer. Hmm, that sounds an awful lot like a sting operation to lure drug dealers to jail to me.

Who would ever participate in such a thing?

The big idea behind it was—whenever a drug dealer in Tennessee got arrested without having that stamp on them, the state would not only prosecute his toothless ass for being a drug dealer, they would also try to collect the additional sin tax money owed as well. LOL.

If you think the Tennessee lawmakers were on crack when they came up with this sin tax, get this: 22 other states have enacted drug collection laws similar to the crack tax in Tennessee. And some of these other states throw in prostitution for good measure—so prostitutes also have to voluntarily show up at their local state revenue office and fork over a portion of their john money? Based on what? The honor system?

Um, yeah, I love the movie *Pretty Woman* as much as anybody, but even Julia Roberts's hooker-with-a-heart-of-gold character isn't going to show up and pay that one.

Eventually the "crack tax" was shot down by a Tennessee Court of Appeals in 2009, but here's the twist: The Tennessee State Revenue Commission said they'd been enforcing the law for years, and by 2007 had already collected over $6 million in revenue! Wow. Maybe this crazy crack tax really works?

Before you get too excited about the prospects of a nationwide crack tax that would reduce our national deficit by a trillion dollars, turns out, the $6 million was not collected by anonymous drug dealers paying the stamp fine on the honor system. The money was actually collected post-arrest, as the tax was used as another excuse to confiscate drug dealer–related property, possessions, and homes, under the premise that they owe *even more* to the state for not paying the crack tax.

Even though the state of Tennessee collected $6 million from drug dealers, I feel like this is another case where money-strapped lawmakers are reverse engineering new ways to collect more tax money under the guise of a morality fee. When will we stop voting the morality police into office?

Because this new reality feels an awful lot like we're back in 1764. Anyone want to dump some tea into Boston Harbor with me in protest? Paging the Beastie Boys, if any of you are still alive, please report for patriotic duty, STAT.

IT'S A BILLION DOLLAR RACKET—FOR YOUR OWN GOOD

I can hear what some of you idealists are saying: Hold up. Yes, these laws sound crazy, but aren't these legislators looking out for our best interests?

Sure, I will agree that some of their hearts may be in the right place. I mean, look around at our nation right now. Americans *are* dropping like flies at an alarming rate due to excessive everything: smoking, boozing, prescription drug taking, and yes, sugar addictions. Diabetes is at an all-time high. More than a third of our nation is obese. So yes, there is a good reason to be alarmed at our growing health epidemic. No one wants to end up a nation who is so fat and unhealthy that we can't leave our Barcaloungers like in that movie *WALL•E*. I totally get that. But rather than allow us to address this health problem on the community level, with our families and physicians, white-hatted government officials continuously try to save us from ourselves.

I've seen firsthand how these so-called "governmental solutions" work—and (try as they might) they just don't. For example, research has shown that when the price of a "sinful" good spikes, consumers just substitute an equally sinful good in its place. One study revealed that smokers who live in tobacco high-tax states are more likely to smoke cigarettes that are longer and packed with a higher concentration of tar and nicotine. These findings were especially pronounced among young people aged 18–24—the switch to cigarettes with more tar and nicotine is so huge for young smokers that the tax increases actually end up increasing their average daily tar and nicotine consumption.[26] Meanwhile, taxes on sugary drinks often cause people to switch to other high-calorie drinks, including beer. So you're off sugar but now you're too drunk to work out! Fat, drunk, and stupid is no way to go through life, son.

But putting aside the effectiveness of sin taxes for a moment— do we really want smug bureaucrats in state capitals (or worse, Washington, D.C.) using our hard-earned tax dollars to attempt to alter or control our behavior? If you're over 18 and want to chain-smoke until your eyes roll into the back of your empty skull while simultaneously stuffing your face with cake and chugging Dr Pepper . . . you should have the freedom to do that, dammit! Sure, that wouldn't be the smartest path in life. But your path is yours to choose or to ruin if you wish. That's the joy of freedom—sink or swim on your own terms.

Of course, all of this is assuming that the bureaucrats actually have noble intentions (a pretty dumb assumption to make). Here is the poorest kept secret behind all of these new sin taxes: *Most legislators don't give a fig about anyone's health.* They will all pay it lip service, but they really just want an excuse to pilfer more dollars from your wallet. If you want a play-by-play of how it works, here is how every sin tax racket operates in virtually every community that has enacted one.

Let's say a state, county, or city government official wants to increase revenue but they don't want to raise sales taxes or income taxes because that would piss off their voter base. So they wonder: *How can we get more tax money without really asking for it?* Ta-dah! Sin taxes are born.

Our elected officials add extra taxes to everything in life that could be potentially dangerous to our health—from sugary drinks to cigarettes—and spin it as if they're doing it *for our own good.* But no one talks about the bloated diabetic elephant in the room—which is sin taxes may sound good in theory, but they rarely pay off in reality. Sometimes, they actually make the situation worse.

And that's not even considering the effect they have on local businesses that sell these taxed items. Heartland Institute senior policy analyst Matthew Glans wrote, "Sin taxes have a strong detrimental effect on local small businesses; when they are implemented, retailers and wholesalers find themselves with decreased sales, as consumers seek to avoid the tax by purchasing products outside the county, city, or state imposing the tax. While sin taxes do sometimes result in increased revenue over the short term, they often lead to an even greater increase in expenditures, which often cannot be supported by the tax over the long term, thereby creating budget shortfalls."

This is all pretty damning evidence for sin tax proponents—but I'm not finished trying to give these lawmakers the benefit of the doubt. So let's take a minute and try to visualize the best-case scenario here. Say our country magically cleans up its act and starts to eat healthy again. Imagine we all swear off junk food, begin working out like maniacs on one of those Suzanne Somers Thigh Master things until we're all totally shredded like that dude who keeps dying in *The Leftovers*. Do you really think these sin taxes would just go away?

As our former smug British oppressors would say, "Not bloody likely."

This whole sin tax thing is huge freaking business.

As I mentioned, the revenue from sin taxes alone in the United States was a whopping $32.5 billion in 2014, which is like the GDP of a relatively large country. Do you really think our government is going to kill this sinful cash cow just because we all stop guzzling milkshakes? Again—not bloody likely. Sin taxes have become a permanent profit arm for many of our local governments; they now make up nearly 4% of our entire nation's total tax revenue.

Let that sink in for a minute while I take a sip of this Slushee . . .

SIN TAXES ARE THE REAL CRIMINALS. LOCK 'EM UP!

I have finally given up trying to justify these lawmakers' thinking. I don't like any sin taxes, but I can at least begin to understand why they are imposed on adult things like boozing, smoking, illegal drugging, and gambling. But when did sinning get downgraded to kid's stuff like drinking soda pop? That's what bothers me the most.

As for all of the Americans out there who just can't control their own bad habits—I hate to break it to all of you idealists, but no sin tax is ever going to change their lifestyle. Just ask the Brits about that.

Except Aiden, man . . . I'm on a mission with that kid. Next time I see him, I'm straight stuffing him with banana chips and yogurt raisins: All. Day. Long. No more double-fisting piles of sugar on my watch. That much I did promise his mom after Aiden threw up chocolate all over her the second I dropped him off. Ugh. What did you expect? His great-great-great-great-great-great-grandfather fought for his right to party! #USA.

SEVEN

CELL PHONES

YOUR SMARTPHONE IS WAY SMARTER THAN YOU

> Although some taxation is necessary,
> all taxation diminishes freedom.
>
> —*George Will*

Imagine it's your job to track a million ants. But the ants aren't all in one place, just waiting for you to tag them and turn them loose—oh no; these filthy little buggers have a 10-year head start on you, and they're scattered throughout every town, city, and state across the country. Oh, yeah—also? Every single ant has been given autonomy and a human level of sentience, offset by a taste for greed and obfuscation. And they will have each enacted their own tax policies.

Spoiler alert: The ants I'm referring to are humans. And now you see what we're dealing with when it comes to tracking down cell phone taxes.

"The problem with taxes on wireless is so many different jurisdictions impose taxes and fees," said Scott Drenkard, an economist with the Tax Foundation.

Over 95% of adult Americans own cell phones.[1] But when these millions upon millions of people pay their cell phone bills, only a fraction of the money they shell out each month actually goes to their mobile phone service. They're paying far more than they bargained for, for things they didn't agree to and arguably don't need.

That's because local, state, and federal governments, 911 systems, and even local school districts slip hidden taxes and fees into our cell phone bills that end up costing the average American cell phone consumer an extra 18%.[2] So a monthly phone bill that ought to be $60 costs around $70.80. Every month.

Think about that for a second: $10.80 in your phone bill, every month, that's not even going to your cell service. That's $129.60 per year.

Granted, $10.80 a month isn't going to put an end to the world as we know it—although that's two fewer pumpkin spice lattes for you—but consider this: Out of 100 hidden taxes, on everything from airplane tickets to fishing, cell phone taxes are the *highest*. For a family living paycheck to paycheck, or a young person out on their own, that's some serious change. Add up these taxes on each phone line, and a family of five might wind up paying a month's mortgage (or more) per year without even realizing it.

CELL PHONE TAXES: THE PONTIAC AZTEK OF BILLS

We're all familiar with the four largest cell phone service providers: AT&T, Verizon Wireless, Sprint, and T-Mobile. These giants receive an estimated annual revenue of $126 billion from providing cell service. This is what we actually *pay* for voice, texting, email, and data services. On top of this, the 18% hidden tax adds up to a whopping *$22.68 billion*. That's the GDP of a small country! And it comes straight out of the pockets of people like you and me.

But you know that's not where it ends. If the taxes on your cell bill add up to "just" 18%, you may actually be *lucky*. The poor suckers in cities like Chicago and Baltimore have it far worse, shouldering hidden taxes as high as 35%![3]

Competition in the wireless industry has led to significant reductions in average monthly bills. But thanks to *increases* in government taxes and fees, the total cost of the average American's cell phone bill has remained relatively static. Example: Between 2008 and 2015, the average price of a monthly cell phone bill dropped from $49.94 to $46.64. Yay! But during that same time span, the tax rate increased from 15.5% to 18%. Boooo.

Our nation's tax system is founded on a progressive system, meaning the more money you make, the more you can afford to pay in taxes. Cell phone taxes do just the opposite, imposing a disproportionate burden on low-income individuals and families. Because the rates for cell phone taxes are universal—got a phone, pay the tax—people like students, lower-income families, and the elderly are forced to pay a bigger share of their income. To, say, Oprah, $129.60 a year in cell phone taxes means nothing. But for a recent college grad making $10 per hour, trying to pay off $100,000 in student loans, that's a huge bite out of their cash flow.

So where, exactly, is all that extra money going? Good question. But it brings up an even better question: How does one find the answers, when cell phone taxes remain largely hidden?

Next time your cell phone bill shows up in the mail, take a good look at it. The federal 5.82% wireless tax is about the only tax that is consistent across all cell phone bills. But state and local governments use phone bills to ratchet up taxes and fees to insane highs—trying to decipher what they all are and who benefits from them is like trying to solve a Rubik's Cube with six extra sides. In New York City, for example, a wireless customer could be paying up to 12 different taxes and surcharges. Imagine that your bill comes and this is what you see:[4]

- State sales tax: 4.00%
- Local sales tax: 4.25%

- MCTD sales tax: 0.19%
- State excise tax (186e): 2.50%
- MCTD excise/surcharge (165e): 0.30%
- Local utility gross receipts tax: 1.49%
- State wireless 911: 2.55%
- Local wireless 911: 0.64%
- MCTD surcharge (184): 0.07%
- NY franchise tax (184): 0.38%
- School district utility sales tax: 1.50%
- Universal service tax (federal): 5.82%

Total transaction tax: 23.69%

Some of these items are relatively easy to explain. And some are so intentionally nebulous, you need a magnifying glass to see the fine print.

New Yorkers have to pay a Metropolitan Commuter Transportation District (MCTD) tax to fund the MTA. That's right; your monthly cell phone payment helps keeps the subway running. This tax (and a related surcharge) is just one of many that give New York the third highest cell taxes in the nation.[5] If you live in the Big Apple itself, cell taxes run you an incredible 27%.

Illinois, Maryland, Montana, and New York charge an excise tax *on top of* the sales taxes. These excise taxes are often paired with a utility gross receipts tax, which heads right back into the levying agency's general fund, rather than a special one for communications improvements. The levying of such taxes is often on the city level, with Washington State allowing local utility franchise taxes up to 9%. Los Angeles and Sacramento users pay a similar utility user tax, and so do over 150 cities in California.[6]

Like a demon version of the Energizer Bunny, the taxes and fees keep going, and going, and going. The District of Columbia charges a "Telecommunications Privilege Tax"—about 9% of the tax goes into the Ballpark Reserve Fund, a slush fund for Nationals' park.[7] They're on top of the NL East and they need a subsidy? Come on. There's also the rampant misuse of the Universal Service Fund that we discussed with cable taxes—in Mississippi, this fund gives telecom companies an over-tenfold increase in subsidies to wireless providers.[8] You pay the tax, and the big operators rake in far more than it costs to provide the service to rural and previously under-served areas.

Most states (and some cities) impose 911 fees, supposedly to fund expenses for the 911 system and operations. Seems legit . . . if the money actually went where it was supposed to go. Take what happened in 2014, when the Chicago City Council increased the 911 fee on wireless consumers from $2.50 to $3.90 a month. The stated reason for the fee hike? *To avoid a property tax increase.* And what's worse is that the 911 tax is considered a "per-line" tax; on a family plan with five lines, the total fee would be $19.50 per month.

And how about the School Utility Surcharge? In Albany, New York, a high school social studies teacher named Jennifer Justice noticed a $2.74 School Utility surcharge billed to her account and couldn't figure out what it was for.[9] Because she was a teacher, she was invested in finding out whether that money actually went to schools in any fashion. She contacted AT&T for answers and was told they *didn't know* where the money went. Verizon had no answers either.

Turns out, New York's School Utility Surcharge tax has been around longer than cell phones. Enacted in 1965, the tax allows small city school districts to impose taxes of up to 3% on utility bills including gas, electricity, refrigeration, and phone service.[10]

Since it's so hard to find out where the money goes, most claims of foul play are impossible to prove. What are you supposed to do when the phone companies and professional researchers claim they don't have the answers?

Take another look at that list of charges and taxes on the New York cell phone bill. Now understand that every single state has its own variation of that list. Every. Single. State. Some are longer, some shorter, but all of them have their own system for what gets taxed and how, as well as varying levels of transparency when it comes to where that money actually goes. So, Sherlock, there's not just one set of questions that need to be asked. There is, at minimum, *one set of questions for every state in the union.*

THE SECOND CITY, FIRST IN CELL TAXES

Until recently, the mating habits of Australian sea turtles got more attention than hidden cell phone taxes. And deservedly so; taxes are pretty boring. But serious research is starting to expose the truth about big cities that jack up their residents' cell phone bills by more than 25% with hidden taxes and fees.

Chicago is home to the highest wireless taxes in the nation (why am I not surprised). Residents in the Windy City pay 35.42% in wireless taxes every month.[11] A family of four paying $100 per month for their wireless plan would be on the hook for an additional $35.42 in taxes.

While most of the taxes injected into residents' bills are given fancy, important-sounding names (like the "911 Emergency System Fee"), others are just blatant attempts by city officials to rake in more revenue. In addition to the federal 5.82% wireless tax, plus a slew of other state- and city-imposed fees, Chicago levies a monthly $4 per line fee for "general revenue purposes." (I mean, the least they could do is *try* to make it sound like a real thing.) So a family of five pays 20 bucks a month, straight into Chicago's general fund, where city bureaucrats can spend it on just about anything they damn well please.

Officials in the city realize that cell phone bills are an easy way to increase revenue, largely under the radar. Fees for 911 have been exploited continuously. In 2008, the city doubled its wireless 911 fee from $1.25 to $2.50 per month. Why? To help fund its Olympic bid (yes, really).[12] You remember the Chicago Olympics, right? Oh, yeah—they lost that bid. Funny thing, though—that 911 tax never got reduced. In fact, it was *increased* a further 56% in 2014, causing Chicagoans' phone bills to rise by $16.80 *per phone line* per year.[13] So, a typical family plan with four lines saw an increase of $67.20 per year. The reason for the 2014 hike? To "save" pension funds for city workers (uh, what does that have to do with 911 services again?).[14] The funds from the tax go straight into the Laborers' Fund, and in its first year alone that increased 911 fee generated $110.8 million.

And now, three years later, Chicago mayor Rahm Emanuel is pushing *yet another* wireless tax hike as the city continues to struggle with its bloated employee pension funds.[15] Emanuel had previously promised Governor Bruce Rauner that he would steer clear of property tax hikes—but he didn't say anything about that 911 fee! The mayor's proposal would be a 28.2% increase—from $3.90 a month to $5 for every phone line. The increase is expected to bring in an annual $27 million to help the city meet its financial "obligations." At the time of this writing, Emanuel's bill is awaiting Governor Rauner's signature.

As Chicagoans discover the cell phone tax scam that their city is pulling, many get angry. And rightly so. One city council member, who opposes the misleading 911 hikes, told the *Chicago Sun-Times* that the city is already "seeing an increase in people using addresses where they don't actually reside" to avoid these taxes. "There's a point of diminishing returns on this," he said. "And we may actually be getting there with this increase."

When combined with the already high taxes of Illinois, Chicago residents are *really* getting screwed. It's bad enough they have 3 trillion inches of snow every year and are constantly playing second fiddle to the city that never sleeps. Ah well. At least they won the World Series that one time.

THE RISE (AND RISE) OF CELL PHONE TAXES

Phone taxes existed long before cell phones were invented, of course. I know it's hard to believe, but human beings were alive for thousands of years without being connected 24/7. And for as long as phone lines have been monetized, the government's been sticking its paws into the pot and taking whatever it can grab.

The first phone tax was introduced in 1898 after the Spanish-American War as a solution to the federal budget deficit. The tax was short-lived, though—it was repealed a few years later, in 1902. A number of similar taxes came soon thereafter under the guise of emergency. In 1914, before the United States even entered World War I, President Wilson instated a 1-cent tax on all phone calls costing more than 15 cents. The tax lapsed in 1916, yet in 1917 a similar 5-cent tax on 15-cent or higher calls and telegrams was introduced to fund our involvement against Kaiser Bill. This tax was phased out in 1924.

Modern phone taxes derive from Congress's Revenue Bill of 1932, which has been reauthorized a stunning 29 times. The tax was originally used as a means of making up for lost revenue from the Great Depression. Over time, federal taxation went from long-distance calls to *all* calls, including local dials. Would-be "temporary taxes" flushed coffers during World War II, with long-distance calls above 24 cents slapped with a staggering 25% tax. Instead of phasing the tax out after the war, it continued on despite a 1953 Gallup Poll listing it as the most disliked tax in the nation. Following a number of losses in court, the IRS finally suspended long-distance phone excise taxes in 2006, yet left them in place at the local level.

Cell phones gave us the freedom to continue our important conversations no matter where we were—grocery store checkout line, back of a cab, during a boring stretch at work—but they didn't free us from federal or state taxation. In the '70s and '80s not many people owned cell phones (they were expensive as hell and looked like massive bricks), but states and the feds smelled a cash cow. The feds instituted a 5.82% Universal Service wireless tax on those who could afford cell phones, claiming the funds were necessary to pay for services that cell phones needed to operate, such as rural telephone infrastructure.[16]

But the truth is that there was never any need for that 5.82% tax. Even in the earliest days of the cellular industry, there was an abundance of companies anxious to build cell towers, especially in the most sparsely populated regions. If an operator built the only tower in a given area, they could charge outrageous roaming fees to out-of-state cell phone users. Remember roaming charges? They were often $2–3 per minute. Between those inflated charges and the Universal Service tax, wireless customers were getting ripped off from the beginning.

Back in the day, this wireless bill-cramming predominantly targeted only the rich people who could afford to buy cell phones. But cell phones are no longer a one-percenter luxury—today they're a straight-up necessity for anyone who has a job or a family they need to stay in touch with. Everyone has one and yet the fees haven't budged. Well, actually, they have—they've gone up.

Often taxes at the local, state, and federal levels are laughably outdated. Some of our federal excise phone taxes are derived from the *telegraph* taxes we used to pay. And a variety of taxes that were ostensibly put in place for emergencies have been repackaged and expanded to plug holes in broken budgets.

And let me remind you, the money doesn't go where you think it goes. In 2008, New York used just 6 cents out of their $1.20 911 fee for actual emergency calling services.[17] A portion of those fees went to almost $1 million in spending by the New York National Guard at various hotels and a swanky steak and seafood restaurant. A Nassau County assemblyman called 911 fees "the goose that lays the golden egg."[18] And a recent audit found that *none* of New York's 911 taxes went toward call centers or upgrades.

I feel safer already!

LET THEM EAT WIRELESS DATA CAPS

There are only so many times I can reference Ben Franklin's old axiom about death and taxes. But damn if he wasn't spot-on with that sentiment. These days, our smartphones literally put nearly every shred of human knowledge in the palm of your hand—and yet they still can't begin to help us understand the startling and bizarre ways our devices are taxed in order to fill the government's pockets.

There are soooo many examples. Utah inserts wireless "control fees" into residents' cell phone bills . . . to pay for its poison control centers.[19] See, instead of announcing a new Poison Control tax, and letting the citizens vote on it, they just slip it into the cell phone bill where no one will notice!

Some states have even taken legal action to ensure that their taxes and fees continue to go unnoticed. In 2007, Texas filed a lawsuit against Sprint.[20] Why? Because the corporation, when issuing its bill, listed a state tax as a line item on its bill rather than hiding it from customers.

You can't even escape this shameless bill-cramming in states with no sales tax, like Alaska, which has a higher-than-average 17.9% state-imposed wireless tax. Same with New Hampshire—my home state, which proudly boasts its 0% sales tax and looks down its nose at its neighbor state, Taxachusetts—which slaps its residents with a 14.68% wireless tax. On the left coast, California taxes callers for the full amount on discounted services. If AT&T offers you a $100 monthly plan for $75, you still have to pay tax on the $100. A class action suit alleges that the state has been overcharging gabbers since 1999.[21] If successful, cell users will only have to pay taxes on the sticker price of the service.

Oregon has the nation's lowest wireless tax rate: 8.84%. Ironically, its neighbor Washington State is home to the *highest* wireless tax rate: 25.42%. But make no mistake—Washingtonians can't escape the high fees by buying a phone across the border in Oregon. The Mobile Telecommunications Sourcing Act of 2002 demands that taxes be levied at the address of the customer's "place of primary use."[22]

If I was feeling mischievous, I could make this chapter four times longer than it already is. But I think I've made my point here.

I know it's not as fun as Instagramming your brunch or confusing your mom with your Bitmoji avatar, but we *have* to educate ourselves on these fees that add up to millions and billions.[23] I didn't write this chapter to convince you to give up your iPhone and 4G LTE. Honest. Keep searching Pinterest for DIY craft projects you'll never do. But I *do* want you to feel the righteous fury caused by being screwed so thoroughly by a government that regulates you with one hand and picks your pocket with the other.

They can come for our soda. They can come for our pets. They can come for our gasoline, and they can even come for our paychecks. But messing with our inappropriate group text about Ryan Gosling? Oh, hell no, Uncle Sam!

Can you hear that, you old bastard?

EIGHT

LEISURE

HAVING A GOOD TIME? PAY THE TOLL!

> Cursing? There's only one bad word: taxes.
> Any other word that is good enough for
> sailors is good enough for you.
>
> —*Ron Swanson*

Welcome to the "Fun Taxes" chapter, where no one is really having fun, except the sniveling Tax Monster. I recently stopped being a total workaholic and took some much needed "mental health" weekends out of town, which is when I realized that taxes followed me everywhere I went, even when I was (supposedly) having fun.

Taxation on leisure activities has largely gone unnoticed because we hardworking Americans just want *two freaking free days a week* where we can pretend we're not helpless pawns in the game of life. Sure, with big-ticket purchases, most people will carefully go over the fine print before dropping down some serious cash—but how about buying a movie ticket? Or checking the fine print on a restaurant bill? If you're like most people, you probably just let that slide. You'll say, "Ah, forget it, life is too short to quibble over a few bucks." Sound familiar?

IS THAT A FLY IN YOUR FIESTA SALAD?
NO, IT'S A HIDDEN SURCHARGE!

During a few long weekends away from the grind I wanted to get out of town, so I used some airline miles I had saved up to see friends in different parts of the country. I won't detail all the hellacious hidden fees that went into traveling right now (dear God, that's already its own chapter)—but my first stop was San Diego to soak up some rays and see a friend. I was ready to drink in San Diego like a modern-day Veronica Corningstone—until I got tricked into paying extra for it.

When I landed, I wanted to enjoy a good meal at a restaurant. If you live in Cali, you may have seen the mysterious surcharges that have been popping up on restaurant bills since 2017.[1] Apparently, these fees go toward paying for California's rise in the minimum wage. When I got out my calculator (and totally turned off my lunch companion)—I ran the numbers and found this hip San Diego restaurant was serving up a *6.9% hidden surcharge.* That's one big bite out of my Big Salad.

The worst part about the surcharge was the sneaky way the restaurant did it. I wasn't told about it when I ordered or when I was given the bill. I had to root around on the check to even notice it was there.

How does the state of California expect restaurant owners to absorb the new cost of this government-mandated rise in wages without firing employees, cutting back hours, or shutting up shop completely? The answer to that question is: They expect restaurants to pass the cost on to their customers.

Turns out, I got off easy with my 6.9% hidden fee—it could have been a lot worse. Some other California restaurants have already put a 20% service charge on their bills! California hotels and rental cars already do as well, but most California restaurants are not going that far . . . yet. I stress *yet*. For now, most restaurants are asking customers to pay a 3–4% surcharge, until, of course, the minimum wage rises again. In 2014, it was $8 an hour. In 2017, it was $10.50 an hour. By 2021, it will be $15 an hour (mandated by the state).

Do you think those mysterious California restaurant surcharges will keep going up? Yeah, me, too . . .

The good news for us crusaders is the San Diego city attorney is looking into the legality of these surcharges—she's investigating the *language* restaurants are using to explain the hidden fee, which is important because several San Francisco restaurants have already gotten in trouble for telling their customers that a surcharge was going to employee health care, when not all of it was.[2] California restaurant owners, I feel your pain, but I suggest you start explaining this hidden fee to you customers. Stop trying to sneak it in!

Of course, this hidden surcharge-o-rama can be traced back to some well-meaning government officials working for the state of California. If they really wanted to solve this problem before it ever got started, they should have counted tips as wages—but who am I kidding? Logic is never going to be high on the list of priorities in California with "Governor Moonbeam" in office (Jerry Brown).

So here's what will happen because of this wage hike: A lot of mom-and-pop-owned restaurants will shut their doors. Restaurant owners will slash employee hours. Then, soon after that, restaurants will completely automate, firing most non-robot employees. Computer screens will become our waiters. "Counter service" restaurants, which employ no servers at all, will become all the rage—and we will begin to see a chain restaurant explosion all around the United States. We've already seen this start to happen in Seattle, where a $15 per hour minimum wage was implemented in 2014.[3]

Guess I'll start going to *a lot more dinner parties* when I visit California. Ugh . . . and all I wanted was a Big Salad.

TEXAS, YOU'RE SO DEAD TO ME . . .
RIGHT AFTER I FINISH THIS OVERPRICED DRINK

A few months later, on my second weekend getaway of 2017, I visited Austin, Texas, to cut loose for a couple of days. Once I arrived, I arranged to meet some friends at a local restaurant. On my way out the door I thought, *I'm not going to need my trusty calculator. This is Texas, where income taxes have been outlawed. How bad could the Tax Monster get here?* Answer: still pretty bad.

I immediately ran into another crazy law that added an 8.25% tax on my tab for no apparent reason. *Et tu, Texas?*

This was my first exposure to a hidden cocktail serving tax *anywhere*. It's a new kind of sales tax for every establishment in Texas that sells liquor in addition to beer and wine. They call it the ordinance HB 3572, and it went into effect in 2017. Its goal is to provide more "transparency and equity between restaurants and bars that sell only beer and wine, and those that also sell mixed beverages."⁴

On the surface, this new tax law claims to level the playing field between establishments that serve booze versus those that only serve beer and wine, but really it's just another way for restaurant and bar owners to push their tax bill on to customers and make more money. It also benefits the state of Texas, too . . . what a surprise?

Uh, no. Not in the least.

Before the new tax law passed, Texas establishments serving mixed drinks had to pay a 14% "mixed beverage gross receipts tax" directly to the state for every cocktail, glass of wine, or bottle of beer sold. Instead of making this clear to customers, most establishments secretly added the 14% tax directly on to the cost of a drink, so customers had no idea they were paying it.

Now, thanks to the new law, all establishments selling liquor only have to pay 6.7% of their gross cocktail profits directly to the state (much better than the full 14%, right?). Sure, for the booze sling-ers—but what about the customers? Does anyone in their right mind think these boozy establishments will suddenly cut the price of their cocktails now that the state reduced their tax bill from 14% to 6.7% per drink served? I'm no expert in human nature, but I do know greed is a powerful motivator—so, I wouldn't hold my breath ex-pecting that to happen anytime soon. Nice try though, idealists. And if you think that's bad, the new law also gives booze-selling establish-ments the green light to drop an *additional* "mixed beverage sales tax" of 8.25% on customers! So Texans who love to suck down margaritas in their favorite Mexican restaurant are now paying the original 14% tax that was built into the cost of their margaritas *years ago* plus an additional 8.25% "mixed beverage sales tax" on top of that for a grand total of a 22.25% hidden surcharge on every single mixed drink pur-chased in the state.

Texas, I thought I knew you.

To end this story on a typically outrageous note—guess what?

The state of Texas is pulling the strings on this racket; they're the puppet master who (surprise, surprise) is also getting a bigger cut of the profits with this law change.

When HB 3573 was originally passed into law, the state comp-troller's office said it did not expect "much of a revenue stream from this new law"[5]—really? Is that your final answer? Because Dallas-based *D Magazine* already let the cat out of the bag on your diaboli-cal plans: "An argument could be made that some small restaurants avoid a mixed beverage license because of the current high costs. The reduction (in taxes paid by the restaurant or bar) could sway them to add a license, resulting in more taxes and licensing fees for the state . . . Also, only a fraction of the drinking public are aware of the amount of sales tax added on a check . . . This could generate even more revenue for the state."

So, sneaky Texas lawmakers are in on this racket, too?

Of course they are!

Enjoy your tax break, Texas booze slingers—and be sure to give your state congressman a free drink next time he or she comes in, and don't forget to charge them 22.25% extra for it. I'm sure you will.

PROGRESS IN MIAMI!

Who would have ever predicted the city of Miami—the town that brought us *Miami Vice* and *Scarface*'s coked-out Tony Montana—would be the voice of reason?

In March 2017, while spending another long weekend in South Beach getting fed daiquiris intravenously, I read the Miami Beach Commissioners had just shut down a hidden tax racket, which got my attention real quickly. They voted unanimously on a measure requiring outdoor restaurants to disclose some of the hidden charges they've been adding on to customer bills.

"There's rampant shenanigans going on," declared Commissioner Michael Grieco.[6] Of course we have long known that South Beach is a popular destination for rampant shenanigans—it's just not furtive consumer taxation that we had in mind.

Rejoice, drunken retired Miamians in Bermuda shorts, keep those Metamucil screwdrivers coming! Now all the outdoor cafes you love to play mahjong in will be forced to disclose any hidden service charges, gratuities, or taxes that were previously added to your bill with no explanation.

Grieco said the measure came after a photo of a restaurant bill was sent to him by a Miami Beach resident: "Right now, sales tax on Miami Beach for food and beverages is 9%. The photos I saw were restaurants that were applying a tax of more than 10%." He visited a number of Miami Beach restaurants himself, and said he verified these hidden taxes are everywhere. "If you were not paying attention, you were getting taxed. Let's say, it's a dollar or two more, but aggregate that out and that's the fleecing of a lot of customers. When you look at your bill and it says 'service charge'—service charge and gratuity are two different things. A gratuity goes to the server. But a service charge is something different . . . If it goes purely to the server, then they're applying a tax where it can't be applied."

Since the measure was approved, the Miami Beach city manager has the power to shut down any outdoor cafe that refuses to comply. So it's a brand-new day on Miami Beach, right? The hidden Tax Monster has been vanquished forever!

Drinks on me! Ding-dong the Tax Monster is dea—Wait, what?

Don't get too excited, Miami mahjong players . . .

Even though the ordinance is in effect, the "find the hidden tax on your bill game" will not end (entirely) for Miami residents.

Why not? You gotta understand, the authority of the Miami Beach Commission isn't exactly like Sonny Crockett's and Ricardo Tubbs's—their jurisdiction *only applies to outdoor cafes* because they fall under the city's jurisdiction. So, other restaurants—which *are not* outdoor cafes—could certainly "voluntarily comply" with the new ordinance, but what are the odds that will happen?

TAXING HOW WE SPEND OUR FREE TIME, CHICAGO?

Even though the frustrating Tax Monster had haunted me at every stop on my "Fun Tour," I decided to give it another shot and attend a concert with some old college friends in Chicago.

What could possibly go wrong here? Ugh.

Chicago pretty much frowns on any type of legal fun you want to have within their city limits, unless, of course, you are willing to pay a tax for the privilege of doing it. I ran into a bizarre hidden tax I never knew existed called an "amusement" or "entertainment tax."[7]

You may think when a city creates an entertainment tax law they mean taxing booze, gambling, drugs, or prostitution—all Chicago "fun time" traditions since the Al Capone days—but you would be wrong about that. No, nowadays, it seems Chi-Town prefers to go after its upstanding citizens and local mom-and-pop businesses.

It started in 2015, when the city (no doubt egged on by former Obama lackey and current mayor Rahm Emanuel) stepped up their tax game to absurd levels, going on a bureaucratic rampage to tax fun in all forms all over their corrupt land. Now, two years later, Chicago citizens and business owners are up in arms about it. Companies are suing the city of Chicago over it, everyone hates the new law, and for good reason.

I first encountered Chicago's so-called "amusement tax" when my friends and I went to buy our concert tickets. We got hit with normal sales taxes plus the hidden 9% amusement tax.[8]

Since 2015, every Chicago business owner who owns, manages, or operates "amusements" or places in Chicago "where amusements are conducted" must collect a 9% tax for live theatrical, musical, and other cultural performances held in an auditorium, theater, or other space whose maximum capacity is more than 750 people. Ticket resellers to live events are ordered to collect the tax, too. The amusement tax was *not* approved by the city council—the Chicago Department of Finance created the new tax by "administratively clarifying two existing city taxes."

I smelled a stinky Tax Monster scam.

What is the point of this tax? Can anyone in the city of Chicago tell me? Anyone? . . . Anyone? . . . Mayor Rahm? . . . Guh.

Turns out, all revenue collected from Chicago's amusement tax goes to . . . drumroll . . . *ye old general fund!* As you know, this means city bureaucrats can spend it however they please.

Believe it or not, there is a happy ending to this story (sort of): Mayor Rahm's amusement tax law, as it applies to ticket resales, went over so poorly with the people of Chicago the past two years that he reduced it from 9% in his 2017 city budget down to 3.5%. Way to bang the drum of protest, Chicagoans!

Chicago isn't the only city charging extra for fun. Baltimore is home to a 10% amusement tax, which brought in $5.5 million to the city's general fund in 2016.[9] As if people in Baltimore weren't struggling enough to have fun. Baltimore's tax applies to charges for admission to any venue showing a movie or sporting event—it also applies to merchandise and refreshment at any place where "dancing, music, or other entertainment is provided." And don't forget that these taxes are charged *in addition* to sales taxes!

Back to my Chicago trip. When it comes to taxing fun, the city doesn't stop at the amusement tax—we've only scratched the surface, folks. I haven't even gotten to the really weird part where the city somehow got the bright idea to make all the biggest online video, music, and gaming companies like Netflix, Hulu, and Spotify pay their amusement tax, too. Not only that—Chicago says their amusement tax also applies to cloud computing services and online subscription databases (like financial service databases and Amazon Web services).[10] How in the hell does a financial service database end up on the amusement tax list? I can't even begin to explain the logic behind this!

But that's not all.

After Chicago targeted streaming services, they went after Chicago bars and restaurants, by levying a 9% amusement tax surcharge on their satellite TV feeds.[11] Has everyone at City Hall lost their ever-loving minds?

Not only is this move absurd, it's not even effective. The revenue generated will not be reinvested into improving anyone's internet service. And here is the kicker: The city of Chicago predicts the 9% levy on "electronically delivered amusements" will only generate $12 million a year for the city of Chicago.[12]

That's it? Is a measly $12 million in revenue worth all of this bloody outrage, considering the city's proposed 2015 budget was $7.3 billion dollars?

Thank goodness there is one group still fighting back and they are total geeks. God bless the nerds! The Entertainment Software Association (ESA) is suing the city of Chicago on behalf of the video game industry, claiming it violated the "Internet Tax Freedom Act." They call the tax program "illegal, harmful, and without precedent across the country."[13]

Um, yeah, I tend to agree with the gamer geeks on that.

Some giant names in the gaming industry are behind ESA like Sony Interactive, Microsoft, Nintendo, and Warner Brothers Interactive—so perhaps they will have the legal firepower to take down the Chicago Tax Monster and his greedy minions, after all.

Good for you, gamer geeks!

MOVIE TAXES: THE WORST THING TO HAPPEN
IN A THEATER SINCE JOHN WILKES BOOTH

Ok, so Chicago clearly hates Netflix—but what about good ole-fashioned movie theaters? The day after the concert my friends and I decided to catch a flick at the nearest theater, and wouldn't cha know it . . . We got taxed on our movie tickets! Turns out that when it comes to extracting tax money, old styles of media are fair game for the insatiable appetite of *el diablo de taxes* (if my ninth-grade Spanish holds up).

Americans are shying away from movie theaters. Part of this is due to the rise of Netflix, but much of it is also due to the rapidly rising cost of a ticket to say nothing of the brutal price of a box of Goobers. One of the major drivers behind the insane prices? You already guessed it . . .

States go out of their way to sneak taxes into movie theater tickets. In 31 of the 46 states with sales tax, they nail you on the way in.[14] Some states charge even higher. Connecticut's "Admissions Tax," for example, allows cities to tack up to 5% *on top of* the 10% percent state tax already levied on movie tickets. The tax passed in 2016, and theaters say they've had to hike their rates; it's the cost of doing business, since their margins are already thin. A few years earlier, North Carolina raised its movie ticket tax from 1% to 4.75%![15]

In 2014, the movie theater chain AMC changed its ticket pricing to include sales tax.[16] Prior to the change, AMC didn't charge the full sales tax; instead, the chain would gradually increase the cost of tickets with the tax hidden from consumers. As tax pressure increased, AMC made it an added fee on top of the ticket price, instead of folded in and out of sight. Rather than small, planned increases, moviegoers got hit with a sudden price hike.

AMC recently won a landmark court case against the state of Texas.[17] They argued that the state overcharged on both sales and franchise tax by not allowing the chain to deduct the cost of running the theater from its profit computations. With the victory, Texas has to pay the theater chain back $1.1 million. AMC only has 20 theaters in the state[18]—that means each one will get back about $50,000. If you live in Texas, that's money that came out of your pocket when you made that regrettable decision to watch *Transformers: The Last Knight*. The extra franchise taxes the state charged the theaters were passed on to consumers through higher ticket and concession prices.

To rub salt in the wound, Texas originally feared that if AMC's calculation of overtaxation was used for all service-based businesses in the state it would mean Austin would pay out $6 billion in refunds and take in $1.5 billion less in its annual tax haul. We're talking half an aircraft carrier of money—and a lot that shouldn't have been taken out of our hands in the first place.

All of this adds up quick. Texas leads the nation in movie ticket sales per capita.[19] Add in a sales tax and franchise taxes, we're dealing with an effective surcharge that prices many out of going to the theater.

Making matters worse is that whether you go to the theaters or not, you might still be paying a subsidy to the industry via your income taxes—28 states give "film tax credits" to Hollywood production companies. Many other states and cities grant similar incentives like grants and tax rebates. Tax credits remove a portion of the income tax owed to the state by the production company; most often, the companies receive a dollar-for-dollar credit for a number of film-related expenses. California tripled its "Hollywood tax credits" to $330 million to help the industry.[20] Other states followed suit. They're not terribly effective either.

- California estimated they have a net negative economic impact.
- In Massachusetts, for every dollar in credit it gave back just 13 cents in revenue. The cost per Bay State film job? Over $128,000.
- Several states scaled back their incentives. North Carolina did after it spent $30 million for only 55–70 new jobs. Best-case scenario, state taxpayers shelled out over $400 grand to big film companies for each temporary job. Yay, crony capitalism!

Not only are these film tax credits ineffective—they can also spawn bad behavior. When *House of Cards* threatened to leave Maryland, where the series is filmed, the state ponied up under pressure.[21] Maryland governor Martin O'Malley, who ran for president for 10 minutes in 2016, coughed up over $10 million in tax credits. Overall, the show received almost $40 million in credits. *Veep* received almost $23 million from Maryland. Once California offered more in credits, the production moved there. Since 1997, Maryland's credits provided $300 million to HBO projects alone! Netflix, the mom-and-pop video streaming company that produces *House of Cards,* would have to make due on the paltry $9 billion gross it made last year.[22]

Bottom line: Large, profitable corporations receive heavy tax incentives, partially funded by money coming right out of *your weekly paycheck.*

So I have to pay for the movie to be made through tax credits *and* through sales and franchise taxes? What a crock! I just wanted to watch *Star Wars* in peace. That way I can get one evil empire on screen and another taking dollars from me I didn't even know I had.

FINALLY, A HIDDEN TAX THAT WORKS?

A few weeks after my Chicago trip, I flew to my home state of New Hampshire to hang out with family. There was no way the Tax Monster would find me out in the boonies! After getting royally ripped off all year, *I needed to kill something* without getting thrown in jail. So I drove out to my Uncle Darren's hunting reserve in the woods to see if I could take my frustrations out on some vicious beast with razor sharp teeth. That, or a duck. Yes, I've been known to fire off a few rounds at some varmints, which may come as a surprise to some of you—but I'm a card-carrying carnivore who has no problem taking out a critter that gets in my way. Deal with it, vegan America—I told you I'm a country girl at heart. This is what we do for fun.

As I pulled up to buy a hunting permit and some ammo at a gun store near my uncle's land, guess who showed up to tax my blood-thirsty ways? You guessed it . . . my old friend, the hidden Tax Monster.

The guy behind the counter told me about a federal law, which I had no idea existed (even though it's been around since 1937), that slapped an 11% tax on my ammo purchase, as well as an excise fee on my hunting permit.[23] These taxes would have remained hidden in the total cost of the two purchases if the counter guy had not mentioned them. But once he did, I stood there stunned. *Don't we have a constitutional right to hunt and fish? Why are they taxing this fun activity? Shouldn't firing weapons be our God-given right? Didn't our Wild West forefathers guarantee that—along with our right to pack heat in our local Whataburger?*

Well, yes and no.

Being *me,* of course, I checked this out—and there is nothing in the U.S Constitution about hunting or fishing (my bad) but 19 states do grant their residents the right under their state constitutions to hunt and fish. Vermont became the first state to do it back in 1777. In 1996, Alabama became the first state in the modern era to amend its constitution to make hunting a state constitutional right. Now, several other states are following suit. California and Rhode Island already have fishing rights on their constitutions, while Indiana and Kansas will be voting on it soon.[24]

I had to understand more about this hidden tax, so after I paid the Tax Monster's toll once again I went out to our family's backyard and sat there waiting to shoot the great grandson of Daffy. I waited . . . and waited. Then, after a while, I got bored and started Googling on my phone, and found the law behind this tax is called "The Pittman-Robertson Act," or the "Federal Aid in Wildlife Restoration Act" of 1937, which charges an additional 11% tax on all purchases of rifles, ammunition, and even archery equipment in the United States. You may ask: Where does all this federal tax revenue go? Great question, my young Padawan learner.

The reason this law has been in place for 80 years is not because the revenue goes to pay for more hunting reserves, or help pay the medical bills of people like Dick Cheney's hunting partner. No, the revenue from this hidden tax goes to fund conservation efforts in all 50 states. More specifically, the money goes to support the Fish, Wildlife, and Parks departments in your state, which fund conservation projects, hunter education, fish restoration, aquatics education, boating access, as well as Parks and Wildlife law enforcement.

Believe it or not, hunters (one of the more maligned demographics in our nation) played an important role in getting this law passed way back in 1937—and hunters seem to be perfectly happy to pay this tax today. Why is that?

Because it's actually going toward a good cause! In 2016 alone, $361 million was collected from this law. Since it was first instated in 1937 more than $2 billion has been collected from hunters and fisherman across the country, which is the single biggest source of money collected nationally for wildlife.[25] Hey, that doesn't sound too bad. I like nature and would like to preserve it. Maybe this fee is actually, dare I say, kind of good?

Every once in a while, you find some taxes that actually go toward a worthy cause. You may disagree with me on this particular issue, but I believe conservation-minded hunters and fisherman have done more to help wildlife populations than any other segment of our society.

So for all you hunters out there who (like me) feel like you get a bad rap—whenever some well-meaning tree hugger accuses you of being "part of the problem," you can tell them politely to go suck an egg because you donate to wildlife conservation every time you buy a hunting license, gun, or box of ammunition. And all you anglers out there can say the exact same thing. You contribute money to conservation every time you pay the 10% tax on all fishing poles, or the 3% tax on a tackle box or an outboard motor for your boat. And all you crazy bow hunters like Ted Nugent? I'm sure you'll tell the haters to suck it without my prompting, because you also contribute to wildlife conservation every time you pay the 11% tax on every bow, quiver, and arrow you purchase.

I'm still not a fan of the Tax Monster but it seems, at least to this intrepid reporter, that all the revenue from this tax really does go back to the states for things like wildlife management, conservation, hunter education, and aquatic conservation.

I guess the world isn't a disgusting cesspool of corruption?

Maybe some things still do work in our government?

Maybe my idealism is still intact, after all?

Someone alert the failing *New York Times!*

But first, can someone tell me when it's "Tax Monster Hunting Season"? That troll may be buttering me up this chapter, but I'm still carrying around a silver bullet with his name on it.

NINE

SHARING ECONOMY

YOU'RE SHARING WITH MORE PEOPLE THAN YOU REALIZE

Death, taxes and childbirth! There's never
any convenient time for any of them.

—*Margaret Mitchell*

I love to share stuff, don't you?

Young people love to share *so much* that millions of us rely daily on sharing apps like Uber, Lyft, Airbnb, VRBO, Postmates, and Etsy.

But the government is already regulating and taxing these sharing companies, while fining individuals who use these services the wrong way. Some cities are actually filing *criminal charges* on individuals just for using sharing apps. This is not some future hellscape I'm describing—it's already happening! Cities and states around the nation are passing laws right now that hurt sharing apps, while protecting their corporate constituents (like the hotel and taxi industries).

The "sharing economy" is the peer-to-peer–based process of buying, selling, or sharing goods and services online or through apps. The revenue from these services is estimated to skyrocket from $14 billion in 2014 to $335 billion by 2025.[1] Sharing services create thousands of flexible jobs while providing a higher-quality, less expensive, and more convenient product and service than their traditional competitors like taxis or hotels.

Many cities, as well as states like New York, Massachusetts, and Wisconsin, are hell-bent on regulating the heck out of the sharing services. Meanwhile, other states like Texas, Arizona, and Florida want to empower them with fewer rules.[2]

Which side is going to win this shared app civil war?

The battle is just getting started.

THE TRICKLE DOWN TAX MONSTER JUST DISCOVERED AIRBNB? NOOO!

Take a vacation to any major U.S. city, and you'll discover hotel prices are off the rails these days. Just one night in a hotel in New York or Washington, D.C., can easily set you back over $300. That's why many people today use home-sharing apps like Airbnb, VRBO, FlipKey, or HomeAway to book a room when they travel. These services offer a win-win situation: Homeowners rent out their properties on a short-term basis for a side income, while travelers enjoy rates that are almost always more affordable than a hotel.

This trend is no flash in the pan—in 2012, Airbnb only had 120,000 listings, but by mid-2015, it already had 1.2 million listings![3]

But in some cities, it's already impossible to book a room on sharing apps unless you want to risk being treated like a freaking criminal and slapped with a fine. State and city bureaucrats see the soaring popularity of these services and continuously seek out ways to get in on the action. Here are the most popular reasons government workers give for regulating the sharing economy:

1. *Greedy landlords* are evicting long-term renters so they can charge higher rates to Airbnb's short-term vacationers.

2. Streams of partying Airbnb travelers are *violating zoning laws* by transforming quiet residential neighborhoods into revolving hotel districts.

3. The government has a *lack of oversight* and an inability to collect taxes on sharing app users, which is by far the most important reason!

I know I'm simplifying a bit here (bullet #1 can be a real problem[4]), but all of these issues sound like property owner problems to me—what do they have to do with regular, law-abiding people who just want to rent one freaking room at an affordable rate? Why should we have to pay more because a few bad apples are abusing the system?

Every time a city or state regulates a home-sharing company like Airbnb, the cost of compliance always trickles down to you and me—the consumers. You've heard of Ronald Reagan's "Trickle Down Economics" theory, right? Well, think of this as "trickle down" overregulation. Sh*t rolls downhill . . . and its only getting started.

Cities like San Francisco,[5] Portland,[6] New York,[7] Los Angeles,[8] Santa Monica,[9] Miami,[10] Austin,[11] New Orleans,[12] Maui,[13] and Spokane,[14] as well as states like Wisconsin,[15] have passed (or are about to pass) legislation to tightly regulate home-sharing apps. The new laws being created also fine homeowners thousands of dollars for advertising their houses or apartments on short-term rental sites—making it *a criminal act for residents to share their own homes.*

Some cities are doing the right thing for their citizens by shutting down heinous abusers of Airbnb. Los Angeles recently cracked down on a landlord who kicked out long-term tenants to create Airbnb hotels.[16] But in many other instances, efforts to squash home-sharing services are just money grabs by local authorities—like in the case of Nigel Warren, a New Yorker who got fined thousands of dollars for renting his single bedroom in the East Village on Airbnb for only three days![17]

Politicians regularly use "fairness" and "safety" as excuses to intervene so they can appease their base of constituents (like hotel and taxi industries, as well as the residential voters who donate to their campaigns). But their sneaky little secret is by passing all these "do-gooder" laws, these bureaucrats are also raking in some serious cash for their city's general funds.

The city of Palm Desert, California, passed a law in 2012 that legalized short-term rentals of up to 27 days . . . as long as the property owners obtain an annual $25 "Short Term Rental Permit" and pay an 11% "transient occupancy tax" to the city.[18] Call me jaded—but do you really think the landlords in Palm City just eat the cost of getting a permit?

Also, who pays the 11% occupancy tax?

The consumer does, of course!

After Palm Beach got the ball rolling, two other cities decided to strike back against home-sharing services. In 2014, San Francisco and Portland (Oregon) passed "Airbnb laws" that require people who rent out their homes to register as hosts, carry insurance, and pay a brand-new tax in their cities: a 14% "Transient Occupancy Tax" in San Francisco, and an 11.5 % "Hotel Tax" in Portland.[19]

How is this law working out for those cities?

So far—not great. Few hosts in either city have followed the new laws or even bothered to register for the required permits.[20] In Portland, less than 10% of all short-term rental hosts had applied for permits by the deadline,[21] which underscores one of the most Pollyanna-like aspects of regulating home sharing—*how the hell do you enforce home-sharing laws?*

Miami Beach, Florida, apparently knows how. The city recently passed a law so officials can now *fine people up to $20,000* for renting out a single property for less than six months. So far, Miami Beach has levied $1.59 million in fines against short-term landlords.[22] Why not? It's a huge untapped well of taxable profits just waiting to be exploited, right?

Ugh.

DO YOU USE AIRBNB? YOU MAY BE A CRIMINAL!

Leave it to New York to have the toughest Airbnb laws in the nation.

My friend Kelly has been renting out her hip pad in New York City on Airbnb for years—but in the eyes of the state, she is now considered a lawbreaking criminal subject to thousands of dollars in fines . . . just for renting out her single apartment.

New York's state law has always outlawed short-term rentals, but there was no concerted effort to enforce these rules until 2016. That year, Governor Andrew Cuomo signed a law that fines people up to $7,500 for advertising short-term rentals on Airbnb.[23] Why did Governor Cuomo finally decide to start enforcing the state law with fines?

To Cuomo's credit, there are some New Yorkers who are abusing the system. In 2017, NYC mayor Bill de Blasio busted a landlord in Bushwick who was cramming 34 people into nine bedrooms.[24] This slumlord jack was slapped with an $11,000 fine—and he totally deserved it. But what about my friend Kelly, and the thousands of other people in the city who rent out their single rooms in good faith? Do they all deserve $7,500 penalties, while the Bushwick slumlord got fined only $11,000?

For regular New Yorkers who rent out their single homes $7,500 is crazy high. And Airbnb agrees—the company recently filed a lawsuit against de Blasio, claiming their users' constitutional rights had been violated. Airbnb believes more than 40,000 hosts could be subject to these $7,500 fines![25]

Let's put a pencil to that: If all 40,000 New Yorkers, like my friend Kelly, who rent out full homes or apartments on Airbnb got hammered with a $7,500 fine . . . that would be an injection of $300 freaking million right into New York City's general fund! Now do you see why the cities are cracking down? Cha-ching! Do you think Mayor de Blasio and Governor Cuomo are planning on rounding up 40,000 law-abiding citizens and fining them for trying to make some extra income to pay for their ridiculously overpriced New York apartments?

I'm kinda joking here, but I wouldn't put it past those two.

Just ask New York City resident Nigel Warren.[26] In 2013, *before* the Cuomo law passed and the city wasn't consistently enforcing its short-term leasing law, Warren got nailed with a $7,000 fine. All he did was rent out his bedroom on Airbnb for three nights while he was away on a trip. His roommate was fine with it and his Airbnb guests didn't party like rock stars. But when Warren returned home, he discovered he'd been fined five times by "special enforcement officers from the city" for running an "illegal transient hotel."[27]

Five fines for renting one bedroom for three nights?

Yep. One. Freaking. Bedroom.

What's even crazier is that Warren's fines could have climbed to over $40,000! He had to hire an expensive lawyer and appeal his case all the way to New York City's Environmental Control Board, which took forever . . . but they eventually reversed Warren's fines. So there is hope for the future?

The moral to this story is: Share your home on Airbnb at your own risk, New Yorkers! You *might not get caught* if you're not a slumlord—but it's still illegal, and if you're one of the unlucky ones like Warren, a mysterious "special enforcement officer" from the city may show up on your doorstep.

BEWARE: LODGING TAXES ARE
COMING TO YOUR AIRBNB BILL

Not surprisingly, the only issue nearly every lawmaker can agree on (when it comes to regulating Airbnb) is they need to start collecting "lodging taxes," "occupancy taxes," and any other tax they can dream up for room-sharing customers.

These taxes are already trickling down to the price you pay for a room, and it's only going to get worse. Today, 200 cities around the world force Airbnb to insert lodging taxes into renters' bills. Over $110 million in lodging taxes have been collected from Airbnb users since 2014![28] If you've rented a room in San Francisco, or Portland, or Washington, D.C.—you have already paid an Airbnb lodging tax.[29]

Another big U.S. city gearing up to drop a fresh Tax Monster on Airbnb is Los Angeles. In 2016 the room-sharing app agreed to fork over at least $5 million in *back* lodging taxes to the city of Los Angeles.[30] The city claimed they were owed for allowing all of the unregulated rental business to go on for years.

It's technically illegal in California to rent a home for less than 30 days, yet nearly half of the state's Airbnb users are in Los Angeles. This brings up a slightly awkward situation for the city—LA is *collecting lodging taxes off an act that's considered illegal by the state of California.* LA officials understand that room sharing has a significantly positive impact on the city's economy; so instead of enforcing the state ban, they decided to tax it. The 948,000 visitors that Airbnb listings attracted to LA between 2015 and 2016 directly contributed to over $1 billion in economic activity to the city![31]

All you have to do is look at how LA's yuppie cousin Santa Monica is treating room-sharing users to see how strikingly differently our nation's cities are addressing this issue. In 2015, Santa Monica eliminated 80% of its Airbnb listings by instituting some of the toughest regulations on short-term rentals in the nation.[32] These rules require anyone listing a home on Airbnb in Santa Monica to live on the property during the renter's stay, register for a business license—which typically costs hundreds of dollars—and collect a 14% occupancy tax from users that is payable to the city.[33]

Santa Monica bureaucrats claim the regulations are necessary due to the increase in housing prices as well as a shrinking housing supply. Well, if that is the real reason, Santa Monica's Tax Monster has worked like gangbusters—it shrunk their Airbnb listings from 1,700 to 300.[34] Gee, I know where *I will not be staying* next time I visit Los Angeles.

THERE IS HOPE: SOME STATES ARE
FIGHTING FOR OUR RIGHT TO SHARE

The good news is that some states are actually fighting to protect your right to share. The first state to pass a law that protected a sharing economy company from local municipalities was Arizona.

In 2016, Arizona governor Doug Ducey signed a law that stops city governments from prohibiting property owners from letting another person pay to stay in their home. Before the law passed, popular tourist cities in Arizona like Sedona, Jerome, and Scottsdale had just about completely banned shared vacation rentals—but not anymore thanks to The Gov.

"This law is a huge win for property owners statewide. Gone are the days when you could face jail time and thousands in fines for renting out your house to tourists," said Christina Sandefur, the executive vice president of the Phoenix-based Goldwater Institute and author of the model bill the law was based on.[35]

Florida is lining up to be the next state to protect Airbnb and the like. In 2017, Florida state senator Greg Steube introduced a bill that would stop city governments from regulating Airbnb into extinction.[36] The bill follows the blueprint of Arizona's law.

We'll have to wait and see how the Florida vote shakes out, but I found it illuminating to hear Senator Steube call out a few of the sneaky moves city governments pull on homeowners to dissuade them from room sharing. He said: "I have seen dozens of local ordinances regulating short-term rentals. The range of regulation includes $10,000 a day fines, government inspections with only one hour of notice, exorbitant licensing fees, special utility and water assessments, excessively restrictive time frames for use of private pools, and requirements for privacy and noise-buffering fences."[37]

Nice job, trying to shut this crap down in Florida, Senator Steube. I wish there were more people in government like you!

WHY DO WE HOLD UBER TO A HIGHER STANDARD?

Now that you know how cities and states are cracking down on room sharing, I want to expose the flawed thinking behind the excuses bureaucrats use to regulate ride-sharing companies like Uber and Lyft. Liberals like Bernie Sanders love to slam Uber as an "unregulated" company with "serious problems." But financial disclosures during his 2016 presidential run revealed whenever old Bernie's campaign required a taxi . . . they used Uber instead![38]

Haters complain that Uber doesn't classify its drivers as full-time employees or offer them any health care or 401k benefits.[39] Yes, it would be amazing if every Uber driver got benefits, but how many other companies in 2017 are handing out benefits to part-time, low-skill employees in the United States? Why hold Uber to this insanely high standard if no other companies are doing it?

The vast majority of people who drive for Uber do it as a part-time job on the side.[40] Uber and Lyft have provided hundreds of thousands of flexible jobs and transformed how millions of people get around town. Drivers get to make their own work hours, while passengers get a safer, cleaner, and, for the most part, less creepy ride that's more comfortable, more private, and more reasonably priced than a taxi. Sure, Uber and Lyft are still working out the bugs in their systems, but 81% of their drivers like working for them.

Of course, our local government workers see the situation quite differently. Some cities want to force sharing companies to hire workers full-time instead of classifying them as independent contractors. Uh, hello—97% of their contractors say they're satisfied with the flexibility of their jobs, and have no interest in becoming full-time employees![41]

Another issue lawmakers worry about is consumer safety. How dangerous is taking an Uber compared with taking a taxi or limousine?

Surprisingly, no city collects information about assaults against passengers of taxis or Ubers . . . so who the hell knows! "There's no way to search for that," said Neva Coakley, a spokeswoman for the Boston Police Department. "We don't collect that kind of data." Neither do the cities of San Francisco, Chicago, New York, or Washington, D.C.[42] This means that those horror stories about ride sharing being unsafe are purely anecdotal. If cities don't track assaults where they happen (in a taxi or in an Uber or Lyft), there is zero real data to back up the claims Uber or Lyft drivers are less safe than taxi or limo drivers.

Are city lawmakers just so out of touch they have no friggin' clue what the "shared economy" even means? *Probably.* Most won't acknowledge that the "gig economy" exists because it provides a system that operates the way young people (both riders and drivers) want it to operate. Most local lawmakers seem more interested in "helping" Uber employees who (in reality) don't want or need rescuing—they like where and how they work.

STATES ARE AT ODDS OVER HOW TO REGULATE UBER

Despite the flaws in our government's rationale for hating on ride-sharing apps, it hasn't stopped 41 states and 69 cities from regulating the hell out of them.[43]

Let's start with our old pal New York, which seems to have it out for Uber and Lyft. By all reports, NYC's "Taxi Cartel" desperately needs a government bailout lest it risk total extinction, due to competition from ride sharing.[44] Could the city's hatred for Uber and Lyft have anything to do with protecting "the Cartel"? Some New Yorkers sure think so—because the state just keeps adding more regulations and fees on ride-sharing services.

In 2017, three New York State agencies issued "emergency" regulations, which forced all ride-sharing companies to fill out an application to operate in the state. The application includes a mandatory fee of $100,000 payable to the DMV. Cha-ching! And I haven't mentioned the annual renewal fee of $60,000 the state of New York now charges these companies to operate. All the money goes right into the state's general fund.[45]

Double cha-ching!

New York also has new rules and a hefty new fee for individual drivers. It can now take up to three months, as well as 60 hours of personal time and $3,000 in freaking fees, for drivers to obtain a license.[46] Compare that to Orange County, California, where drivers are only required to pass Uber's background check, which takes less than two hours and costs 10 bucks.

New York is the only city in the nation where Uber and Lyft drivers are required to be fingerprinted.[47] You might assume required fingerprinting is a good thing (the safer our drivers, the better for us, right?). But in reality, this is just another unnecessary, government-required step that adds extra costs to companies who have to perform them (as well as to drivers who use their own resources to submit the results). Uber and Lyft already conduct their own background checks on drivers. These checks, performed by private contractors, are proven to be effective at weeding out bad applicants with criminal backgrounds.[48]

Not only all that, but if ride-sharing companies are forced to adopt more rigorous background checks—which include fingerprinting—drivers can sue Uber or Lyft on the grounds they are being forced to submit to fingerprinting, as if they were full-time employees (rather than independent contractors).[49]

New York should take a page from the Texas playbook. In 2016 Uber and Lyft were run out of Austin, over a city law mandating fingerprinting for all drivers . . . but now the services are back.[50] You can thank Governor Greg Abbott for their return. He passed a law in 2017 that overrode city laws, like the one in Austin.

Now Texas has an across-the-board, statewide regulatory law allowing ride-sharing companies to operate. But there's a catch: These companies are now required to buy a permit from the Texas Department of Licensing and Regulation (TDLR) and pay an annual $5,000 fee to operate throughout the entire state.[51] Sure, a $5,000 fee stinks to high heaven, but it's still better than the $60,000 annual fee New York State charges.

ONE CITY IN AMERICA HAS THE RIGHT IDEA

I'm no high-and-mighty lawmaker but I've got a creative solution that might solve this mess—why not level the playing field by cutting the regulations on the hotel and taxi industries rather than heaping additional regulations on the sharing companies?

One city is already taking my advice—the salt-of-the-earth town of Rochester, New York, appears to be one of the only cities in the nation with its head screwed on straight. When the marauding ride-sharing services rode into town in 2017, instead of dropping a ton of new regulations on Uber and Lyft its city council members thought outside the box. They decided to level the playing field in a totally different way: by removing some of the regulations they used to place on traditional taxi drivers.[52] The Rochester City Council stated, "They recognized the change in the transportation market and wanted to give taxicab owners and drivers greater flexibility to compete for business."

Now that is an idea I can get behind!

I'll be keeping close tabs on how this program works out but one thing is for sure, next time I'm in Rochester, I'd like to buy everyone on the city council a drink!

PART TWO

ADVANCED ADULTING

TEN

CARS

ANIMALS ON WHEELS MUST PAY

To compel a man to furnish funds for the propagation of
ideas he disbelieves and abhors is sinful and tyrannical.

—*Thomas Jefferson*

Road trip!

Have you ever bought a car before? Or hung out with your mom
while she traded in the minivan for a cute convertible? (Hey, she
doesn't have to cart *your* lazy butt around anymore. Why shouldn't
she score some sweet wheels?) Buying a car is one of the biggest bait-
and-switch operations foisted on us by the "American Dream." This is
supposed to be the ultimate symbol of "making it"—status. Money.
Freedom. Taking on the open road. We imagine it as this quintessentially *American* experience.

But the truth is, buying a car is one of the most stressful, confusing, and utterly exhausting "adult-y" things you'll ever have to endure.
Why?

I'll give you two guesses. *Hint:* It has to do with the government,
and a dump truck full of hidden regulations that jack up the price of
your car, about which you can do absolutely nothing.

Like I said, buying a car? Quintessentially American.

"WHAT CAN WE DO TO GET YOU INTO THIS CAR TODAY?"

There are currently more than 253 million cars on the road in the United States—and every single one of them is being driven by a sucker. And yes, that includes you if you own or lease a car. Even if you snagged a "great deal," or spent months doing your research, you're still getting snowed. We tend to lay all our car-buying negativity at the feet of those slimy car salesmen. And sure, they play a part . . . But to be honest? The rigmarole a car dealer has to go through just to be able to sell you a car in the first place is *staggering*.

Long before you or I ever set foot onto a car lot, these much-maligned dealers have endured a series of tasks that would make Sisyphus weep. Let's look at a small sample of all the government regulations a dealership must comply with *before* they get to slap a sticker price on a car. Some of these regulations apply to *all* businesses, so it's not like the auto industry is being singled out. On the other hand, many of them are costs that the auto industry bears alone. But all of them affect the price of the car you want to buy.

I call this, "Government Regulation of the Auto Industry—A Play in 90 Million Acts and Acronyms":

Americans with Disabilities Act (ADA)

Equal Pay Act

Genetic Information Nondiscrimination Act

Affordable Care Act

Consolidated Omnibus Budget Reconciliation Act (COBRA)

Mandatory workplace posters such as "Your rights under the FMLA"

FTC Repossession Rule

Federal Child-Support enforcement regulations

OSHA training

Clean Air Act

Clean Water Act

Resource Conservation and Recovery Act

Comprehensive Environmental Response, Compensation, and Liability Act

Department of Transportation (DOT) training for hazardous materials-handling procedures

National Highway Traffic Safety Administration (NHTSA) alteration and tire-placarding rules

NHTSA Tampering Rules

NHTSA tire regulations

NHTSA Safety Belts

DOE/EPA Gas mileage guides have to be present in every dealership.

This isn't even *close* to being a full list of the hoops that manufacturers and dealers have to jump through just to open up shop. But I got tired, so let's move on.

I'm not trying to lead a "love your car salesman" sensitivity training here. But I *am* saying that those shady practices they're so well known for aren't the real problem—they're just a symptom. When the government says that cars have to be a certain way, prices and production costs go up. Simple as that. It costs *money* to make a car.

It costs *more* money when the government starts saying, "Make *this specific kind of car,* or we'll shut you down. It must look a certain way, sound a certain way, and perform a certain way, or you're going out of business, auto dealer."

When prices and production costs rise, job growth goes down. And when job growth goes down, dealers will do *anything* to sell their cars and stay in business.

THANKS FOR NOTHIN', RALPH NADER

Between 1900 and 1965, automakers put tens of millions of vehicles on the road . . . with almost no interference from the federal government.[1] That's right—federal bureaucrats haven't *always* had their noses in the automobile industry. And yet somehow, cars produced in this period of no regulation were still fitted with modern and standard safety features like windshield wipers, turn signals, and headlights. The auto industry self-regulated via the Society of Automotive Engineers, a group of people who actually worked in the business, and it was effective. Cars weren't falling apart or causing accidents at alarming rates; people weren't dying in car crashes at record high numbers.

Enter Ralph Nader in 1966. Nader—an attorney at the time—published a book called *Unsafe at Any Speed: The Designed-in Dangers of the American Automobile.* In his "bombshell" book, he argued that GM's Corvair cars were unsafe because they had a tendency to roll . . . and therefore the entire car industry needed safety regulations! The book prompted a national dialogue and a push toward regulation that eventually resulted in Congress giving birth to a new government agency: the National Highway Transportation Safety Administration (NHTSA). Federal do-gooders at the NHTSA have tightly regulated the automobile industry ever since.

Ironically, in 1972, the very same agency Nader prompted into existence issued a report stating: "Corvair compares favorably with contemporary vehicles used in the tests . . . the handling and stability performance of the 1960–63 Corvair does not result in abnormal potential for loss of control or rollover." Simply put, Nader's book was based on inaccurate information—there was nothing wrong with Corvair models after all.

Since the '60's, the feds have found countless other ways to tightly control the car industry. The economic burden of federal regulation has risen dramatically over the last 50 years, and the nation's manufacturers have paid the price (and then passed that price on to you, the consumer). It didn't take long for the bureaucrats at the Environmental Protection Agency (EPA) to get in on the regulatory action, too.

Regulations on vehicle fuel emission have made it significantly more expensive to produce cars in the United States, which forces dealerships to jack up prices so they can continue making a reasonable profit. The EPA's Clean Air Act, for example—mentioned earlier in the Supreme List of Acronyms—regulates air emissions from cars "to protect public health and public welfare and to regulate emissions of hazardous air pollutants."[2] Well, that doesn't sound so bad, right? I guess . . . but consider this: This regulation will come to an annual compliance cost of $65 billion by 2020.[3] Yep, you read that right: That's BILLION, with a *B*.

And the EPA is continuously pushing for *more* laws that will increase vehicle prices even higher.

"Tier 3," which sounds like the title of a really awesome horror movie but is actually the name of a boring set of EPA rules, was passed in 2014 under President Obama. These rules impose strict vehicle-emissions mandates on car manufacturers and their customers, requiring emissions reductions of methane by 80% and decreases in particulate emissions by 70%. Put simply: Tier 3 was supposed to reduce toxic air pollution. Sounds like a noble cause, but it comes at a steep cost. The EPA itself estimates the cost to consumers and manufacturers from this regulation to be $1.5 *billion* annually.[4] Other studies have estimated even higher burdens.

You're probably thinking, "Well, yeah, it's annoying to pay more for my car, but I guess I don't really mind if these regulations are saving the planet by reducing harmful emissions. Preserving the Earth for future generations and all that." Yeeaahhhh. See, the thing is, much of the time, these expensive EPA standards *aren't even effective at lowering fuel emissions.* Once again, a well-intentioned government fails. Shocker!

Corporate Average Fuel Economy (CAFE) standards also impose fuel-efficiency regulations on the automobile industry.[5] The Obama administration increased CAFE standards significantly, requiring automakers to increase fuel-efficiency standards to 54.4 miles per gallon by 2025.[6] If an automaker's average mileage fails to meet the CAFE standards, they get slapped with a hefty fine ($5.50 per 0.1 mpg, multiplied by the manufacturer's total domestic production). Some companies, like BMW and Mercedes-Benz, opted out of the new regulations by simply choosing to pay the penalties. Either way, though, these CAFE standards can end up costing car companies hundreds of millions of dollars per year.

But there's plenty of evidence showing that CAFE standards *don't do anything to help the environment.* The rules were first introduced in 1975 during the first "oil crisis," to reduce America's dependence on imported oil. But our dependence on imported oil increased significantly *after* CAFE standards were implemented.

The standards also led to the rise of gas-guzzling SUVs, since mileage rules for "light trucks" (the category that SUVs and minivans fall into) were set to a lower mileage standard than smaller, fuel-efficient cars.

CAFE standards are basically just an inefficient stealth tax on driving. Drivers end up paying more, car companies make *less,* and the Earth is still screwed. You think Mother Nature is sitting around clapping for the government? Think again.

The biggest and most unfortunate effect of the fed's "well-intended" regulation of the auto industry is that these rules incentivize dealers to sneak in hidden fees to make up for higher production costs. I learned this myself after I moved to Texas from New York, and bought my first car. When I first arrived at the dealership, it seemed like there were some great bargains on new vehicles. But my bank account was in for a rude awakening. I ultimately ended up paying much (much, much, much) more for my car than the sticker price said I would.

DUDE, WHERE'S MY DOCUMENTATION FEE?

Buying a new car should be—*could* be—as simple as going to the grocery store and taking something off of the shelf. But imagine that every time you wanted to buy a box of cereal, you had to pass through a showroom and sit down with the cereal gatekeeper. The cereal gatekeeper would then confuse you with fancy jargon and verbal footwork, essentially *refusing to sell it to you* until you agreed to pay more than what the price tag says.

When I went looking to buy my first vehicle in Texas, I saw the perfect car for me—sitting in a lot, just waiting for me to come give it a test-drive. So I sat down with the salesman, ready to get in my new car and drive into the sunset like a happy moron.

I was buying my new car at a great bargain price (or so I thought). Just as I was about to sign on the dotted line, my sales guy said there was "one more thing." He said he'd forgot to mention a few formalities—and he had an invoice in his hand.

I looked to see what he was yammering about, spread out the invoice . . . and was absolutely horrified by what I saw. For starters, most states charge a sales tax. If you buy a car in Texas, you will pay a 6.25% sales tax on the purchase of any vehicle. Not a big deal when we're talking about a box of cereal. But when you're buying a car that costs, say, $20,000, that's another $1,250.

Also, that 6.25% in Texas isn't even *close* to the ceiling of what sales tax can be. If I had driven to California, Washington, or New York to buy my new car, I would've paid about 8.5% in sales taxes. Meanwhile, New Hampshire (my home state—Live Free or Die, baby!), Oregon, Delaware, and Montana have zero sales tax.

What's that sales tax used for? To the surprise of exactly no one, it goes into the federal government's general fund. That's the catchall, anything goes, whatever-is-necessary-for-the-good-of-the-state fund.

Back to the car lot. There were more shenanigans on this invoice. Another line item. He wanted me to pay "documentation fees," which include fees for processing paperwork, storing documents, registration, and title work. These fees are similar in some ways to the "startup" costs that some gyms charge to activate your account, when you know full well that "activating an account" means someone entered your info into a computer and pushed a button.

In Texas, there's no cap on a documentation fee, so they can charge whatever they want. But even in many states *with* caps, you could still expect to pay up to $250.[7] There's no clear way to tie these fees directly to regulations, but remember—the dealer is in the business of making profits. The more regulations the government imposes, the more creative dealers have to be to turn a profit anyway. Enter add-ons. If *you* were a dealer in a state with an uncapped documentation fee, and you were scrambling to turn a profit, don't you think you might hit that as hard as you could? Of course you would!

I paid all the ridiculous add-on nonsense fees and got the hell out of the dealership, wondering if I should feel as violated as I did. I was only one mile away when I realized I'd completely forgotten about insurance. And property tax. I was going to be paying monthly insurance on this car, and yearly property tax, for as long as I had it.

I also forgot about buying gas. The government gets 18.4 cents for every gallon that you buy, and there are additional fuel taxes in some states (remember chapter 1?).

"DO YOU KNOW WHY I PULLED YOU OVER?"

As if the costs of buying a car aren't enough, you'd better hope you're never pulled over. Traffic fines make a certain amount of sense, in terms of keeping the roads safe, but most local and state governments have exploited these fees to rake in massive amounts of revenue. Get caught going 31 MPH in a 30 MPH zone with out-of-state license plates? Good luck against the graft machine!

Speeding tickets are big business—nationwide, drivers receive over 100,000 tickets *per day* and provide over $6 billion annually to municipalities across the country.[8] The revenue from these fines goes to a variety of sources, including administrative offices and city pensions. In New Jersey, for example, part of your ticket is supposed to go to the police "Body Armor Replacement Fund"—but in 2016, politicians diverted $400,000 for an unrelated call center for the state's Department of Human Services.[9] In Missouri, a $3 surcharge goes directly to the pensions of 125 former sheriffs.[10] They're a politically addictive form of revenue—and used as a cudgel against drivers.

Cameras are an increasingly popular (but constitutionally dicey) way of collecting money from speeders. One town in Ohio was court ordered to refund $3 million in tickets illegally handed out using cameras.[11] In new Miami, every violation comes with a ticket of up to $180—and the accused have no chance at a day in court as there is no police officer to testify against the accused. Worse, the city outsourced the enforcement to a private vendor.

Cities and law enforcement often use their power against anyone who even warns of abuses by cities and states against drivers. This goes well beyond traffic cameras. A Texas man was arrested in 2013

for violating a local ordinance after he held a sign that read simply
POLICE AHEAD.[12] A year later the charges were dropped but the police kept his sign.[13] In 2012, a Missouri motorist flashed his lights to
warn other drivers of a speed trap. He was ticketed and threatened
with up to $1,000 in fines and points on his license. The city dropped
the charges, but the driver fought back, bringing the case to federal
court. A U.S. District Judge eventually ruled that yes, you can flash
your high beams to warn upcoming traffic.[14]

Traffic stops are often used as a convenient segue to other fines for
things like broken headlights and unstuck registration stickers. The
Supreme Court declared these stops unconstitutional in 2015,[15] but
they still continue today. There are hardly any protections for drivers—and that's just what government agencies want. Until a 2015
court decision, California charged drivers contesting their traffic fees
with special fines, including having to pay all unpaid prior tickets
before even allowing a court hearing. Meanwhile, the state canceled
four million drivers' licenses due to unpaid or partially paid traffic
fines.[16] Only in 2017 did California actually stop this unproductive
and punitive practice.[17]

Many states implement a number of automatic charges on top of
the initial ticket, as well. California charges a 20% surcharge on all
traffic fines, and tacks on a number of other fees that can add hundreds of dollars to the total cost.[18] These include heavy surcharges
on each ticket written in the Golden State—$40 for court opera-
tions, $35 for a criminal conviction assessment, $4 for medical air
transport, $55 for requesting traffic school (not the cost of the class
itself), $100 for a "State Penalty Assessment," $50 for a Court Facility Construction Penalty, $50 for a DNA ID Fund, $20 for a Medical
Services Penalty, and a night court fee of a whole dollar. These should
all sound like a racket—because they are.

The revenue collected from such fines is deposited straight into
California's general fund. Some of these fines go toward causes as

diverse as the California Beverage Recycling Fund and the Fish and Game Propagation Fund.[19]

On average, 80% of the money paid by Californians after a ticket is written doesn't even go toward paying the ticket itself—instead, it goes toward added fines and charges.[20] Get slapped with a $100 speeding ticket? Prepare to pay a total of $500 to the state. The state's original charges were much more modest—in the 1960s, drivers paid a 5% surcharge with each traffic ticket to fund driver's ed. But government only grows; today, California collects billions every year, with $10 billion in uncollected debt alone.

The situation is so bad, even Governor Jerry Brown—Moonbeam himself—said, "Loading more and more costs on traffic tickets has been too easy a source of new revenue. Fines should be based on what is reasonable punishment, not on paying for more general fund activities."

And make no mistake: This racket isn't only happening in Cali. New York charges you $100 per year for three years if you accumulate six license penalty points in 18 months.[21] If you get any more points beyond those six, you pay $75 per point for the following three years. Most of the fines don't even go to local roads and bridges. Often only 5–10% goes to the local city, with the rest headed to your state's general fund.[22]

Parking tickets are no better, but the fines are often small enough that they go unchallenged in court. Washington, D.C., gave out over $17 million in improper parking tickets over the last few decades. In St. Louis, angry ticketees sued the city for writing unwarranted and unnecessary tickets.[23] When a former city counselor requested information in 2014 regarding a potentially defective parking meter, he was told it would cost $1,700 for the city to provide the information.

Over the last several decades, parking violations have become valuable sources of revenue for city and state coffers.[24] Municipalities around the nation are well aware of this, and continually increase fine amounts to keep the money coming. Pensacola, Florida, raised its fine for parking in front of a fire hydrant in 2009 by 900%, from $10 to $100. One Boston suburb mandated that each police officer write at least one parking or traffic ticket per shift.

Here's the bottom line: The government will take whatever it can get, and if it's going to reap the greatest possible profit, it needs you to stay ignorant. If you convince yourself that you can't possibly purchase a car on your own, you'll be forced to rely on people you can't trust. But if you spend some time getting ready, you can march into the dealership like you know what the hell you're doing.

Owning a car IS pretty cool. You just have to get past all this government interference to finally enjoy it.

ELEVEN

PETS

THE HIDDEN COST OF UNCONDITIONAL LOVE

> The art of taxation consists of plucking the goose so as
> to obtain the most feathers with the least hissing.
>
> —*Jean-Baptiste Colbert*

Jimmy was my first love. He was always there for me—when I was sick, he'd never leave my side, and if I didn't like my food I could always count on him to finish it. He was always a comfort when I was sad, and he never failed to shower me with love at the end of a long day at work.

Jimmy was . . . wait for it . . . a dog! I know; you're stunned. He was a scruffy little mutt with floppy ears who was rescued outside a Whataburger dumpster in downtown Houston. His farts were powerful enough to knock a vulture off a meat wagon. Nonetheless, he was my little gaseous monster and he brought me so much joy. It's true what they say—owning a pet lowers blood pressure, eases depression, and calms anxiety. And the love and gratitude we feel for man's best friend (and whatever cats are) contributes to a "whatever they need!" mentality when it comes to spending money on our pets.

And that's exactly what the government exploits to bring in more tax revenue. (Cue record scratch.)

I know; I ruin everything good. Even Rover isn't safe! But hey—I'm just the messenger.

There's an ever-growing list of methods bureaucrats use to make money off of your decision to share your home with a wild beast. Some of these are well-intentioned initiatives driven by a "common-sense" approach to ensure pet safety—like the small-town Barney Fife—esque dog warden, who has a legit role in reducing feral populations or preventing rabies. Often, such a position is done without pay or fanfare.

But you *know* it doesn't stop there. City, state, and federal pet regulations (all in the name of "safety," of course) drive up the cost and hassle of owning your furry best friend.

PET LICENSING FEES:
SUPPORT YOUR LOCAL BUREAUCRAT

I'll never forget the day I picked up Jimmy at the pound. I adopted a dog because I was ready to take the next step in my adult life—I didn't want to have kids yet, but I was ready to take care of something other than myself. (Yes, my life is often just a series of hackneyed clichés.) And I'd finally endured enough teary Sarah McLachlan commercials to move me off my couch and into the animal shelter. Driver's license, cash, and several references in hand, I marched into the pound ready to change an animal's life.

I knew the many benefits of having a dog; it's amazing what a good pet can do for a person's health, morale, and general well-being. But as soon as I adopted Jimmy, I got slapped with a bevy of local, state, and federal fees that needed to be dealt with in order to save him from street life.

Before I could leave the pound, I had to cough up a $129 "adoption fee" plus $20 for a pet license. The lady behind the counter informed me that the license is a tag for Jimmy's collar that will "tell everyone that my pet is not a homeless stray." Um—isn't that what my dog's normal collar and tags are? I told her I wasn't interested. "Sorry ma'am, it's mandatory," she replied. I wanted to put up a fight, but I knew it was useless—this *was* the government, after all. So I turned over my last crumpled $20 bill, collected my new four-legged son, and went home.

Most U.S. cities, as well as several states, require dog licenses by law. They typically cost $20–$40 and must be renewed annually. The intended purpose of the tags is to let the public know your dog has an owner, and to help city officials track the number of cats and dogs for "safety concerns."

If you adopt a dog in Seattle, for instance, you'll pay a mandatory $35 pet license fee, which you must renew annually. If you're late to renew the license, you get stuck with a $25 penalty. Don't want to license your dog in Seattle? Too bad—it's the law, and if a city official catches your furry friend without a license, you'll get slapped with one (or more) of the following fines:[1]

- Not having an animal license: $125
- Not displaying an animal license: $54
- Not showing license to an official: $54
- Using another's license: $109
- Removing license without permission: $109

Think the city government won't actually try enforcing these licensing rules? HA! Officials will go to incredible lengths to snoop on citizens for even *possibly* having a pet without a tag. For years now, Seattle has purchased lists of people buying pet food at stores and mailed them threatening letters to register their animals.[2] (Big Brother, anyone?) The letters were a clear attempt to boost the health of the local government's coffers. As the *Seattle Times* pointed out: "The county says its pet-licensing agency, which has been using direct-mailing lists since 2012, made more than $80,000 in profit from pet-licensing revenue from last year's letters."[3]

This brings me to an important question that you're probably asking: How do local governments *spend* our pet-licensing fees? Is the money used to save abused and homeless animals? Or provide better care in shelters? Or anything remotely pet-related?

Well . . . that depends on where you live. Most municipalities will claim that the money goes to animal shelters—but pet-licensing fees also provide an easy, steady stream of revenue for city and state governments facing budget crises. Pennsylvania, where dog licenses are required by state law, has its own Bureau of Dog Law Enforcement Office. And it's not an adorable and hilarious group of crime-fighting dogs (although someone should really make that happen). The office—which is funded almost entirely through pet-licensing fees and license-related penalties—claims its mission is to ensure "the welfare of breeding dogs and puppies in commercial breeding kennels."

On paper, that sounds perfectly acceptable. But in 2009, Pennsylvania State officials were struggling to balance their budget when they thought of a brilliant idea: They transferred the $4 million sitting in the Dog Law bank account straight into Pennsylvania's general fund.[4] *Voilà!* Budget problem solved.

Pennsylvania's bureaucracy is massive and expensive, with nearly 73,000 full-time salaried employees who each enjoy comfortable salaries and pension plans.[5] The state shells out $4 billion per year for salaried payroll alone. Given the state's enormous annual expenditures, PA struggles with budget issues year after year. In order to balance their budget, officials continue to divert funds from the Dog Law bureau to the state general fund, where the money can then be spent on just about anything. In 2015, the state collected $6.5 million from the sale of a million dog licenses.

Meanwhile, state politicians continue to complain that the Dog Law bureau is underfunded. Their solution? Raise the cost of pet-licensing fees! Of course, these same officials don't acknowledge that pet-licensing fees rarely support the bureau's work.

Think the bureaucrats in Pennsylvania are the only ones funneling pet-license fees into a general fund? Aw, buddy. You should know better than that by now! Turns out, government workers all around the country have realized how easy it is to take advantage of responsible pet owners. Numerous cities, large and small—including Honolulu[6] and Des Moines[7]—deposit pet fees directly into *Ye Olde General Fund*.

I wish I could say "I'm shocked!" But I'm not. And you shouldn't be, either.

Turns out I'm not the only one who rails against the thought of asking the government's permission to give a homeless dog a loving family. Despite extensive efforts by state and local governments to force residents to pay pet-licensing fees . . . many Americans still just *don't*. In Seattle, officials saw a small uptick in licensing after they sent those threatening letters in the mail—but even after the increase, only about 23% of pets in in the city are licensed.[8]

And it's not just American citizens who seem to hate (or ignore) dog-licensing laws. The UK banned dog licenses in 1987 because they were "held by only around half of dog owners." Despite charging the equivalent of just 50 cents per tag, the British government could only get half its dog-owning residents to comply with their license law. The UK's official Kennel Club remains opposed to dog licensing to this day—in an issued statement, the Club warned that "it is the responsible dog owner who will end up paying a further tax on dog ownership, whilst the irresponsible will continue to flout the law. Licensing has been tried before in the UK and it has neither been enforceable nor has it been effective."[9] EXACTLY! Get it together, 'Murica.

Will American bureaucrats learn from our British friends across the pond? Hahahahahaha—you're funny.

GOVERNMENT-SPONSORED
DISCRIMINATION, DOGGIE STYLE

There's no doubt pet-licensing fees are the pits—but they are worse if you own dog breeds pegged as "dangerous." In an oh-so-noble effort to protect us from "vicious" pets, many municipalities charge higher license fees for owning certain breeds.[10] Little Rock, Arkansas, for instance, requires pit bull owners to obtain a special permit, a city license, and a window sticker on an annual basis.

In most cities, large and small, owners applying for a license are asked to identify the breeds of their dogs, trusting that those breeds will remain legal in years to come. Yet it's not uncommon for municipalities to outright ban entire dog breeds. One of the largest and most egregious is Denver's ban on pit bulls.[11] Since the ban was passed in 1990, the city has put down over 3,500 pit bulls at a cost of over $250 each.[12] Since Denver's law was put in place, it has withstood numerous battles in state and federal court—on each occasion, the ban has prevailed. Denver's consistent legal victories have helped many other cities put similar laws in place. Dozens of locations have breed-specific restrictions, which have been decried by animal control officials as "canine racism." In Alabama alone, *six* towns ban pit bulls.

Given the pit bull banning trend, you'd think the dogs have been mauling and biting humans, fighting with other dogs, and eating babies. But they *used* to be America's darlings—and if you've ever met one, chances are he's been a total sweetheart, right? Before the mid-'80s, stories of pit bull attacks were rare. So what changed?

For one, dogfighting made a comeback in the '80s. Given pit bulls' strength and tenacity, they were typically the dog of choice. The breed has also been the preferred guard dogs for drug dealers and gangs. A highly publicized attack in 1987, when a pit bull guarding a California marijuana crop mauled a two-year-old to death, put the breed at the center of controversy.[13] By the summer of that same year, over 30 communities passed legislation against pit bulls. Yet numerous studies have shown evidence that pit bulls aren't even the most dangerous breed[14]—government action is often due to the *perception* of danger, rather than the reality of it. Is it possible that the blame for some pit bull attacks rests squarely on humans? One animal official told the *Houston Chronicle,* "Many pit bull attacks are due to a skyrocketing number of poorly bred and badly trained dogs raised by backyard breeders, who are trying to cash in on the pit pull's growing reputation as a cheap but deadly effective guard dog, particularly in urban areas."

And it doesn't stop with pit bulls. Many other supposedly "dangerous" breeds (rottweilers, Alaskan malamutes, Doberman pinschers, to name a few) are prohibited in various locations across the nation.

Do-gooder bureaucrats don't just stop with dogs, either. They regulate the hell out of all kinds of pets, and some restrictions appear to lack any sort of logic (try to hide your surprise). For example, it's illegal to own a jackrabbit in Kentucky, even though the animal is hardly considered "dangerous wildlife." You have to pay a fee and get a permit to own a pet rabbit in Indiana.[15] And if you get caught with an unregistered bunny? You can face fines up to $500 and be charged with a misdemeanor! You can't take a French poodle to an opera in Illinois.[16] *(Author's note: this is now on my bucket list.)* Imagine the State Senate Committee that discusses and advances these things. It's almost like they were invented by the imaginary Law Enforcement Dogs, right? *No rabbits! We hate rabbits! And poodles are dumb!*

MITTENS' FANCY FEAST IS TAXED UP THE A**

Next time you're at Petco stocking up on dog chow (or whatever nasty stuff cats eat—I wouldn't know), take a close look at your bill—you'll notice a sales tax on your Kibbles 'n Bits. Pet food has been subject to sales taxes for years in the United States. Oddly enough, though, sales taxes on animal food only apply to animals that are not suitable for human consumption.[17] WTF? How does the government define "suitable for human consumption"? The answer is exactly what you'd expect from the government (*read:* It makes no freaking sense whatsoever). Food eaten by dogs and cats is taxable; but food eaten by horses *is not* taxable, since by law horses are classified as "livestock"—and livestock is typically consumed by humans.

Um . . . When's the last time you ate horse? You're a monster!

Like so many other taxes and fees, pet food taxes end up hitting low-income earners the hardest. Nearly 44% of all U.S. households have a dog, and 35% have a cat. Yet horses—a pet of the elite—are exempt from the tax. Think about everything you need to keep a pet horse: a barn, riding equipment, and plenty of land for the horse to run. Not to mention all those oats and carrots they eat. It's no surprise that horses are associated with wealth.[18] Now don't get me wrong—I don't want to tax horse food, but some consistency would be nice.

Some states take it a step further, tacking on *even more* fees to dog and cat food beyond just the sales tax. In 2013, Maryland passed a pet food "fee." The state claims the funds collected will help cover spaying and neutering costs for pet owners who are on welfare (such as food stamps or Section 8 Housing).[19] The cause has been applauded by do-gooders in the state, yet the collected revenue does nothing for the responsible pet owners in Maryland, who pay their own way for doing the right thing (in fact, it punishes them, since they're the ones paying the fees). And considering recent history, how long until that tax revenue goes right into Maryland's "general fund"?

Many states create pet food regulations, intended to promote safety, that end up raising costs—meanwhile, many of these regulations are laughably ineffective. Illinois, the Bankruptcy State, has one of the harshest set of pet food safety regulations. That didn't stop a pet food manufacturer there from selling several varieties of dog food chock-full of pentobarbital[20]——a drug vets use to put our canine companions down.

There are also *indirect taxes* on pet food. State taxation and regulation regimes lead the pet food industry to set up shop in more business-friendly areas. Great news if you're in one—lookin' at you, Texas—bad news if you're not. One of the top-quality suppliers of pet food, Blue Buffalo, decided to place and expand a major complex in Missouri.[21] If you live in a high-tax state, the cost to ship pet food to your house is added on right there—on top of normal production costs and the pet food sales tax, of course.

But it's not just regulations and taxes at the state level that are jacking up the price of your dog chow—our buddies at the federal Food and Drug Administration (FDA) want a piece of the action, too. While the agency says it doesn't directly regulate the Kibbles 'n Bits headed into Jimmy's bowl, it still finds a way in. The ingredients and even the food colorings in every bag of pet food require approval from the FDA.[22] These animal food mandates cost the industry *$100 million* annually——and of course, the costs are passed down to pet owners like you and me. Lucky us!

13-YEAR-OLD PET SITTERS ARE CRIMINALS

Did you think it was only Fido's pet food that's being taxed? Oh, puh-lease. When our local officials find something to tax . . . they won't stop until they squeeze out as much of your money as they can.

Depending on where you live, you may face special taxation on activities surrounding regular animal care. New Jersey requires vets to charge sales tax for many services,[23] adding yet another layer (and expense) to an already-difficult profession. Florida pet owners pay sales taxes on vet services as well as boarding, grooming, and items like nail clippers, brushes, and soaps. The state legislators in Tennessee decided that the charges for bathing a pet are subject to sales tax, while charges for grooming are not. Why? Because, according to the state's Department of Revenue's website, bathing a pet is categorized as "laundering or dry cleaning tangible personal property," which is a taxable service in the state.

But New York City, true to form, is leading the way when it comes to Draconian regulations on pet services. According to the city Health Department, dog sitting is *illegal*. Yes, seriously.[24] A city law bans anyone without an official kennel license from all pet sitting, boarding, feeding, and grooming for a fee. The department insists that this ban is for residents' own good, because officials conduct inspections of all licensed facilities to make sure animals would be secure and safe. Right . . . Because I'm really going to feel safer leaving Jimmy at a "facility" than in the care of the 14-year-old kid down the block who loves the dog more than life, and knows his walking route, and whose family I've known for years.

But here's the worst part about NYC's law: Even if my 14-year-old pet sitter (or any other private citizen) *wanted* to comply, it would be impossible—private households are banned from obtaining a kennel license. Go on vacation for the weekend and leave Socks with your friend? Penalty fees for violating the law *start at $1,000*.

New York's pet-sitting ban is just one example of how occupational licensing—which costs U.S. consumers $203 billion per year[25]—is often a thinly veiled government protection racket. Bureaucrats pushing the kennel-licensing law tell residents they're doing it because they care about the "little guy," when the ban only protects commercial pet boarders who might be put out of business from the new competition. The city's *real* incentive might have to do with the fact that in order to obtain a kennel license, you must pay to complete a city-run "Animal Care and Handling Course."[26] When you're done with that, you need to pay hundreds of dollars in "Permit Fees" to the city (which you'll have to renew annually) and fill out paperwork so that the government can collect sales taxes off your boarding business.[27]

That's a lot of work (and money) just to feed your neighbor's cat for a few days.

Until recently, most New Yorkers were completely unaware of the city's pet-sitting ban. But an incident involving the pet-sitting app "Rover" has spurred an outrage among residents. Rover matches pet owners with pet sitters, offering a win-win situation: The pet owners get convenient, reasonably priced care for their animals, while the sitter makes money for watching Fido in the comfort of his or her own home. Like Airbnb, but for dog sitting. Most dog-boarding services in Manhattan cost well over $60 per night, while rates on Rover start at around $20 a night, so the app's popularity exploded quickly in the Big Apple.[28] Nearly 100,000 pet owners registered in the city, as well as 9,000 sitters, who made over $4 million per year. Everything was going well . . . until 2016, when the Health Department's general counsel attempted to squash Rover's presence in the city. He sent a stern letter to the app, warning that its 109,000 NYC-based users were *breaking the law* and could each face thousands of dollars in penalties.

Several apartment residents were subsequently slapped with violations for pet sitting through Rover. But the app isn't going to go down without a fight, and it's leading the effort to get NYC's kennel-license law overturned. Rover's general counsel John Lapham told the New York *Daily News,* "If you've got a 14-year-old getting paid to feed your cats, that's against the law right now. [Many] places right now continue to make it easier to watch children than animals, and that doesn't make any sense."

Seems like common sense to me! I'm rooting for Rover. Perhaps there's hope for NYC's pet sitters, after all.

Unlike the taxes discussed in some of the other chapters in this book (everyone needs to use transportation, eat food, and live somewhere), there *is* a way out of all these pet-related fees and taxes—don't get a pet. (Don't give me those sad puppy-dog eyes; you know it's the truth.) But that's basically like saying, "Your mental and emotional well-being (not to mention the life of a sweet, loyal pooch) aren't worth it."

But we all know that's not true—the joy and love that pets bring into our lives is *priceless*. Which is why, just like all the other taxes and fees in this book, we roll over . . . and pay the price.

TWELVE

HOUSE

BUYING A HOME? YOUR DREAMS ARE IN ESCROW

> The problem is not that the people are taxed too little.
> The problem is that the government spends too much.
>
> —*Ronald Reagan*

Welcome to the high-octane world of middle adulthood! Your formative years are behind you, the days of all-night benders and taco-eating contests have reached their conclusion, and now you can get down to the serious business of L-I-V-I-N'. And to do that, you've got to plant roots. For most people, that means buying a house.

Things aren't how they used to be. If you talk to anyone from the "Greatest Generation," you'll find that many of them built their own houses. I have a friend whose grandpa got married at age 20, then spent the next two years building his house out of bricks with his new wife and sleeping under the stars. This requires a level of grit and know-how that many young people today just don't have.

But times have changed. Now, instead of physical strength, a willingness to live without HBO Go, and a solid understanding of things like structural engineering (LOL), homesteading requires different skill-sets—including knowing how to buy a home without getting absolutely massacred by hidden taxes and fees.

I don't think anyone really believes that buying a house is simple or easy, but let me tell you—it's a whole hell of a lot harder (and pricier) than it used to be and needs to be.

But why?

IF IT MOVES, TAX IT. IF IT KEEPS MOVING, REGULATE IT.

Bureaucrats tell us that all housing regulations are necessary, well-intended measures to ensure the health and safety of the home-buyer. But tight regulations act as stealth taxes, increasing the cost of housing and putting the government in a position where it can't be questioned, held accountable, or pressured. That's a step toward totalitarianism, not freedom.

On average, city, state, and federal regulations on building account for 24% of the cost of a home![1] Excessive rules, typically put in place under the guise of promoting safety, make it harder for the average American family to afford a home.

In some states, the burden is worse than in others. In Minnesota, a state law requires all new homes to include childproof windows. Such windows, which won't open more than three inches unless un-latched by an adult, must be present in every new home . . . even if no kids will be living there. This required "safety feature" costs around $1,000 to implement per house.[2] Minnesota law also requires homes to have "automatic air exchanges" and an extra two inches of insulation in basement walls. Locals blame all of these excessive regulations for Minnesota's absurdly high housing costs. The state's latest code-book affecting residential homes is *567 pages long.*

Complying with these regulations isn't so burdensome to the wealthy—but it can be financially crippling to middle- or lower-class families.

Homebuyers pay an average of *$29,000 more* for a home in Min-nesota than they would for the same house in neighboring North

Dakota. This significant price difference is the direct result of Minnesota's housing rules. The two states have the same culture and the same weather . . . Except one votes for regulation-loving bureaucrats.

State regulation has gotten to the point where each individual component of a home must meet strict guidelines. In New York, for instance, anyone who wants to construct a new house over two stories and of a certain size needs to pony up for an in-home sprinkler system. This can cost over $25,000. And if you're not on municipal water, your well pump just got a lot bigger and more expensive.

The same goes for additions and improvements to your existing home. The list of small projects requiring permits in many cities is long enough to make you cry.[3] Whether you're adding a porch, installing a patio cover, building a deck over 30 inches high, updating windows, moving 10 cubic yards of earth, or replacing a water heater . . . well, make sure it meets local zoning rules. Want to add a deck to your home in Prince William County, Virginia? Get ready to comply with 17 pages of regulations.[4] Put a sign on your own property in Chicago? $200 fee.[5] Build a fence that's slightly "too high" in Macon, Georgia? Take it down . . .[6] If you don't, you're going to have a lot of fun over the next two years paying fees to the local planning or zoning board seeking a variance.

Each state and city has a different way of using the collected fees. In many cases, the money goes right into a general fund, but it's often put back into the departments in charge of zoning and codes. This creates a feedback loop incentivizing writing more tickets.

Ultimately, these fees are an easy way for state and local governments to fill their coffers. Why else would officials charge a $1,000 "rezoning fee" to put a shed in your yard, like Winston-Salem, North Carolina, does?[7] Or a $7,500 fee *per parking space,* like Newburyport, Massachusetts, does?[8] Salaries, office supplies, and equipment can effectively pay for themselves with one creatively defined regulation!

It's not just state and city regulations that increase housing costs—the feds want a piece of the action, too. Many federal housing regulations are geared toward environmental causes. Hey, don't you support a place for Bambi's friends to frolic?! You don't hate the environment, do you?

Take out your wallet, Sucka!

New EPA regulations cost the overall economy over $100 billion annually.[9] Few Americans understand that these regulations add an average of $85,000 to the construction of every new house built in the United States.

One of the most idiotic and burdensome EPA rules effectively outlaws old-style residential woodstoves; in 2008, the agency ruled that the smoke pollution from woodstoves violated the federal Clean Air Act. Now the EPA is stepping up their enforcement efforts, affecting people in Alaska the worst.[10] Burning wood in the state's interior is about the only feasible way to stay warm in the winter, when it can reach −50 degrees Fahrenheit. Heating oil is difficult to ship to some areas of Alaska, and natural gas isn't available in parts of the state.

But the feds don't seem to care—they've threatened to revoke Alaska's transportation funding if the woodstove "noncompliance" continues. Out of fear of losing the federal funds, state and local authorities have threatened to impose hefty fines on residents who continue to put woodstoves in newly constructed homes. Homebuyers are stuck with an unfortunate choice: use costly heating oil or cough up cash for the woodstove fine.

Other EPA regulations are just as costly for consumers, like the Department of Energy's 2014 rule requiring non-weatherized furnaces in homes to be switched out for "more efficient" models.[11] The total cost for homebuyers? *Over $12 billion.*[12]

For many older homes, compliance is grandfathered in on a whole gamut of rules and regulations. For many homeowners-to-be, it's often easier to buy an older house and get it up to snuff than to build a new home that meets all these new "For the Environment" rules.

What about proven health hazards? Surely by now, we're all on board with eliminating the dangers of things like lead paint and asbestos.

Most people understand the dangers of lead paint—van Gogh went nuts from nibbling at his own paintbrushes, and ended up short an ear.[13] But the way our government has handled the problem is just as crazy-making. An Obama-era rule to remove lead paint when found on site seems pretty straightforward—until it isn't. For years, the standard practice was to simply cover or paint over the offending lead paint, thus preventing it from getting in the mouths of tots. But the new rule change, forcing a labor-intensive removal process, at least doubles the cost of repainting.[14] Contractors need special licensing, equipment, and ability to isolate and remove the paint chips. And if you hire a contractor that doesn't abide by the new standards, guess who pays $37,500 for every violation? (Hint: It's not the contractor.)

And if there's nature's cotton candy, asbestos, within a country mile of your domicile? Be sure to set aside a half-year's salary to have it removed (that is not an exaggeration—it costs upward of $20,000 to remove asbestos from even a small building). A 1989 EPA rule effectively bans asbestos and requires extensive remediation on existing property.[15] Does that mean that I want asbestos? Of course not. But the market did a far more effective job of removing it from Americans' homes than the EPA's own rule, which was partially struck down in a 1991 court ruling.

What if I don't want to worry about lead paint and asbestos? I'll just build a brand-new house! Yeah . . . welcome to the confusing and maddening world of regulatory "soft" taxation.

Have an old, functioning septic tank you want to reuse? Forget it, it doesn't matter that it still works fine—it doesn't meet the new state regulatory code. If you're within a stone's throw of mountains that feed a city's water supply, like New York's rural Catskill Mountains, you need approval from local officials, the State Department of Health, and the New York City Department of Environmental Protection. Congrats on winning the consolation prize of digging up your septic tank, paying a consultant to inspect the site for contaminants, and paying for a new, less efficient, more expensive replacement.

NANNY-STATE MCFEE AND THE MYSTERY OF HIGH CLOSING COSTS

Let's beam into the near future together: It's time to close on your new place in New York. Buckle up for some nasty closing costs!

Government Recording Charges—*CHA-CHING!*

The sale of the home, and the transfer of ownership to lucky you, means that the paperwork has to be officially filed with a recorder's office. By recording a real estate purchase or sale, the deal becomes part of the public record. Which means that most of the time, an inquisitive person can look up any property and see who owns it, when it was purchased, and the property's tax assessment. Sometimes it also shows the number of bedrooms, bathrooms, lot size, and more. Sounds like a wonderful tool for potential stalkers and burglars, yes? There's no opting out of the snooper-enabling policies—or the fees.

The costs of government recording charges in New York break down as follows:[16]

- Recording fee: $40
- Recording and endorsement page: $5.00
- Per page $5.00

That's not going to break the bank, but these aren't short documents. Once you're looking at the pile of pages that is a housing contract, you'll understand why the government does this. One, because it can. Two, because it's free money for them, taken away from you and me. But wait—there's more!

Tax Service Fee—*CHA-CHING!*

This one is pretty minor, but it's the little things, tons of them, that peck away at your wallet (and your soul). The tax fee verifies that all of the previously owed taxes on the property were paid. The fee comes in around $50.

Transfer Tax—*CHA-CHING!*

The vast majority of states charge some sort of transfer tax, which is stuck on people who sell their homes. Some rates are relatively low, like Colorado's 0.01% tax, while in other areas the rate is closer to 2%, like parts of West Virginia. Adding 2% on top of the other closing costs and sheer borrowing for the house stacks up quicker than you thought. That comes out to $4,000 on the sale of a $200,000 home. That's real money. I know, you're reading about *buying* a house. But you don't think the current landowner is going to eat this cost, do you?

Mortgage Tax—*CHA-CHING!*

Did you think we were done? Prepare to pay a tax on the largest sum of money you'll ever borrow! If you plan to move to Alabama, Florida, Kansas, Minnesota, New York, Oklahoma, Tennessee, Virginia, or Washington, D.C., you'll shell out for this extra-special mortgage tax just for the privilege of signing your life away. You're dealing with up to another 0.35% if you buy your house in Florida. Beaches are nice. Holding on to my money is nicer.

Mandated Insurance—*CHA-CHING!*

If you took out a loan for a house, you have to pay insurance on your mortgage. Even worse, there's no rest for your payment schedule. In 2013, the Obama administration changed the Federal Housing Administration's rules regarding when you could stop paying. Prior to the change, it was at 78% repayment; after the change, it was at 100%.[17] The Obama White House also added a poison pill for the incoming Trump presidency. Knowing the new president would freeze regulations put in place at the 12th hour by #44, Obama's HUD declared just 11 days before the end of his term that they planned a mortgage insurance rate cut of 0.25%. When Reince Priebus suspended all of the overarching regulations, this was swept up with them . . . just in time for the press to declare Trump raised the cost of owning a house[18]—even though the reduction never took effect.

The Mortgage Itself—*CHA-CHING!!!*

Yes, through the mess of papers and actuarial charts, the mortgage itself is more complex than a season of *Lost*. After the 1920s housing bubble collapsed, FDR's New Deal set up a number of alphabet soup agencies to foster home ownership. Not every single agency was a disaster, some of them run counter to their stated goals.

Enormous public-private monsters like the Federal National Mortgage Association (Fannie Mae) and Federal Home Loan Mortgage Corporation (Freddie Mac) not only back mortgages at the federal level, they also play important roles in social engineering. They are the biggest of the "too big to fail" agencies, and come with inherent dangers. The two were among the largest contributors to the 2008 crash and guarantors of those absurdly risky subprime mortgages. Now, with $5 trillion in public debt backed, the bubble grows bigger than ever. Your home's value is directly tied to how everyone else manages their responsibilities. If the Great Recession is any indication, maybe renting doesn't sound so bad for now. Screw the white picket fence!

I'M GLAD THAT'S OVER . . . OH, WAIT.

Whew! You've made it, and now you can finally enjoy some of the benefits of being a homeowner. Singing in the shower without worrying that the upstairs neighbors can hear you. Putting your feet on anything you want. Walking around naked. You know, the normal stuff. Oh! And how about that sweet home mortgage interest credit you get to write off on your taxes? Deducting that interest means less in taxes, right? Well . . . not always.

Before home ownership, when you filed your taxes, the standard deduction was always better than any itemization you might try. Think about it like this: The standard tax deduction is a set amount that the government can't tax. In 2016, single taxpayers (and married couples who filed separately) were able to claim a $6,300 standard deduction. This is staking your territory and saying, "Hands off, Government!" Choosing the standard deduction isn't quite a "set it and forget it system," but it allows you to check one box instead of many.

The downside to standard deductions is that you can miss out on money you might be able to get if you *itemized* your taxes with *itemized* deductions. Now, the IRS encourages you to run both sets of numbers and choose whichever option gives you the biggest deduction—the deduction that will save you the most money. See? When the IRS isn't caving in to Scientology, they're not all bad! Just mostly bad.

Itemized deductions can result in more money for you, but that's because they're way more complex. I don't want to stray too far from home taxes here, but here are a few examples of common expenses that qualify for itemized deductions:

- Mortgage
- Property, state, and local taxes
- Anything you give to charity

So you can see how if you had a huge mortgage, or if you gave a ton of money to charitable causes, you'd have a greater amount of nontaxable income. This can be a great reason to itemize—and with a tax code that is 74,000 pages long, not even the most brilliant CPA can find every loophole.

Also, housing prices vary wildly, resulting in different treatment from one homeowner to the next. The vast majority of that mortgage deduction goes to families making over $100,000 a year. This means that a first-time homeowner of a small duplex in Kansas can only deduct their modest interest payment, while the thrice-refinanced home still underwater in Las Vegas receives a much larger deduction. Why? Because there's more government profit to be had from bigger mortgages! It works better for the government to pretend everything's fine with the finances of King Vegas and ignore the Peasant of Kansas, because Kansas can't generate as much money in interest! It's despicable, and obvious, and yet . . . there's no opting out without reform. See the depressing, wretched pattern?

It doesn't stop there. The federal subsidy on state and local taxes helps blue states jack their tax rates even higher. Imagine that! A tax loophole that allows states to tax their suckers—er, residents— at even higher rates! Currently, federal taxpayers can deduct those costs from their overall burden. This enables the states with the highest income and property taxes to keep their rates sky high. Since many of these property taxes are not progressively scaled, a large landowner ends up paying the same rate as a small pig farmer. Why should a mechanic in Indiana or a mom with two jobs subsidize the taxes on an investment banker's second home in Greenwich, Connecticut?

During the economic crisis of 2008, this type of policy socialized risk while privatizing earnings. When the housing market crashed, thousands lost their homes as they went underwater. However, the big banks received bailouts. At every turn, our friends in the federal government handed our tax dollars to those that caused the issue in the first place. Money going in through backed loans and securities, money through promises of Section 8 assistance on new construction and through the troubled-asset relief program (TARP).

Have you ever felt like you're playing Three-card Monte against the big banks and the feds? Well, keep a close eye on your cards because the Dodd-Frank legislation institutionalizes the risk further and makes it even more likely that such a banking collapse will happen again—and this time it will be all the more spectacular.

If you find all this tax and legal mumbo jumbo confusing, you're not alone. And it's designed to be this way to keep you more unaware, confused, and broke. All you have to remember is this: Government bureaucrats design new regulations and impose new taxes to raise more money and grow their own agencies. Whether the new regulations make sense or whether the fees are fair are moot points.

Well, damn. This home-owning thing hasn't been as tranquil as you hoped. Because even after you're all settled in and paid up, you still have to deal with property taxes. And highly taxed utilities. And insurance. And there will always be that constant threat of a new safety or environmental regulation that will force you to pay dearly for something you don't expect, want, or need.

You didn't really think this was your house, did you? You hand over control of your own property to an unelected bureaucrat, and you hand over money to fund the agencies salivating at the chance to fine you.

Don't say I didn't warn you.

THIRTEEN

VACATION TAXES

RESORT ROBBERIES

> When it comes to taxes, there are two types of
> people. There are those that get it done early, also
> known as psychopaths, and then the rest of us.
>
> —*Jimmy Kimmel*

Every year, one in three American families takes a vacation 50 miles or more away from home. Whether you dig traditional Griswold family trips or hip sojourns to places where the DJs spin and cucumber water flows—*your vacation will be chock-full of hidden taxes.* It doesn't matter where you go or what part of the world you visit, the Tax Monster will be lurking on every chaise longue, at every water bar, at every resort, on every cruise, and in every amusement park.

I recently got some time off from work—what to do? Screw adulting, I went to Disneyworld! I hadn't seen my cousin and her kids in a while, so I planned to meet them there. As I thought about my upcoming vacation, I felt all the stress melt away—*It doesn't get any better than this; life is amazing!* But of course, as soon as I bought my plane ticket my good vibes were bombarded with taxes.

PLANES, TRAINS, AND AUTOMOBILES: A TAX STORY

If you skipped the Griswold family traffic jam on the highway and flew to your vacation destination instead, your airfare was riddled up with taxes. Boy, did I find that one out fast.

My $204.65 plane ticket to Orlando had $28.05 in taxes added—that's a 14% tax rate! I thought that was high . . . But it turns out I was *lucky*. Up to 25% of each plane ticket can go directly to the federal government in the form of taxes.

WTF? Where is all that money going?

To start, every domestic flight is subject to a 7.5% "passenger ticket tax" levied by the Federal Aviation Administration (FAA). On top of that, the agency slaps a $9 surcharge on flights to or from Alaska or Hawaii, and a $4.10 "Federal Segment" fee on all flights within the Lower 48. Each airport you step foot in (even for a layover) means another $4.50 Passenger Facility Charge to pay for airport maintenance, also mandated by the FAA.

All these taxes and fees collected go straight to the FAA. The agency is relentless in its thirst for money—it's also funded by a 7.5% tax on the value of all credit card mileage awards (gadzooks), a 21.8 cent per gallon jet fuel tax, and a 6.25% tax on the transport of domestic cargo or mail.[1]

With this steady stream of cash, the FAA has rapidly ballooned in size and decreased in efficiency. The agency's budget has doubled since 1996, as did its personnel costs—even though its workforce fell by 4%![2] This means that on average, each FAA bureaucrat has gotten a *100% increase in compensation* over the last 20 years—on your dime!

Hey, let's be fair . . . Maybe these bureaucrats really worked their asses off and deserved a generous raise. LOL! Not likely . . . The FAA is one of the most wasteful agencies in the federal arsenal! Not once but twice the late Senator William Proxmire awarded the FAA with the "Golden Fleece Award," given to federal agencies that go above and beyond to squander public money.[3] The agency received the award for wasting millions—no, billions—on a regular basis. For example, an FAA-headed satellite navigation system called "Next Generation Air Transportation System" is 12 years behind and has a cost overrun of over \$1 billion. The project is slated for a 2025 completion.[4] What are the chances technology will have changed a little by then?

For decades, the FAA has thrown responsibilities out the window when funding is threatened. Take what happened in 1981 when thousands of FAA employees went on strike because they wanted higher salaries. President Ronald Reagan ultimately fired these strikers (hah! Gotta love Reagan), but the incident almost brought air traffic to a halt. A more recent incident occurred when Congress proposed a 4% budget cut in 2012—in response to the proposal, and in an effort to prove a point, the FAA threatened to furlough 10% of its air traffic. This action would have delayed nearly 40% of daily flights.[5]

Okay, so the FAA inflates airfare with various taxes and fees—what else is lurking in each plane ticket?

Since the feds know it's much harder to say no to anything with the word "security" in it, the Transportation Security Administration (TSA) slaps on a \$5.60 "September 11th Security Fee" for each leg of every flight, including each layover. The FAA can charge you up to four times for this one fee in any one trip. Sure, most people are probably willing to pay a little extra to make sure terrorists don't get on planes. But the TSA is laughably ineffective at keeping us safe—agents have a pathetic 95% failure rate when detecting bombs and weapons![6] Meanwhile, the agency is rife with waste and abuse.[7]

But wait—there's more.

If you're flying into the United States from another country, get ready to pay an additional \$7 for a "U.S. Immigration and Naturalization Fee" (even if you're an American citizen). The Immigration and

Naturalization Service uses these funds for air and sea operations in their budget. Nothing like a little international taxation to start your dream summer vacay.

Traveling overseas? Tack on another $12.50 for Customs and Border Patrol, $35.40 in departure and return taxes (FAA), over $3 for an Animal and Plant Health Inspection Service Fee (USDA—yeah, that USDA), and any foreign taxes, and you have an idea of how much it costs to go on vacation outside the country.

Each time you wait for a layover, you get fee'd again! And remember, every person with you is on the hook for the taxes in their own tickets. Traveling as a family of five? Pay the fees and taxes five times over.

Check out this example of a domestic flight from New York City to Miami, with a layover in Atlanta:

Base Ticket Cost	$300
Excise Fee (FAA)	$22.50
Federal Segment Fee (FAA) for four airports	$16.40
Passenger Facility Charge (local airport) for four airports	$18.00
September 11th Security Fee (TSA) for four airports	$11.20
Taxes and Fees	**$68.10 (almost 23%!)**
Total Cost	**$368.10**

THE RENTAL CAR TAX REALLY HERTZ

Back to my Disney trip. After I enjoyed a $14 plate of 99-cent snacks on the plane and touched down in sunny Orlando, I was ready to drop the top on a rented convertible and feel the wind in my hair. Well, that feeling lasted about 10 seconds after I shuttled over to the rental car place and found the Tax Monster hiding in my trunk, under the hood, and in the driver's seat of my rental car.

I'm not even talking about a fancy sports car, either. I never fig-ured a couple of days behind the wheel of a stick shift Toyota Yaris would add up so quickly.

Forty states impose special rental car taxes.[8] A further 15 allow city government taxation on top of that. These tax rates and fees range from 1.5% in Alabama to 14.2% in Minnesota!

How are the collected funds used? It depends on the state and city. I paid the $2 per day fee Florida puts into its "road fund."[9] In Daytona Beach, renters get stuck with a $2.50 fee (in addition to the state fee) that is used for airport "upgrades" including comfy ad-ditions to its lobby and concession areas. Okay, I don't like paying these fees, but at least that stuff is related to travel—in other places, though, rental car taxes go toward completely unrelated projects. Las Vegas, for example, is considering a rental tax to support the build-ing of a culinary institute and arts center.[10] If you're in Boston, you fork over a $10 tax to pay for convention center repair. Dallas puts its 5% fee into its American Airlines Center, where the Mavericks play (c'mon—it's not like the NBA doesn't have money!).

Most states collect a regular sales tax *on top of* these rental car taxes, giving you a double whammy.

Renting straight from the airport or certain locations might ex-pose you to even more fees and hidden costs.[11] Denver got in some hot water for charging an airport surcharge for cars rented outside the airport.[12] This is beyond the city's 3.5% sales tax and 7.25% special car rental fee and Colorado's $2 per day tax. I never figured Rocky Mountain High meant vehicle taxes.

STAYING AT THE CHÂTEAU L'GOUGE

I'm not going to keep complaining about my Disneyworld trip. It was actually a lot of fun and I didn't let the Tax Monster get the better of me. Florida has its advantages—like no income tax—but alas, all good things must come to an end. Several months later it was time to catch up with some family in New York City. Check out all the taxes I had to pay for a measly one-night stay in a Big Apple hotel:

- Room Rental $276.00
- NY Sales Tax (8.875%) $24.50
- Occupancy Tax (5.875%) $16.22
- Hotel Room Tax (flat fee) $2.00
- Hotel Room Unit Tax (flat fee) $1.50
- Misc. Tax $1.33

I paid $45.55 in taxes and fees on a $276 room. The biggest tax on the bill is the 8.875% New York Sales Tax. Oh, the good old sales tax, it's the gift that keeps on giving, the "catchall" classification for any Tax Monster scheme.

Next, I paid a 5.875% Occupancy Tax. What is this mysterious charge? It's just a tax hotels charge in order to grease the wheels of their partners in crime (i.e., their local governmental officials who make the laws that benefit them). In this case, it's New York City. Occupancy taxes have been bringing in the big bucks since 1970, when the city began levying them. In 2016, these taxes brought in $546 million, or about 1% of the city's overall annual tax haul.

In 2009, the city raised the occupancy tax from 5.00% to the current 5.875%. The increased rate was supposed to be temporary—well, we all know how that usually turns out. The city council kept it in place as a valuable means of funding the general fund instead of cutting costs.[13]

The New York–imposed $1.50 Room Unit Tax is often referred to as the "Javits Tax" after former Senator Jacob Javits. (Note to any aspiring politicos: If a tax is named after you, you probably weren't doing your job.) The Javits Convention Center in Manhattan has received almost a half *billion* dollars for renovations since the fee's implementation in 2005. The *New York Post* referred to the renovations as a "facelift for a corpse."[14] One year after a new roof was put on, it was already leaking. New York plans another $1.5 billion in changes to the building, paid for through a continuance of the hotel tax.

Make no mistake: Occupancy taxes are not unique to New York. Over the last generation they've become an "easy" tax for legislators to enact. They primarily charge nonresidents and can be justified as some sort of boon for tourism. Twenty-five states and Washington, D.C., charge a hotel tax, which ranges from 1% in Nebraska to a gob-stopping 15% in Connecticut.[15]

Many cities and counties also charge the traveler their own taxes on top of state fees. Why wouldn't they?! There's nothing you can do about it. Travelers will fork over 13% in Palm Springs, 15% in San Francisco, and 17% in Houston.[16] A $100 hotel bill? Prepare to give H-Town and its surrounding local governments 17 extra dollars . . . simply because they want it. A portion of Houston's hotel tax was instated as a "temporary" measure to cover the cost of hosting the 1992 Republican National Convention. Not only did the GOP lose that year, but so did visitors—the tax never went away.

Some city governments put the collected revenue into a dedicated fund for encouraging tourism—but the higher the rate, the lower the number of renters and hotels willing to come. It's a nose-face spite thing going on, and we're expected to pick up the tab.

Home-sharing apps like Airbnb bend down the price of spending the night somewhere new. But as you already know, state and local governments are doing everything to clamp down on the sharing economy.

All of these changes and fees have profound effects on who decides to stay where. When lawmakers can effectively "outsource" the pain of taxes to visitors, their understanding of the true effects of such levies declines. It's always much easier to increase tax rates when your own constituents aren't paying the bill.

PAYING VISA FEES WITH YOUR VISA

After lots of domestic traveling, I decided it was time to head someplace new. London's always had a certain call to it, especially since it doesn't involve picking up a new language to ask where the nearest bathroom is.

It was time to renew my passport and I decided to also pick up a supplemental "passport card" for easy travel to Canada and Mexico. Since the feds had to run all sorts of background checks and a mugshot-esque photo, I expected to fork over a couple of Hamiltons for the trouble. But the State Department decided they wanted Bennies where tenners should do.

An adult passport renewal is now $110.00. I wanted to speed up the process, so I checked the box for expedited service—that added $60. Add on an extra $25, if it's your first passport, for an Acceptance Agency Fee. The passport card added $55 to the total. So . . . here I am, out $250, on an Expedia deal that adds just a few bucks more.

All this money goes toward the State Department's budget.[17] The State Department's mission goes well beyond UN peacekeeping and vaccinations in the Third World. State has one of the worst reputations for cost overruns and abuse. Here are a few of the many (many, many) ridiculous things your passport fees helped fund in 2013, the most recent year for which data is available:

- $400,000 in booze for State Department employees
- 12,000 wineglasses at $85 a pop
- $1 million on a granite sculpture that "resembles stacked piles of paving stones"[18]
- $450,000 to send two comedians to India on a tour entitled "Make Chai, Not War"[19]

Ugh.

While I was in London, I wanted to buy a few items for my family. I soon realized that anything other than trinkets would be almost impossible to get through customs without a heavy duty. For goods within certain value parameters, you have to pay customs duties. For booze after the first bottle (exempted from tax), you get slapped with $3 in excise taxes[20] and about another 3% in customs duties. Hauling more than a carton of cigarettes back home will also result in steep excise taxes.

You paid local tax for the items and now Uncle Sam has to make sure that you give your offering to the Tax Monster.

TAX MONSTER, YOU NEED A LONG VACATION

While this chapter has focused on the cost of travel-related taxes on your vacations, don't forget that extra government charges on travel also burden people and companies that travel and lodge for business and other nonentertainment-related purposes. It's a whole other subject in itself—but that's no fun. Let's close by thinking about vacations again.

Can you imagine if vacation taxes ever went the way of the dodo bird?

All those billions of dollars in taxes would no longer be handed over to the government. The money would stay in our pockets, which would give us freedom on vacations. It would also give more money to the local hotel operators, restaurant owners, and small businesses that make our vacations possible, who could then reinvest back into their businesses, hire more people, and (yes) help grow our economy.

I don't know about you, but a Tax Monster–free paradise sounds a lot like the vacation spot I've been searching for, one that's truly worthy of our hard-earned vacation dollars . . . Now, if I could just find it on Google Maps.

FOURTEEN

EDUCATION

IF $200,000 IN TUITION WEREN'T ENOUGH

An unlimited power to tax involved, necessarily, a
power to destroy; because there is a limit beyond which
no institution and no property can bear taxation.

—*John Marshall*

Learning is free—it's schooling that's expensive.

My younger brother recently started college, which got me
thinking of my future. Eventually, I'll have kids of my own and they
will probably attend college. By then, the cost of education will most
likely have an extra digit at the end, as tuition prices continue to
grow far faster than the rate of inflation.[1] I'll pay for a portion of
my kids' tuition—but they'll end up paying for the rest with loans,
which will take decades to pay back.

Everyone knows that the costs of secondary education are spiraling out of control. But the underlying reasons are often obscured.
How will the education landscape look in 20 years? What are the
primary drivers of these costs? Are there reasonable solutions? As I
researched, I clutched my purse a bit tighter and began discovering
one of the worst financial scams affecting American families.

STUDENT LOANS: HOW THE GOVERNMENT
ENSLAVES KIDS AND DESTROYS THEIR LIVES

The bane of my friends' existence—student loan debt didn't open the doors they wanted; instead it placed a ball and chain around their future. Sometimes it's hard to sit with a straight face as they come up with every excuse for their predicament other than the real cause of their financial mess. "Hey, it couldn't be the government's fault," they tell me. "Heck, they were nice enough to at least loan me the $200,000 I needed to go to college. Otherwise, I would never have been able to go in the first place! Thank God for student loans."

But now they can't pay back those same loans, because, you know . . . Greedy businessmen are taking advantage of them. Or the economy just sucks. But it's certainly not *their fault* that they can't pay back their $200,000 debt with their newly minted degree in Art History!

Born in good intentions, the federal student loan program seems necessary due to high tuition costs. Private and public colleges cost an average of $29,000 and $22,000 per year, respectively. Many prominent universities, like Tufts and Boston College, will set a family back by over twice that amount.

It's not the big bad banks that reap the most profit from loan programs, it's the federal government. The feds fund more than 70% of all student aid. Put more accurately, *your tax dollars* fund more than 70% of all student aid. Most students can qualify for as much money as they think they need to cover the cost of their education, including housing, no matter how high the price tag. This enables colleges to raise tuition rates each year with impunity—and without anyone even complaining—because no matter what they charge students will always be able to finance it with government money. And by "government money," I mean your money—taxpayer dough.

I earned my bachelor's degree from Emerson College, a small but well-respected liberal arts college in Boston. It set me back at least

$150,000 in tuition, room, and board. And yes, I am still making payments of $800 a month on those student loans.

While attending Emerson, my roommate Carla would constantly moan that she needed more government student loans—she was not happy that she was maxed out. She would complain, "It's not fair that the stingy government limits what I can borrow while tuition prices across the country are soaring!" I nodded my head in compliant, ignorant agreement.

What Carla and I hadn't figured out yet is that the government student loan program is precisely what is causing soaring tuitions across America.

Imagine, if you will, an America where every college student is allowed to borrow $1 million for college. Now, every student can afford any college they want. Once colleges understand that money is no longer an issue, they immediately pump money into advertising and marketing to attract as many of these new "millionaire" students to their campuses as possible. They also build gorgeous dormitories—mini Taj Mahals—to impress prospective students and their parents. The gymnasiums become spectacular and enormous; every high-end workout machine is available. The dining halls are impressive and the meals are to die for. Salaries for professors and staff skyrocket to six figures across the board. And, of course, to pay for all of these goodies, tuition rates increase to levels once thought absurd.

This is precisely what has happened to secondary education in America. And why not? Money is no issue! The government lets kids borrow as much as they want. Eventually, tuition will rapidly rise to that magic $1 million student loan level. At that point, there will be political pressure for the government to raise loan limits, and the obsequious politicians will comply. Student loans will continue to rise, and the cycle will continue.

Today, student loan debt is at $1 trillion and it continues to go up. Many of these new college graduates have degrees in History or

Philosophy that are unlikely to get them a career enabling them to pay off this debt. As a result, young graduates like Carla will become indentured slaves to their government for decades to come. Such a financial burden will hinder young people from pursuing their dreams; from buying their first house, their first car; and from saving for their retirement. Debt-enslaved millennials are also more likely to put off starting a family[2]—which, in turn, delays the next generation of taxpayers and their revenues. (Yes, this is the kind of thing that keeps me awake at night.)

Bottom line: Young graduates have been handed a 30-year mortgage without a house. Meanwhile, professors like Senator Elizabeth Warren will continue to make $400,000 per year for teaching one class at Harvard University.

The federal government made a $41.3 billion profit from student loan interest in 2013 alone;[3] that's a higher profit than all but two companies in the entire world, Exxon and Apple. It's quite a sweet little racket they have. The government issues the loans, backs those loans, sets the student loan interest rates, and collects all the profits. Even better, unlike bank mortgages or consumer loans like credit card debt, the government does not forgive your loans even if you're desperate and file bankruptcy. Al Capone and John Gotti never had such a sweet deal.

Even "Income Based Repayment" plans, touted under the Obama administration, lead to further problems for all students involved—not to mention John and Jane Q. Taxpayer—including higher tuition across the board. Graduates unable to pay off their loans may get it waived after 20 or 25 years.[4] "Waived" is a weasel word here—it means that the true cost gets passed to the taxpayer, once again.

Income Based Repayment plans are an intermediate step for supporters of "free" college. Bernie Sanders built his 2016 presidential campaign support around such a promise. I will give him this—he does know a lot about colleges. His wife ran one (Burlington College) until May 2016, when she became the subject of a federal investigation for alleged bank fraud.[5] (Investigators are also looking into whether Bernie used his influence to help her with this suspected scheme.[6])

Loan debt almost tripled in the last 10 years—from $480 billion in 2006 to almost $1.4 trillion in 2016—as politicians from both parties tripped over themselves in faux action. Part of the issue is that student loan debt completely ignores the principles of the free market. Students receive taxpayer-subsidized loans regardless of credit history, with artificially set interest rates, and with zero regard to the earnings potential of their secondary education. Should we be providing student loans for engineers and computer programmers? Many Americans would say yes—it's a good investment in the nation's future. But should we also be subsidizing loans for students studying Art History? How about Russian Literature? The University of Connecticut offers a degree in Puppetry; should we be offering taxpayer-backed student loans to students who want to pursue a degree in Puppetry? The answers here are not as clear.

What studies do you think had the most growth within America's university system over the last 20 years? Engineering? Computer science? Nursing? After all, these are where the jobs are in the 21st century. If you made this logical assumption, you would be wrong. The field seeing the most growth over the last two decades has been . . . *drum roll please* . . . GENDER STUDIES!

Gender Studies degrees increased 300% since 1990.[7] Such degrees have their place in academia, but often not in the private sector. In fact, Gender Studies graduates can expect an average salary of just $15,000 per year five years after graduation.[8] That's about half of the average haul of a Philosophy major(!). Today's liberal arts graduates have an average unemployment rate more than double that of education, science, and engineering majors.

Bachelor's degrees in "Lesbian Gay Bisexual Transgender and Queer" studies are also becoming popular now. And what will you learn? Wikipedia gives us a hint: "Queer studies is not the same as queer theory, which is an analytical viewpoint within queer studies that challenges the putatively 'socially constructed' categories of sexual identity." You can learn exactly what that means by getting your degree in LGBTQ studies at Brown University for a mere $40,000 a year, fully subsidized by taxpayer-backed student loans!

There is massive inflation happening at almost every college in the nation. Soon it will be impossible to pay for that Philosophy degree while working at Starbucks. The expectation that every student of varying backgrounds, abilities, and motivations *must* go to college is cancerous. It's effectively a cultural mandate that devalues the end results of that education at a steep fiscal cost.

WASTE: THE MOST EXPENSIVE PART OF COLLEGE

Whether it's a television show, a breakup, a book, or six figures in college debt, time has a way of clarifying things. Your fancy but unprofitable college degree seems less impressive when you're under your bathroom sink at 2 a.m. with a roll of duct tape . . . *again*. Your last disposable dollars went to pay back that Stafford student loan. No plumber this month.

At this point it makes sense to ask: *How did I get here? Why does my checking account balance never have two digits before the decimal point?* Lesson in hand, my family applied it heartily to little bro's quest for quality education.

Various tours, research, and glossy pamphlets led the way in my brother's search for the right college. Finally, we came upon a quaint University of California campus that seemed to have it all. With great hope and excitement in our hearts, my mom, brother, and I piled in the car and set off for his "dream school." For the sake of the university, which he chose not to attend, I will eschew its name. If you're really curious, its NCAA team sucks, anyway.

When we entered the campus, the construction scene was busier than the Hong Kong skyline. How could a school with several thousand students afford a new student union building, two brand-new lecture centers, three sprawling dining halls, and a revamped gym built just nine years ago?

For all of the talk about cuts to education funding, the money spent on campus "improvements" was right here, shoved in our faces. Modern art pieces indistinguishable from junkyard trash littered the campus. Breathtaking chandeliers were dangling from ceilings in every empty room and every library. Spectacular stone fountains were on display everywhere.

And as the college tour with my family continued, our enthusiasm for the institution waned. Perhaps it was our pragmatic upbringing—we are a thrifty family from central New Hampshire—but these ostentatious displays of unnecessary luxuries just didn't seem right.

Secondary education wasn't always like this.

So what happened? Waste is one of the key parts of a tuition bill. Unfortunately, anything—and I mean *anything*—can be deemed "essential."

Some examples of "educational investments" at today's universities are laughable. Colleges drunk on cash embark on insane spending, paying for high-tech student centers, fancy administration offices, and other amenities that are downright outrageous. Examples include:

- A $15 million water tower and fountain renovation at the University of Albany[9]
- A planned renovation of Berkeley's student union that will cost over $650 per square foot[10] (more than quadruple the average cost of commercial construction[11])
- An $85 million upgrade to Louisiana State University at Baton Rouge's student gym, including a lazy river, a climbing wall, and a rope course[12]

- A $140 million renovation to Ohio State University's rec facilities, including a 250-foot hot tub[13]
- A miniature golf course just for Clemson University's football team (they "saved" money by having *only* nine holes)[14]
- A $46 million health club at Virginia Commonwealth University in Richmond, which includes a state-of-the art climbing wall, an "aquatic center," four full-sized basketball courts, and a whirlpool[15]
- A *$450 million* renovation to Texas A&M's Kyle Field[16]

The spending spree isn't showing signs of slowing down. As the colleges compete for notoriety with your tax dollars, the situation only grows worse. Meanwhile, today's millennials are saddled with $1.4 trillion in student loan debt, and state governments are billions in the hole. Largely from paying for all of this nonsense.

THE INFAMOUS TITLE IX

One of the key buzzwords at colleges is *diversity*. There are different ways to say it. There's often the word *social* in front of a hackneyed version of it. However, it's always there. It's everywhere.

Government-enforced diversity efforts usually backfire. They remove much of the ideological diversity vital to higher education, and instead balloon the cost of tuition. Two of these efforts really stand out: Title IX and "multicultural education." For different but similar reasons, each led to a swamp of spiraling costs and diminishing returns. This isn't the book to discuss the moral foundations of either program, but we can discuss their effects on your bottom line.

Title IX of the Education Amendments Act of 1972 was intended to reduce gender disparities in college settings. Now, in the age when female students well outnumber males in colleges, the implementation of the act should be a quaint anachronism. Instead, the federal government dedicates an entire agency within the Department of Education to Title IX enforcement. Part of that agency's responsibility is levying heavy fines against universities in violation of varying interpretations of the law.[17] Some such fines relate to co-ed sport facility access while others attempt to regulate campus sex life. Over and over, the feds use a heavy hand instead of simple guidance and often levy fines that are more expensive to fight than to pay.

Colleges found guilty of violating Title IX can lose all federal funding.[18] Enforcement often appears selective, and the agency just hired 200 additional attorneys.[19]

Making matters worse, Title IX provisions grew well beyond their intended limits. The law is now used for such things as transgender bathroom rules and campus sexual assault policies. The Obama administration quadrupled the number of investigations into university sexual assault policies even though campus rapes fell precipitously over the last several decades.[20] That led to an explosion in the number of well-paid bureaucrats, both in Washington and on campuses themselves. Title IX administrators earn up to $150,000 each. Berkeley increased their enforcement costs by $2 million alone. The cost is absurd and mandatory for all federally funded universities.

Every public school and college must have a Title IX Coordinator,[21] and in many cases an employee takes this on as an exclusive duty. Each such enforcer requires an office (Harvard has two offices!), and comes with several assistants. It got to the point that the American Association of University Professors protested, stating that the overzealous actions inhibited academic freedom.[22] The group said that student complaints about innocuous comments by professors and "trigger warnings" changed academia for the worse.

Often, Title IX enforcement costs are rolled into an overall nebulous total on tuition bills. However, in 2016, the University of Maryland system Student Government Association (SGA) approved a $34 annual fee, issued to students as a separate line item, to cover a portion of Title IX enforcement costs. An author at the liberal news site BuzzFeed was shocked—*shocked*—that the colleges wanted the costs "passed down" to students.[23] Of course, the BuzzFeed writer didn't realize that the costs were already borne by students and taxpayers, only that they're now visible through the separate line item. Imagine the confusion that would ensue if the writer were to ever crack open a basic economics textbook.

The SGA later withdrew its endorsement of the annual Title IX fee,[24] but many at the university continue to insist that efforts to enforce the rule are underfunded. One University of Maryland Title IX administrator, Catherine Carroll, said that her office doesn't receive enough money, even though it has a *$1 million* budget. "My people are burned out," she told BuzzFeed.

Other state and federally mandated diversity quotas require their own expensive bureaucracies. It's a common theme recurring throughout public universities nationwide: Government-mandated requirements increase costs and government-subsidized loans make it worse. These costs add up, and are directly funded by student loans, state and federal taxes, and parents' bank accounts.

Despite the fact that colleges are more ethnically diverse today than they've ever been,[25] these institutions know that in today's America they are expected to hire campus diversity officials. These jobs will continue to be filled and the job descriptions will continue to grow long after the need for these agencies disappears. And it's all being funded by *our* money.

The average college diversity administrator rakes in over $175,000 annually.[26] Some make well over $300,000. At the University of Berkeley alone, its Office of Inclusion and Equity employs 150 people and spends $18 million per year. That's your tax dollars at work, Californians!

Of course, "inclusion" is important at our nation's universities. But what kind of atrocities are taking place at Berkeley that an army of faculty needs to battle this tsunami of "inclusion and equity" offenses? Is it really such a crisis—or is it just an ever-growing, expensive bureaucracy?

As diversity offices continue to grow at a record pace, prepare to be on the hook for an ever-increasing litany of causes *du jour.*

ADMINISTRATORS GONE WILD

During my brother's college tour in California, I noticed that professors weren't the only ones with offices. There were dozens of offices for positions I never knew existed. Many of the rooms had name placards and empty chairs. What is the Office of Inclusion Review? Why does the vice president of International Studies need two deans, five secretaries, and six student workers?

Consider this: While the number of full-time professors in the University of California system stayed steady over the last 30 years, the number of administrators quadrupled. Since 2000, the number has doubled.[27] The pencil pushers now outnumber the instructors. How is that possible?

A state audit reveals the tip of the iceberg of bloat in the U.C. system.[28] The system has $175 million in reserves yet still plans to raise tuition. What the. . . ?

The U.C. system president Janet Napolitano said the audit findings were false . . . But numbers rarely lie. The college was paying administrator salaries significantly higher than top salaries at other state agencies (which are already well above those of their private sector peers). And why not? When the checks are coming from the government—both federal and state funds—there's no need to concern ourselves with such quaint concepts as "return on investment" or "market rates."

An "Information System Manager," whatever that is, makes $258,000 a year in the Golden State's university system. Several executives around Napolitano received an average of $370,000 per year, plus millions in their retirement pensions.

At colleges around the nation, every fancy new position seems to require a staff behind it. Between 1987 and 2012, colleges added 517,636 administrators to their payrolls.[29] Because we all know that the key to a great education lies in lots and lots of administration!

We can assign much of the blame to the rise of one position in particular: the Provost. This nebulous, important-sounding title is a catchall for various college administrative positions. Assistant to the President of the College? Affirmative Action Long-Term Coordinator for Out of State Students? Deputy Dean for Student Government Affairs? All these employees are euphemistically labeled "Provost." It sounds so much more relevant than "administrator," doesn't it? And each one needs an office and two secretaries.

With each one of these positions comes "mandatory training," "student enrichment programs," "cultural sensitivity seminars," and the like. Each takes time, money, and space that could go to the Economics or Physics Departments or, heaven forbid, be used to hold down tuition rates.

For every dollar spent on instruction, almost two go to other functions, including administration. The median salary for an Associate Provost position across the nation? $135,000.[30]

Of course, in the private sector, you would never see all these absurd administrators and provosts, because assets that don't provide any value to the product (in this case, education) are ditched. But when government money, including unlimited loans, is the primary payer, bureaucracies grow and efficiencies wither.

All of these administrative costs are deliberately hidden from students and their parents. If universities were required to provide students and their families detailed reports of where every dollar was spent, there would be outrage and demands for educational reform.

PUBLIC SECTOR UNIONS: NICE UNDERGRAD
PROGRAM YOU'VE GOT THERE. IT WOULD BE A
REAL SHAME IF SOMETHING HAPPENED TO IT

The alphabet soup of America's public sector (government employee) unions is emblematic of abuse in every level of government. It's even worse in education. For decades, the National Education Association (NEA) played a rigged game with money intended for education. It runs both the labor and management sides of the coin. Public sector unions make every step in college more expensive. From pensions to salaries to tenure to demands for new facilities, NEA-affiliated unions are a primary, yet mostly surreptitious, driver of college costs.

In most public policy debates, blame can be assigned to "both sides." Well, there is no other side here. Teachers unions political contributions reached $33.2 million in 2016 alone, and 93% of that money went to Democrats. Teachers are given little say as to where their "mandatory" union dues go.

So where do these forced union dues go? Not to buying chalk and textbooks, that's for sure. The NEA organized a call for students *and teachers* to skip class to protest Trump.[31] Its New York chapter regularly goes out of its way to massacre cost-effective charter schools that help predominately black students.[32] Unions would love to see all charter schools disappear, because these schools aren't run by the unions—and therefore are not a revenue source for union dues.

Affiliated union bosses control each lever of the game. These include the high-up muckety-mucks at the colleges, education officials, and the donations to state and federal representatives.

Part of the incredible cost of college is due to professor tenure, which essentially guarantees employment until retirement or death, regardless of performance or competency. And it's not just salaries that go along with it. In most cases, professorships come with lifetime health benefits and pensions that pay well above the private sector. In fact, very few private sector companies even offer pensions anymore, because they are simply too expensive to maintain. Even the *Harvard Business Review* called for the outdated and absurdly expensive benefits packages at American colleges to end.[33] One estimate pegs the costs of a 35-year tenured professor's career at between $10 million and $12 million.[34]

Disciplines change with the times. However, byzantine personnel rules and a staid professional culture result in a situation where it is essentially impossible to fire a tenured faculty member. Once professors nab tenure, there's less motivation for them to update research or teaching methods.

Tenure policies also create rigid departments and a massive influx of research papers. Receiving tenure and increasing respectability comes from publishing—even when there's little or no interest in the topic. Much of modern academia is now flooded with irrelevant, fake, or faulty academic journals.[35] There are now 141,000 academic or scholarly journals worldwide. Take the infamous case from 2017 of the hoax paper titled, "The Conceptual Penis as a Social Construct."[36] Two authors under pen names and from a fake research organization submitted the paper, which was duly published by the *Cogent Social Sciences* academic journal. To demonstrate the fact that journals often accept nonsensical articles, the authors included over 20 cited sources in the paper, some of which were later proven to be completely fictitious. The article was written to highlight society's "hypermasculine dominance" as a cause of climate change.

Useless academic publications increase the final costs of education in two ways: One is the salaries we pay professors to do such "research." Another is that the time they take off to do it, in paid sabbaticals, reduces course access for students. "Research-for-the-sake-of-research" is an entrenched obsession designed to market a professor's academic prowess by promoting the number of papers he has published.

In a given year, a full *40%* of history professors at Harvard won't be in the classroom. They'll be paid to not teach. What are all these professors doing during their time outside the classroom? Many are writing papers on obscure topics, which go on to be published in journals that often don't even fact-check the received work.

It's like the old Soviet joke: *We pretend to work and they pretend to pay us.* My brother's student loan payments will subsidize professors he will never meet to do research no one will ever read. If no one reads this "research" once it is published, then what is the value to students? And if there is no value, why is so much money going into it?

THE UNICORN: A MODEL WHERE THE COLLEGE COSTS GO DOWN

Colleges that don't have the luxuries of extensive state support and unlimited student loan dollars will often see costs per student *go down*. An example can be found at many of America's community colleges. With a disproportionate number of older, part-time, and parent students,[37] there is less room for error at these institutions. Many of the enrollees have been around the block a few times and know this may be their only shot at a solid education. Mommy, Daddy, and Uncle Sam aren't there to save the day.

Why do community colleges often work better than their public four-year cousins? Prestige projects, over-unionization, forced diversity, and political radicalization are not priorities at community colleges. Degrees are sculpted around practical careers and professors have real-world experience. They're also often ignored by state legislatures, which is good, as this reduces mandates and administrative bloat.

Tuitions are held in check at community colleges because of the types of students enrolled. At two-year community colleges 61% of students applied for federal aid, compared to 71% of students at public four-year schools; 69% of community college students worked while pursuing their degrees, far higher than the percentage of students who did so at four-year schools. Almost double worked full-time compared to their four-year counterparts.

Tuition at the average two-year school nationwide averages around $3,400 per semester. This is about a third of the cost at a four-year public school, and the tuition gap only continues to grow.

Of all students that graduate from community college, 59% do so with zero student loan debt. Another 20% do so with less than $10,000. For four-year college students, only 34% graduate debt free, and one out of eight leave with debt of over $40,000.

But when it comes to four-year colleges, the news isn't all bad. Texas, for example, has made tuition reform a priority. State Senator Kel Seliger recently introduced bill SB-543, which would require Texas State schools to meet performance-based metrics—like above-average graduation rates—before being allowed to raise tuition. It's far from a panacea, but it's a start.

Similar tuition reforms are being initiated in state legislatures around the country. They are long overdue.

FIFTEEN

AND YOU THOUGHT $500 FOR
A PILL WAS RIDICULOUS

One thing is clear: The Founding Fathers never
intended a nation where citizens would pay nearly
half of everything they earn to the government.

—*Ron Paul*

Nobody likes to think about it.

What happens if you get T-boned on your way to work? What
would you do if you sprained your ankle at the gym and couldn't
work for three weeks? What if that chronic bellyache turns out to be
the Big "C?"

As terrifying as a massive health crisis can be in and of itself,
it can pale in comparison to the complicated (and expensive) hoops
you have to jump through to navigate the medical system. Lab tests.
Specialists. Wrongful diagnoses. More lab tests, a different special-
ist. The people aren't nice. The wait times are ridiculous, and no one
ever apologizes. And when it's all said and done, you get a bill that
boggles the mind (and wrecks your life even further).

No matter where you sit on the political spectrum, we all agree
on a few things: Health-care costs are out-of-this-world expensive,

going to the doctor pretty much sucks (and often doesn't get you anywhere anyway), pharmaceutical companies are making bank, and Obamacare has caused problems.

Where the various factions start to *dis*agree is on what exactly those problems are, who's to blame for them, and how we got into this whole jacked-up situation in the first place. In this chapter, I'll break down our current situation and how it affects the average taxpayer (i.e., you) and hikes the cost of every doctor's visit.

As this is a hot-button issue for most Americans—especially if you or a loved one has been touched by chronic or terminal illness, preexisting conditions, or serious injury—try to remember, taxes and regulatory fees affect us ALL. They're the great unifier! So, my intrepid reader, let's mix it up.

Rule #1: The government is involved in every discussion you have with your doctor—directly, through stringent and outdated regulations, and indirectly, through taxes.

Picture this: Your adorable little niece gave you a nasty case of the flu. (Thanks, kid.) You avoid the doctor for as long as you can—the great American way—but after two weeks you finally break down and make the appointment. Two hours—90 minutes of which you spend finding hidden pictures in *Highlights* magazine—and one illegible prescription later, you're back home in bed where you belong, feeling all smug and proud of yourself for taking control of your health. You get better, and you forget all about the Niece Flu. Then, about four months later, BLAM! You get a bill for $600. WTF?

There are a number of reasons for the spiking cost of health care, and we'll get into them (goody). But government intervention in the market isn't a new thing, especially after the creation of Medicaid and Medicare in the 1960s. Taxes taken straight from our paychecks subsidize a variety of programs. Many of the causes of recent hikes are directly tied to the Affordable Care Act (aka Obamacare). The ambitious but ultimately poorly conceived and implemented plan had several major goals: to reduce Americans' annual average health insurance premiums by up to $2,500, ensure coverage access for those with preexisting conditions (like diabetes or conditions from birth), and require all Americans to obtain health insurance. Some were covered by an expansion of existing programs, like Medicaid. Others were forced to get coverage by the promise of a penalty if they did not. The penalty was essentially a tax, as the Supreme Court later determined.[1]

Obamacare didn't exactly work out as planned. The average family health insurance plan today is over $17,500 annually, which is nearly *three times* what it was in 1999. Single plans are now more than $6,000; this figure is also triple what it was in the late 1990s.

Before Obamacare, both high- and low-deductible insurance plans played a role in the economy. High-premium, low-deductible plans were perfect for older folks or families more likely to have medical issues. Meanwhile, young people could opt for no insurance at all, or a high-deductible, low-premium plan. Makes sense: Low risk = low premium, right? Before Obamacare went into effect, many people under 40 opted for a "mini-med" insurance policy with a low coverage cap and high deductible to meet emergencies.[2] Now, under Obamacare, such plans are effectively illegal.

Due to the high costs of Obamacare policies, many people are forced to get an insurance policy *for their insurance policy* (yes, really). These "gap plans" fill in any cracks within the Obamacare framework—like that massive deductible you'll never, ever, ever, meet.[3]

The per-user cost is ballooning, too. Between 2006 and 2015, the money spent on insurance premiums and deductibles as a share of national median income leapt from 6.5 to 10.1%.[4] The average worker puts out over $5,000 a year for the cost of a family plan.[5] These increasing costs also force more lower-income Americans to go to the emergency room for basic care, rather than wait around for an appointment they won't be able to afford anyway. Some even go to the ER for routine dental work!

If you're self-employed, or work for a small business, and have to buy insurance for yourself, the situation is grim. Premiums for a single person's plan jumped 99% between 2013 and 2016. Family plans jumped 140%.[6] Deductibles rose at a similar rate—a family can now expect to pay over $12,000 in deductibles, compared to $5,000 before 2013. What good is being covered if you can't even afford your deductible?

Remember, Obamacare is essentially a taxation on health care through regulation. While the health-care bill may not seem like a direct tax, it functions similarly and has the same effects. In fact, in 2012, the Supreme Court upheld Obamacare in a 5–4 decision, finding that the mandate penalty is a tax.[7] Hardworking, taxpaying residents are forced to pay significantly more than they were before, while getting little in return.

Obamacare's restrictions and mandates have been terrible for consumer choice, and great for insurance companies' bottom lines. Many insurance companies can't make a profit in certain regions of the nation, even with federal subsidies. When this happens, the company often stops offering service there. In five states and in portions of others, there is now only one insurance provider with Obamacare-approved plans.[8] In 45 counties, there may be no insurance options at all on the Obamacare exchange.[9] Some states are trying heavy-handed tactics to stop insurers from leaving the market—New York threatened to not pay back patients' Medicaid expenses to any insurance company that leaves the exchange.[10]

A WASHINGTON BUREAUCRAT FLAPS HIS WINGS, AND SOMEONE IN TEXAS LOSES HIS JOB

Health-care subsidies—paid for by hardworking, taxpaying shmucks like you—create a perverse welfare cliff that incentivizes people to remain in receipt of government aid.[11] A family making just under $60,000 per year qualifies for over $5,000 in Obamacare subsidies toward health insurance. If they make just $2,500 more, they lose the whole credit. For struggling families, this creates a hard cap in potential income.

It gets worse for those nearer the poverty line. Imagine a family making $17,000 a year. They would receive up to $10,100 to purchase an Obamacare policy, making their total net "income" $27,100. But the more money they earn on their own, the smaller their credit. By the time they reach $34,000 in income, much of the credit is gone. The family is thereby disincentivized from making more money because no comparable health plan can be obtained for the family for $10,100. What incentive is there to earn more?

For businesses and organizations, the costs associated with Obamacare are often crippling. If a company has more than 50 full-time employees, they are now required to offer full, Obamacare-approved coverage to each worker. This puts companies on the line for at least $600,000 more per year![12] Naturally, this results in small businesses being far less likely to expand beyond 50 employees. Prior to Obamacare, many companies fostered long-term development, mutual growth, and other perks. Now there's more of an incentive to hire transient part-timers or contractors to avoid the costs of providing insurance.

Following the implementation of Obamacare, many companies with fewer than 50 employees stopped offering health insurance altogether. Many of those that offered plans voluntarily before couldn't afford the spikes in premiums Obamacare wrought. Employers with under 10 employees dropped 36% of their policies.

And what if you're ready to leave your position for a better job? Well, the whole game has changed now. The risk of losing any form of quality health insurance has increased to the point of absurdity, deflating job mobility to a dangerously low level.[13] People are more likely to stay at a soul-sucking job they hate than risk the expense and uncertainty of the marketplace or Medicaid.

Here's the point: All of this nonsense is raising your premiums and being subsidized by *your* tax dollars. And it'd be one thing if it was doing what it promised to do—to take care of a greater number of Americans and "fix" our health-care system. But the system is more broken than ever, while our medical costs increase and our paychecks are getting skinnier and skinner to cover it all.

Actually, your paycheck is looking a little sickly because of all of the taxes you're paying. Perhaps you should take it to see a doctor?

WOULD YOU BUY AN INSURANCE POLICY THAT INCREASES YOUR CHANCE OF DEATH?

And now, kiddies, it's time to talk about Medicaid. Millions of underprivileged American families use the program, which subsidizes medical services to make health care more accessible to the poor. Founded in 1965 by President Lyndon B. Johnson, the program relies on both federal and state funds (in other words, your tax dollars). But however good its intentions may be, Medicaid remains one of the most expensive and often counterproductive federal programs. And you're paying for it straight out of each paycheck.

During recent years, the costs of each new Medicaid enrollee have skyrocketed. In 2009, each state had a choice of whether or not to expand Medicaid coverage to the new maximum income level imposed by Obamacare, and participating states set estimates for how many new residents would join the expanded program. California's estimates were off by 400%! Meanwhile, Colorado, Kentucky, Nevada, New York, and Washington saw enrollment numbers that were more than double their initial projections. Making matters worse, the cost of each new expanded Medicaid policy was well over predicted levels. The Centers for Medicare and Medicaid Services predicted in 2015 these new policies would cost $4,281 per enrollee. The next year, the cost increased 49% to $6,366.[14]

Perhaps you're rusty on your Intro to Econ concepts, but as a quick refresher, a 49% increase in cost is bad. And if you're wondering about all those newly insured people on Medicaid, consider this—Medicaid policies are generally inferior to traditional insurance. *But aren't you better with Medicaid over no insurance at all?* The answer's not even clear there.

Medicaid patients generally have worse medical access and mortality rates than people with *no insurance at all*.[15] The reason is pretty straightforward: Demand outstrips supply. Many doctors simply won't take Medicaid, because they only get reimbursed 61% of the amount they would for the same services for Medicare. Even worse, due to Obamacare's Medicaid expansion, government is guaranteeing even less payout for doctors performing the services. The average reimbursement rate projected a 42.8% fall in reimbursements for doctors between 2014 and 2015.[16]

Medicaid enrollees are far more likely to face adverse medical outcomes (or die) than even those with no insurance at all. We're setting up a two-tiered system that hurts patients who don't have access to the free market.

Add to that the wildly incorrect cost projections. In 1987, Congress projected that Medicaid's total cost would be under $1 billion in 1992. They were off by $16 billion[17] . . . that's 1600%! The 2017 fiscal year projected $377 billion in federal spending,[18] increasing to a projected $404 billion in 2018,[19] matched by over $200 billion from the states. That's about 10% of the annual federal budget! It's even worse for the states—they spend an average of 16.8% of their annual budgets on Medicaid.

So what does all this mean to your wallet? Well, it's not good, folks. That cost gets rolled into payroll taxes: 12.4% of your income is taxed to pay for Social Security and Medicaid—half by you, and half by your employer. Unless you're self-employed, and you get to pay the full 12.4% all by your lonesome. Most Americans understand that we need a way to help the poor afford health care—but all that money is getting funneled into a system that *doesn't even work*.

But since Medicaid is an entitlement and has an interested constituency, it's extraordinarily difficult to reform.

JUST SAY NO TO GOVERNMENT DRUGS

Well-to-do Americans loooove to talk about Canada. Amiright, or amiright? "Canada's perrrrfect." With their hunky prime minister, and their delicious maple syrup . . . and their single-payer health-care system . . .

Well, the Justin Trudeau fan club does have one thing right—why are prescription drugs so darn expensive in this country? Isn't the United States a major leader in drug development and research?

Part of the reason is our licensing and patent system. The United States allows for a longer patent period and exclusivity—often 17 or 20 years. This enables drug companies to pour millions into research projects that might not otherwise be worth their time. Many companies in other nations, especially India, copy the original to create knock-off generics that are often cheaper. However, what Canada fanatics often don't understand is that without our unique system, those cutting-edge treatments wouldn't exist in the first place.

The FDA's system is a bizarre mix of regulation and delay. The 1984 Drug Price Competition and Patent Term Restoration Act, signed by President Reagan, allowed for massive investment into the drug market.[20] It *also* encouraged the manufacture of cheaper generic drugs. However, the FDA was so slow to respond to applications that many up-and-coming drugs were mired in years of development hell. Worse, the morass sparked a number of bribes, which unscrupulous bureaucrats snatched up in exchange for speeding things along.[21] Reagan's act also mandated that the FDA was not obligated to release information about serious issues concerning new drugs, including inspection failures and false medical results.[22] One FDA-approved drug, rivaroxaban (marketed as Xarelto), has the highest number of reported injuries of any high-use drug in the country, with over 10,000 hospitalizations and 1,100 deaths.

While generics' share in the prescription drug market shot up from 35% in 1983 to 85% in 2012 (a good thing), the law also allowed drug companies to settle lawsuits out of court (a bad thing). Lawsuits skyrocketed as litigants could "win" cases without ever going to court—the pharma companies wanted no negative press and started settling for "undisclosed settlements." The average medical malpractice payout is now $353,000![23] Did someone say "Tort Reform?"

Just like so many other government initiatives, all of these actions that were intended to lower drug prices have had the extreme opposite effect. A free market approach allowing international trade in meds would solve much of the problem.[24] But Congress blocks it due to concerns about "safety" . . . even though the medicines we're talking about are the same exact ones traded across the border in Canada!

In addition, a number of pie-in-the-sky federal actions spiked the price of meds and inadvertently drowned smaller drug companies. Take a Republican idea—President Dubya's 2003 Medicare Part D plan. This program was intended to increase seniors' access to prescription drugs by providing a subsidy. While this happened, the per-pill price tag ballooned. Pharma companies set their own prices, and with consumer consideration removed, the price checks a free market provides were also removed. Between 2011 and 2015, the average drug covered by the program shot up in cost by 84%, with one up almost 500% in 2015 alone! And this won't end anytime soon. Medicare Part D does not allow the feds to negotiate drug prices, which inflates costs even further.

The Department of Veterans Affairs, on the other hand, *can* negotiate—and their drugs are between 40% and 58% less expensive than the same ones offered under Part D. So if you're a senior who paid into the system all these years, you pay both ways—indirectly (through tax) and directly through copays for more expensive meds. The chief architect of the original bill, Republican congressman Billy Tauzin of Louisiana, left shortly after its passage. And whaddya know—old Billy picked up a $2-million-a-year job as head of the Pharmaceutical Research and Manufacturers of America lobbying firm!

Many of the bureaucrats in charge of Washington grew up in the *Just Say No!* era. I know it's not intentional, but their actions turned the already complex world of drug research, copays, and reimbursements into a psychedelic, David Lynch–style nightmare. It's almost like they *want* us to take drugs.

TAXES WRAPPED IN REGULATIONS
INSIDE OF HEALTH POLICIES

There are many health care–related costs caused by state and national policies. They're visceral—taxes out of your paycheck, insurance rate increases, or fees on your medical bill. However, there are plenty of other tangential costs and odd taxes nibbling away at your paycheck, too.

Because your health insurance is becoming more expensive due to Obamacare, you're already paying more out of pocket. However, a number of hidden taxes are liberally sprinkled all over your life.[25] If you're rich, you're paying 3.8% more on investment income.

Although it's been suspended for now, the Obamacare penalty for not carrying insurance is still on the books. At the time of this writing, the penalty is 2.5% of your income or $695—whichever is higher.

Other taxes include those on insurance companies, high-quality "Cadillac" insurance plans, medical device manufacturers, all of which slash your tax credit if you have high medical bills. One of the most damaging policies is a cap on Flexible Spending Accounts used by families for health care. Of the hardest hit? Parents of special needs children who attend specialty schools. The law even imposes an up-to $50,000 fine on charitable hospitals that don't fully comply with its regulations! *Freaking Saint Jude's Children's Hospital barely missed the penalty!*[26]

Earlier we talked about sin taxes. But have you heard about the "skin tax?" Hold on—I have to take five deep breaths before I start talking about this.

(Breathing . . .)

Okay. As part of the $1.3 trillion needed to fund the health-care overhaul, Obamacare imposed a 10% punitive tax on tanning.[27] Yes—tanning. As in skin, not leather. Democrats in Congress projected the tax would bring in $2.7 billion over a decade.

The effects are massive. The tanning industry itself estimates that Obamacare killed 10,000 salons nationwide and 81,000 jobs.[28] These salons are predominantly woman-owned, with a high concentration of immigrants from Asia. The Obama administration's "war on women" and small businesses was like that emo guy from *Twilight*— pasty, annoying, and sucking the life out of its victims.

So was it worth it from a financial standpoint? Well, instead of the $300 million intake projected in 2016, it was just $99 million. Less than half of all salons comply with the tax as it is.[29]

This case is something of a poster child for sin and medical taxes. It punishes voluntary activities, even though they're perfectly legal. It damages the prosperity of "protected classes." And worst of all, it

takes in far less than projected and doesn't help anybody but the bureaucrats who enacted it in the first place.

We all have to go through illnesses, injuries, and aging. It's part
of the trip on this popsicle stand we call life. I just want to do it on
my terms.

Don't you?

SIXTEEN

DEATH

FREE AT LAST? NOT SO FAST

> In this world nothing can be said to be
> certain, except death and taxes.
>
> —*Ben Franklin*

My Great Aunt Mabel was a hilarious, wild woman.

When Mabel died a few years ago at the age of 91, she left behind a hoarder's paradise that included more than 3,000 Beanie Babies. You couldn't blame the old girl for her eccentricities; she grew up during the Great Depression when people were literally farming dust—so she was incapable of getting rid of things. After she died (because she forgot to take her heart pills), cleaning out her apartment took weeks. Oh, you've never lived until you've sifted through a collection of fortune cookie fortunes from the 1960s and old newspapers from *both* Roosevelt administrations.

Aunt Mabel had no children and no spouse; her only living relative was my dad (her nephew). So when Mable died, we got stuck dealing with all of her possessions, like an apartment she owned in Philadelphia. Being the tax nerd that I am, Great Aunt Mabel's death got me curious about all these mysterious taxes and fees our nation's deceased leave behind for their loved ones, so I went to the library to see if I could learn anything that would help save Aunt Mabel's estate from the clutches of the Tax Monster.

There I was in the estate-planning section of my local library— *oh joy*. What twentysomething wouldn't love a day trip like this? After wandering around the library, I found three bookshelves that were groaning under the weight of a bunch of estate-planning books. There were nearly 100 books about estates, trusts, and wills, as well as about how to avoid financial disaster after the death of a loved one. I was shocked—how can there be so much information to consider when you're simply passing down your assets to your loved ones?

After spending hours perusing the shelves, I finally checked out a book called *Beyond the Grave: The Right Way and the Wrong Way of Leaving Money to Your Children (and Others)*. It was 498 freaking pages long; my God, why is this such treacherous territory? *Beyond the Grave* is filled with chapter headings like:

"If You Do Nothing, The Law Will Do It for You."

"How Does the IRS Knows How Much I'm Worth When I Die?"

"How to Leave More to Your Children and Less to the IRS."

"I Can Get Your Death Tax Wholesale."

"Your Money Is Taxed a Second Time When Your Child Dies."

Heartwarming stuff.

HOW THE PICKING OF DEAD POCKETS BEGAN

Death taxes are nearly as old as death itself. Such taxes were popular in medieval times, when heirs wishing to use transferred property were required to pay the king an estate tax.[1]

What was the rationale?

Today as then, the government—whether it's a king or a congressman—sees the transfer of wealth between individuals as an opportunity to rake in revenue. People in power have a deeply ingrained belief that no one should get anything for free without the government getting a slice of the pie. It's blatant but very simple.

Historically, there has been debate over this flagrant money grabbing by elected officials. In 17th and 18th century Europe, philosophers, economists, and jurists argued about whether people had a "natural right" to transfer property upon their death, free from government intervention. Among all those courtly gents wearing powdered wigs to keep down the fleas, the consensus emerged that property transfer rights are not "natural" but are granted by the government. In other words, it was only by the grace of government that Aunt Mabel could direct (or *will*) that her trunk full of cash be given to my dad rather than being taken by anyone who could grab it. Thus, the government needed to be paid for its oversight of the process.

Remember in the story *A Christmas Carol,* when Scrooge died, his charwoman, his laundress, and the local undertaker stole his possessions and sold them to a criminal? That's anarchy, which the government says it's trying to avoid—for a fee.

The first attempt in the United States to impose a tax on estate property transfers was made under the 1797 Stamp Act;[2] any *document* that concerned a property transfer after death—a will or a probate inventory—was subject to a tax. The tax was imposed to help fund the national defense in the war against France. When the war concluded, the Stamp Act was repealed . . . But then it was resuscitated in 1862, during the Civil War, but this time not just the documents were taxed. Now the actual estate of the deceased person was taxed. In 1864, needing to raise even more money for the war, Congress added a "gift tax" on property transfers made during one's lifetime.

When the war ended the estate tax was repealed, but in 1898 the cost of the Spanish-American War brought the estate tax back for a short time. It was like a zombie—rising from the grave, getting beaten down, and then clawing its way back to life to pay for wars.

Modern estate taxes were enacted by Congress in 1916, during World War I, the same year that the income tax was created. This time, a new rationale entered the discussion: the idea that an estate tax helped redistribute wealth from the rich to the not so rich, courtesy of government intervention. This was something new: The estate tax was no longer aimed at funding a specific project (waging a war) but was being used as a tool for social engineering.

Now the government was saying, "We want a cut of the estate so we can redistribute it to other, unrelated people."

INHERIT A MANSION? PREPARE TO BE
HAUNTED BY THE ESTATE TAX

I will leave the eternal question of what happens to our spirits, souls, energy waves, or whatever you want to call them to the philosophers and theologians. All I can say without equivocation is that as far as taxes are concerned our dearly departed definitely stick around long past their expiration dates. They haunt the earth and torment the living, whispering "IRS" in their ears at the most inopportune moments.

If Aunt Mabel had died with more money, my dad would have been hit with a federal estate tax of up to 40%. Today's estate tax, sometimes known by the more evocative but decidedly grimmer "death tax," is essentially a commission the government charges for transferring assets from deceased wealthy people to their heirs. The IRS offers an exemption that allows estates under a certain value to pass property to heirs tax-free. The 2017 exemption was $5.49 million. So if someone died with an estate valued at $5.49 million, no tax; if the value was $5,490,500, then $500 was taxed. The first $5.49 million was exempt. The federal tax bill passed by Congress at the end of 2017 doubled the estate tax exemption to $11.2 million. However, the new exemption amount is temporary and reverts back to $5.49 million in 2025 absent further congressional action.[3]

Aunt Mabel's estate wasn't worth millions, so my dad was off the hook when it came to the estate tax. Maybe it was this kind of foresight that led Aunt Mabel to sink all of her money in Beanie Babies? Nice thinking, Mabel, but unfortunately your 3,000 Beanie Babies' investment value vanished almost as soon as it began!

The estate tax imposes expensive and burdensome estate-planning costs on to families who are affected (one out of every 517 estates paid the tax in 2017). Yet for all the trouble it causes for these individuals, the estate tax is one of the federal government's least effective means of raising revenue.[4] It only produces $18 billion in revenue per year (yes, that's considered small beans when we're talking about a $4 trillion annual budget).

The elimination of the federal estate tax would have a minimal effect on the federal budget. But the positive benefits could be significant. Of course, the direct beneficiaries of an estate tax elimination would be wealthy families; but there would be an important indirect beneficiary, too: everyone else. Accumulated wealth makes the United States prosperous. When wealth is circulating and invested in the market—as opposed to being taken by the government—businesses grow, workers make more money, and the economy progresses. A tax on surplus capital is a drag on that driver of economic progress.

But this is the government we're talking about. The idea that the estate tax—an easy, albeit relatively small stream of revenue—will be repealed is unlikely. Even Trump, who repeatedly promised to do away with the tax, has hit the pause button on a repeal effort.[5]

Where does the taxed cash go anyway? You guessed it . . . Right into the federal general fund, where bureaucrats can spend it on anything they want including all those bloated pork-barrel projects that members of Congress like to award their states and perks that members of Congress enjoy (like 100% free health care).

THE STATES WANT THEIR SHARE, TOO

If an estate escapes the federal estate tax, it may still get hit with a state estate tax. That's right: government double-dipping. First the feds reach into your pocket, and then your state.

15 states have estate taxes, with their own rates and exemption amounts:

- Connecticut: 7.2–12% (exemption threshold: $2 million).
- Delaware: 0.8–16% (exemption threshold: $5.45 million).
- Hawaii: 0.8–16% (exemption threshold: $5.45 million).
- Illinois: 0.8–16% (exemption threshold: $4 million).
- Maine: 8–12% (exemption threshold: $1 million).
- Maryland: 16% (exemption threshold: $2 million).
- Massachusetts: 0.8–16% (exemption threshold: $1 million).
- Minnesota: 9–16% (exemption threshold: $1.6 million).
- New Jersey: 0.8–16% (exemption threshold: a measly $675,000).
- New York: 3.06–16% (exemption threshold: $3.125 million).
- Oregon: 0.8–16% (exemption threshold: $1 million).
- Rhode Island: 0.8–16% (exemption threshold: $1.5 million).
- Vermont: 0.8–16% (exemption threshold: $2.75 million).
- Washington: 10–20% (exemption threshold: $2.078 million).
- Washington, D.C.: 0.8–16% (exemption threshold: $1 million).

Oh, and in case you were wondering: Yes, the money collected from these estate taxes is almost always swallowed up into each state's own general fund, to be lost in the swirling maelstrom of government accounting.

An estate tax is paid by the estate. It doesn't matter who's named in the will or who inherits the deceased's cash. The estate pays, and then the remaining assets are distributed. But that may not be the end of it! As a beneficiary of an estate, you may have to pay an *inheritance tax* on the cash or assets left to you. In most states that have an inheritance tax, the rate varies depending on the relationship of the heir to the decedent.

In Pennsylvania—Aunt Mabel's home state—my dad got hit with a 15% tax. The rate is lower for heirs who are surviving spouses, children, or siblings. And here's the worst part about state inheritance taxes: Most of the time, there's no exemption amount. Which means that every single time a person dies in one of these states, regardless of how much money they had to their name, the heir gets hit with the tax.

My dad had nine months to pony up 15% of Aunt Mabel's estate, and if he didn't pay—he'd get slapped with a massive penalty and interest. Not exactly the kind of thing you want to be worried about when you're grieving the loss of a loved one.

Here are the six states that have estate taxes. Keep in mind that the rules about who pays what rate vary from state to state.

- Iowa: 0–15%
- Kentucky: 0–16%
- Maryland: 0–10%
- Nebraska: 1–18%
- New Jersey: 0–16%
- Pennsylvania: 0–15%

Sharp-eyed readers will note that two especially greedy states—New Jersey and Maryland—currently sock qualifying estates with both estate taxes *and* inheritance taxes.

As depressing as this all is, it's something that looms in front of us all.

We all think we're bulletproof.

We all think we're invincible.

We all think that we'll be around forever.

But we also know deep down that none of those things are true.

I hate to break it to you, but this whole death thing is something we all have to deal with at some point. But if we educate ourselves on the process, stay vigilant, and speak out against predatory government behavior, one day we might actually be reading the obituary of an unjust system.

#MabelLifeLessons!

PART THREE

WHAT YOU CAN DO

SEVENTEEN

NOT A SINGLE PENNY

IS IT POSSIBLE TO PAY NO TAXES?

I like to pay taxes. With them, I buy civilization.

—*Oliver Wendell Homes Jr.*

In a ramshackle farmhouse in the rugged southeastern part of Alaska, where the black flies are big enough to steal your snowmobile, lives an old friend of mine named Murphy. (Well, actually, his name is something else, but he made me swear to keep his identity a secret.) "Murphy" *values his privacy.* He's not exactly a hermit—he can be quite sociable when the mood strikes him—but he prefers to live a very low-profile existence.

He hates the government, thinks the air force has aliens on ice in Roswell, and wants to give up the least amount of money possible in the way of taxes. A few years back he got fed up with all the costs of living in upstate New York, so he packed up his old van and drove west and then north until he ran out of road. I'm giving Murphy his very own chapter in this book for one reason, and it's not because I want to celebrate his bear-grease-encrusted ZZ Top beard. It's because he tries, as best as he can, to live completely off the grid.

In other words, he wants to pay NO taxes or fees, keep every nickel he earns, and stay off the government's radar as much as he can. And that's what we're going to dissect in this chapter: What would it take for you to *really* get off the government's radar? And is that what you want?

We'll start with the *where*. Living in Alaska gives Murphy a slightly unfair advantage in his quest to live tax-free. Unlike New York (and most other states), Alaska doesn't collect a state sales tax, nor does it levy an individual income tax on *any* type of personal income, either earned or unearned. While some Alaskan cities and towns have a property tax—which can be steep—in the remote and deeply forested borough where Murphy built his own farmhouse, there's NO property tax. And as a special bonus, in Alaska every citizen receives a cash payment each year from the state government, via the Alaska Permanent Fund Corporation. On account of the state's rich oil and gas resources, every citizen of the state receives an annual check for $1,100, cut from the state's trust fund.[1]

Okay, step one: Move to Alaska. We got this, you guys.

Thanks to his location, Murphy has most of the big obvious taxes (the ones most of us see as unavoidable) taken care of. But even in Alaska, Murphy has to really work to keep the government's greedy fingers out of his wallet.

Murphy wanted to escape gas taxes, so he sold his van and bought an old diesel-engined Mercedes, which he converted to run on used cooking oil that he gets from fast-food joints. He had to make some major modifications to the car, including installing a separate fuel tank and fuel line for the cooking oil, and a heater for the veggie fuel tank because the stuff congeals in cold weather—which is like, 99% of the time in Alaska. But the cool thing is that restaurants will give him their used oil for free, because otherwise they'd have to pay to have it taken away. Score!

So the fuel is free, and Murphy doesn't pay the ubiquitous gas tax, which in Alaska currently totals 8.07 cents per gallon of diesel. It's less painful than Pennsylvania's whopping 52.1 cents per gallon, but it's still a tax. Small catch though—technically, running your car on vegetable oil violates federal law. On its website, the EPA says, "Raw vegetable oil or recycled greases (also called waste cooking oil) that have not been processed into esters are not biodiesel, and are not registered by EPA for legal use in vehicles. In addition, vehicles converted to use these oils would likely need to be certified by the EPA; to date EPA has not certified any conversions." *Translation:* From an environmental standpoint, it's illegal to use anything but fed-approved gasoline or diesel fuel (because where would the government get its money from?). In reality though, very few people ever get prosecuted, so this doesn't concern Murphy. Plus, his car's exhaust smells like French fries, which makes him feel like he's back at Rockaway Beach in the summertime.

Step two: . . . Yeah, I don't have the faintest idea how to do any of that stuff. Visit your local Pep Boys. Moving on.

But here's where Murphy is still getting hit with hidden taxes: Since he's chosen to drive a car, he needs a valid Alaska driver's license ($20 paid to the state) and vehicle registration fee ($100). To go *truly* off the grid, he'd have to get rid of his car and buy a bike. Even a scooter or moped requires a $60 registration fee. The only other option would be a snowmobile—no fee for that! Unless, of course, Murphy wants to drive it on public property, in which case he'd have to pay a $10 fee to register it.

Unlike many other states, Alaska no longer has a vehicle inspection program. In Alaska, you can drive any hunk of junk you want, as long as it keeps rolling and is not on fire. In New York, Murphy had to get a safety *and* emissions inspection at a DMV-licensed inspection station every 12 months, or when the ownership of the vehicle was transferred. The annual inspections cost him $37 in New York. Basically, Murphy has figured out the absolute least taxable way to continue driving a car—but even he has to pay a *little*.

Next up, edibles. Murphy lives on a farm and grows his own food to avoid meal taxes. Although agriculture in Alaska poses many challenges—the climate, the short growing season, and generally lousy soil for agriculture—Murphy grows lots of broccoli, carrots, cauliflower, potatoes, peas, spinach, and more. He even brews his own beer, because he likes the good stuff and wants to avoid the federal excise tax on alcoholic beverages.

He also enjoys his own venison, which he bags during hunting season in August and September, and then stores in a huge freezer. To legally hunt in Alaska you need a license, which costs $45 a year. A state law has been proposed that would make it legal to hunt on your own property without a license in any season, but it's currently stalled in the legislature. If Murphy bought his meat at the supermarket, he wouldn't have to pay for a license and he'd be even further off the grid. But unless you live in Alaska, Montana, New Hampshire, Delaware, or Oregon, you'd get stuck with sales taxes at the grocery store.

Murphy's freezer, along with everything else in his home, is powered by solar and wind arrays. Between the two, he's got his energy needs covered for his farmhouse, which, by the way, is heated with a geothermal heat pump—there's no fuel oil, no carbon footprint, nothing. The inside unit is about the size of a dishwasher, and makes less noise than a water boiler. He's managed to completely avoid most utility taxes, but it's taken a lot of work to do it. That's the thing about this romanticized "primal human" life—cave people didn't have jobs or money, because *staying alive was their full-time, year-round job*. And they didn't get sick days or health insurance or long weekends. (Or *weekends*.) And it's basically become Murphy's full-time job to create and maintain a lifestyle that allows him to give as little of his money as possible to the government.

But we're not done yet.

How about the phone? As you know by now, local, state, and federal governments, 911 systems, and even school districts tack on taxes and surcharges to your wireless bill that can increase the cost an extra 17%. Murphy uses a prepaid cell phone, but even that doesn't escape taxation. There are basically two kinds of taxes that telecom providers can collect on prepaid airtime and plan renewals: point of sale taxes, collected directly from the customer when they make a purchase, and telecom taxes that mobile operators are allowed—but not required—to pass on to their customers. When you buy a pre-paid cell phone you may not *see* the taxes because they're built into the price.

If Murphy wanted to truly pay no hidden taxes, he'd throw his phone away and communicate via Skype or some other free internet platform—but he'd have to use the library's internet, because installing his own would be way too *on-the-grid* for him.

One thing that Murphy really loves about Alaska is that he never has to go on vacation; to see stunning scenery or go on a fishing trip, all he needs to do is open his front door. Good thing, too, because he saves a bundle in vacation-related taxes. He doesn't fly anywhere, at least not on a commercial carrier.

Murphy's buddy Fred once came to visit him from New York. When Fred arrived in Alaska, he arranged to take a three-day boat trip to see some glaciers and polar bears. "Have fun, dude, but count me out," Murphy said. "Don't you know about the commercial pas-senger vessel excise tax? Anyone who takes an overnight boat trip lasting more than 72 hours has to pay a tax of $34.50 per person."

Fred looked stunned. "Wow, that's a tax that even New York doesn't have!"

"Up here in the Last Frontier, the government likes to stick the tourists from the Lower 48 with a sweet little surcharge for breath-ing our air."

During his visit, Fred also met Murphy's girlfriend Naomi. Emboldened by a few pints of Murphy's home brew, he said, "You guys have been together five years. Aren't you going to get married?"

"Are you kidding?" replied Naomi as she munched on a piece of Murphy's homemade venison jerky. "In Alaska, a marriage license costs 60 bucks! Nah—we just got a local moose to watch as we pledged our troth to each other. It was very romantic, and the only cost was a bushel of apples for the moose." (True story.)

As Fred flew home in his first-class seat—sipping a bourbon that had been taxed at about 21 cents per ounce—he thought to himself, *Could I do what Murphy and Naomi are doing—live as far off the grid as possible? Could I be happy?*

He's not the first New Yorker to wonder this. Travel to any rugged nature-y place, like Bozeman, Montana, or North Conway, New Hampshire, and you'll find plenty of off-gridders and experimental communes on the outskirts of town. No more $150 dinner bills or skyrocketing rents, no 9–5 schedules or stuffy commutes, no . . . *Game of Thrones*! No iPhone! No Facebook! *No Amazon!*

Here's the bottom line: Unless you want to literally live on a deserted island like the survivors on *Lost*, with no phone and no car, you're not going to escape paying *some* hidden taxes and fees. The government has carefully woven these payments into the fabric of our lives, and if you do pretty much anything in public, or anything that involves a transaction between yourself and another human being, the government will want its share.

Is the answer to move to a remote area, like Murphy and Naomi did, and dedicate yourself to avoiding all taxes and fees? If so, the price—in ways besides taxes—is steep. It's a massive lifestyle overhaul that requires sacrificing pretty much every creature comfort you can think of—not to mention your proximity and accessibility to your family and friends. For Murphy and Naomi, it was worth it. They're so committed to escaping the long reach of the state that they've devoted most of their time and energy to doing just that.

But for the vast majority of "normal" citizens who just want to play Candy Crush during a boring conference call, have a few glasses of wine after work, and binge *Orange Is the New Black* in a well-lit, comfortable living room, that sort of lifestyle just isn't possible—even if you *did* want to do it, which, let's be honest, most of us don't. Not really.

See, giving Uncle Sam the finger is actually the easy way out. Sure, it takes a huge shift in mentality, and requires time, energy, and skills the average American just doesn't have—do *you* know how to convert an engine to run on vegetable oil? 'Cause I sure don't—but opting out is the same thing as *copping* out. Running away from the system is just another way of giving the system your permission to endure.

Real change takes even *more* time and *more* hard work.

EIGHTEEN

PURSUING ALTERNATIVES

IT'S RIGHT TO DEMAND BETTER

> The wisdom of man never yet contrived a system of
> taxation that would operate with perfect equality.
>
> —*Andrew Jackson*

American citizens have been protesting tax policies since the earliest days of our country's existence. In 1791, just a few years after the adoption of the Constitution, the federal government began taxing whiskey to pay off its debts from the Revolution. But (unlike the whiskey) it didn't go down so well with Americans. The same year the tax was enacted, the Whiskey Rebellion sprung up—a good ole-fashioned revolt against sin taxes! Rebels living in Pennsylvania and Ohio began tar-and-feathering whiskey tax collectors (fun!). Their movement picked up steam, and eventually they formed a militia. Marching against the U.S. government under their own flag, the rebels raised hell against corrupt and unfair taxation.

The conflict continued with sporadic flare-ups until it reached a climax in 1794, when more than 500 men marched on the home of a tax inspector in Pennsylvania. George Washington, who was facing pressure from Alexander Hamilton (the tax-and-spend king of the

1790s), responded by dispatching government troops to enforce the tax. Fighting against the might of a powerful federal government, the insurgency was suppressed for several years after that.

Then, in 1800, something uniquely American happened: an election. Thomas Jefferson ran as a low-tax candidate and his platform resonated with voters. Jefferson repealed the whiskey tax as soon as he was voted into office.

So how much have things changed since then?

Well, taking up arms is certainly frowned upon these days. So is tar-and-feathering, although I propose we bring that back ASAP. Other than that, the Tax Monster still lurks. Federal, state, and local officials still take advantage of a surprisingly wide range of relatively unchecked powers to inject hidden taxes, fees, and other regulation-related costs into our consumer spending needs: utility bills, transportation costs, tuition, rents, mortgages, food expenses, entertainment, and more. Elected officials don't *want* us to see the scope of this piecemeal pilfering from your pocketbook. They do it little by little, and spread it across countless everyday life expenses, hoping you won't notice. And mostly, it's worked.

What's more, federal, state, and local governments are spending our money on whatever they please, including bloated and above-market salaries for themselves and their underlings, with surprisingly little accountability for mismanagement, systemic inefficiencies, and downright bad decisions. Our collective inability to recognize and push back against these practices has allowed elected—and unelected—public officials alike to get away with these schemes for decades.

Now that we're equipped with the knowledge of how the system is covertly bleeding us dry, we need to do something about it. But what? How do we even start to dismantle something this vast and complex? Well—the first step in any revolution is this: Know what you want.

Let's revisit one of the first ideas introduced in this book: When it comes to tax policy, we've been consumed with divisive, politicized debates about *what* and *whom* gets taxed, when we need to be focusing on the *how*. Taken another way, we need to concentrate more on the *process* than the *product*. Given the current state of affairs in this country, the two main factions are never going to agree on what and whom (the product). But we can ALL agree on the process, the how. *How* do we expect our government to behave when they tax us? What should they be telling us before they tax us? What are the expectations when they collect that tax? And finally, how do we want them to operate once they've received our tax revenue?

So—what do we want? I have some ideas . . .

1. TRANSPARENCY.

We need to demand that information about taxes and fees be easily accessible and not buried under a mountain of legalese. Officials must be obligated to call a tax what it is. The average American should be able to learn the reason behind every tax, as well as where that money is going. As it stands now, all we have access to are the city, state, and federal budgets, which we're free to pore over if we really want to— but who's going to do that? These abstruse budgets are deliberately designed to hide reality from ordinary people anyway. Bottom line: The government takes up to 50% of our income, and a hefty slice of that is coming from consumer purchases; we should be able to get a clear picture of our consumer taxation in the same way we clearly know what our income tax bracket is.

Greater visibility on taxes, fees, and costs by regulation means greater accountability. For example, a New York City councilman is less likely to vote for an MTA fare hike that increases already-bloated city worker salaries if he will be publicly tied to the vote. If their decisions were made in the clear light of day—and if voters knew how, specifically, their tax dollars were being used—elected officials would need to carefully weigh their support for proposed fare hikes or taxes. And if an elected official *did* cooperate in enacting wasteful taxes, or stand idly by as they were imposed by some other part of the government, a more accessible stream of information would make it easier to hold that official accountable for their decisions—by voting them out of office in the next election.

2. THRIFT.

Most of us can agree on the general premise that we need *some* form of government—federal, state, and local—to provide certain services that benefit us individually and as a society. We need a national military to defend us from hostile foreign and domestic powers. We need public schools and colleges to keep our population educated and competitive in the world economy. Nobody wants a pay-as-you-go military or fire department. Likewise, when you drive your car over a bridge, it would be quite inconvenient if that bridge fell into the water half a mile below.

But here's the thing. If we the citizens agree to pool our money in order to pay for these services and thereby entrust our public officials with the responsibility to spend that money wisely, then we must *demand* that every level of government is lean, efficient, and ultimately judicious and disciplined in its spending. Too often public officials squander our money through unjustified spending like absurd government salaries, unjustifiable federal subsidies, and flat-out waste. Our elected officials continue to spend tax money like drunken sailors . . . because there's zero accountability and zero consequence. Thrift is a natural offshoot of accountability—when we have a clear picture of where our money is going, we can demand sensible spending. Likewise, when the public is able to scrutinize its government, well then, it's in the government's best interest to behave itself, isn't it?

3. FAIRNESS.

We have to demand that taxes be fair and reasonable for everyone. Hidden taxes and fees are not *progressive* (meaning that what you pay does not increase in proportion to your earnings, like the income tax bracket)—they're *regressive*. Let's say two people, Susan and Greg, each need to buy the basics of life—food, clothing, a phone, a non-hooptie car, stuff for their apartment. Say each spends $10,000 per year on these things. If taxes and fees on these purchases add up to 6%, then both pay $600 in taxes. Sounds fair enough, right? Well—no, it's not fair at all. If George makes $40,000 year at a teaching job, then he's paying 1.5% of his total income toward these taxes. Meanwhile, Susan works as a big-shot attorney, pulling in $400,000 a year. That $600 is just 0.15% of her income. It takes a much smaller bite, and she has proportionally more money left over. And poor George is stuck eating $1.50 ramen noodles every night.

Regressive taxes hurt the lower and middle classes the most. And we're not just talking about sales taxes on discretionary purchases (as in, nonnecessities; things we can live without). Taxes are injected into each and every heat, water, electricity, internet, phone, and gas bill—the essential, non-optional purchases.

Transparency. Thrift. Fairness. The three pillars that any successful system of taxation needs to be built on. But how do we get there from here?

THE "GENERAL FUND" SLEIGHT OF HAND

Before we talk about how to move forward, we need to address one of the biggest obstacles preventing citizens from obtaining basic knowledge about how their hard-earned tax dollars are spent: widespread abuse of city and state "general funds." If we want transparency, thrift, and fairness in taxation at every level, we need to see major reform in the collection and spending processes surrounding general fund revenue.

The previous chapters revealed that one of the shadiest and most irritating practices of state and city governments is to set up important-sounding taxes and fees (like pet registration fees or cigarette taxes) that you'd think were designed to benefit something related to what they're called (awww, pets!)—but in reality, the income gets diverted into general funds, where it can be spent on just about anything.

General funds are largely sourced from individual income tax, property tax, retail sales tax, and the state lottery. Other sources include the corporate income tax and other business taxes, alcohol and tobacco taxes, and miscellaneous taxes and fees. States also have trust funds that are supposed to receive money from taxes or fees that are earmarked for certain purposes by law. For example, gas taxes are often supposed to be used only for highway maintenance, not dumped into the general fund. But it doesn't always work that way . . .

In Georgia, two environmental funds received $450 million between 1993 and 2015—but only $264 million went to environmental cleanup.[1] The remaining $186 million was diverted to the general fund. The cash came in part from a fee of $1 levied on each new vehicle tire sold in the state, supposedly created to clean up tire dumps. Millions collected from the tire fee were diverted into the state's general fund by a succession of governors and lawmakers, in an effort to balance the state's budget—and all the while, Georgians were kept in the dark about where their money was going.

For Georgia lawmakers, this was a win-win scenario: They got the money they needed, *and* they were able to avoid raising taxes or having to further cut spending. On the other hand, it was a lose-lose for their constituents: They had to pay a non-optional fee for buying new tires (which is something you have to do or you don't pass inspection), AND they were led to believe that those fees were intended for a specific purpose, while in actuality they were being spent elsewhere.

In Connecticut, money has been siphoned from the highway fund to finance non-highway initiatives for decades. In the 1970s, highway maintenance suffered from a lack of funds, and in 1983 a bridge on I-95 collapsed. With all that money being continuously diverted from the special highway fund into the state general fund, state officials complained that there wasn't enough money to maintain roads and bridges. (Insert eye roll here.) Their solution? Institute tolls![2]

In California, bureaucrats funnel money meant for state parks into the general fund, where it's spent on other, non-park related expenditures. In 2012 the majority of "hidden assets"—a stash of cash that officials at the California Department of Parks and Recreation kept off the books in their annual reports to the Department of Finance—were held in something called the Off Highway Vehicle Trust (OHV) fund. This fund collected cash at the parks themselves, through entrance fees, souvenir sales, and other site-specific sources. State officials reported that the hidden assets in the OHV fund and the State Parks and Recreation Fund totaled $54 million.

Park leaders squirreled away that $54 million for as long as 12 years. This continued even as officials moved to close 70 parks in 2016, to comply with cuts to the state's general fund (I feel like this sentence should have about eight exclamation points).[3] The OHV fund was *supposed* to pay for parks dedicated to all-terrain vehicle usage. But no new parks were ever opened, and the fund was regularly raided and diverted to . . . wait for it . . . the general fund! I know, you're shocked.

In Arizona, a "balanced Arizona budget relies on diverting school funds." Yep, for all those cries of *"But it's for the chiiiiiildren,"* Arizona officials take money from the state land trust—cash that was earmarked mainly for schools—to balance the state's budget via the general fund.[4]

In New Jersey, former governor Chris Christie diverted more than $1 billion from ratepayer subsidies on customer utility bill charges. That money was ostensibly supposed to go toward clean energy programs, but it went straight into the general fund. He also took hundreds of millions of dollars from fee-supported environmental programs, diverted toll revenue from transportation projects, and tried to grab more than $160 million in affordable housing funds.[5] A real gem, that guy.

Such raids and other budget-balancing magic tricks are often critical for state lawmakers to be able to balance their out-of-control budgets without enacting politically unpopular program cuts, or breaking their pledges not to raise taxes (or taking a pay cut themselves).

Examples of general fund schemes like the ones above are countless and happen all across the country. I could go on, and on, and on, and on . . . but I'm tired. Let's talk solutions.

THE WAY FORWARD

If enough young people knew how much of their money routinely went into government coffers without their knowledge, and how that money was getting spent, significant reform would be within reach. But it's incredibly difficult and time-consuming to build a basic understanding of how all this works—especially when you have to work multiple jobs just to make ends meet. In writing this book, it took over a year of research to track down the various ways city, state, and federal governments mislead taxpayers and spend their money on initiatives that are wasteful, vastly overpriced, and sometimes just plain absurd. And that's exactly why bureaucrats love to funnel so much tax money into the general funds; it allows them to spend our money however they please with minimal accountability.

One big step toward increased transparency would be the public availability of simplified budgets for your town or city and your state—including a simple breakdown of which taxes and fees are funneled into general funds and how that money is spent. In this age of digital communications, there's no reason why every citizen can't have access to this information.

Let's say you live in Midcity, USA. Your city budget is $100 million. You can probably go online and access the wonky accountants' version of the city budget, but unless you've got a degree in finance you're probably not going to know how to read it. Here's what you deserve to know, in simple English:

1. Where is my city getting its money from—and specifically, how much does it get from individual citizens and from small business owners?
2. Which funds go into the general fund, and which ones are kept in their own dedicated pots? For example, does my boat excise tax go into the general fund, or is it earmarked for harbor improvements?
3. What happens if the city has trouble balancing its budget? Are services going to be cut, or revenues increased?
4. If revenues are increased, where will the money come from? Tax hikes must be publicly known—not stealthily imposed on citizens via hidden fees.
5. And finally, how are our tax dollars spent? City, state, and federal funds must account for and clearly disclose how they use every dollar received. This includes simplified breakdowns of government workers' salaries and benefits.

Point five is especially critical. Many Americans don't mind paying a little more in taxes, because they simply assume that their hard-earned money is going to the "greater good." But too often, citizens are unknowingly overtaxed (often through hidden taxes and fees) to fund above-market government salaries and pension plans. A federal government worker receives compensation that is 30–40% higher,[6] on average, than the pay of a worker who has the same job in the private sector. And federal employees are insulated from recessions, enjoying job security regardless of the state of the economy. Aligning federal compensation with market rates would save taxpayers more than $47 billion every year.[7] And that's only on the federal level! State and city workers also make far more in salary and benefits than workers in the private sector. As of 2013, the most recent year for which data is available, employees in the private sector received an average of $29.11 per hour in compensation, while state and city government workers received an average of $42.09 per hour in compensation.[8]

The average public salary and pension for each position, and how those salaries compare to the private sector, should be easily accessible information to taxpayers. And if there is an overall increase in public employee salaries, residents deserve to know how those increases compare to the rate of inflation as well as the rise in private sector salaries.

Bottom line: Taxpayers must demand that every city and state government create simple, transparent reports showing citizens who aren't accountants—namely, just about everybody—where the money comes from and where it goes. The reports should also include all revenue collected from hidden fees on consumer spending that essentially function as stealth taxes. They should be just like the nutrition labels on the food we buy: mandatory, standardized, and legally obligated to contain truthful information.

What's the alternative? Continued opacity in municipal budgets results in public employees who enjoy cushy salaries with no accountability, systematic overpayment for goods and services, and straight-up waste . . . all being funded by YOU! While wastefulness is obviously bad, lack of transparency and accountability also opens up opportunities for people to game the system. It's already happened in the past. Have you heard of Rita Crundwell? She is perhaps the most audacious female thief in American history.

No, she did not rob a bank—she robbed the city of Dixon, Illinois. From 1983 to 2012, she was the comptroller and treasurer of the city. Over the course of 22 years, Crundwell embezzled $53.7 million from the city's bank account.[9] Her scheme was amazingly simple, and if the system had been even a *tiny bit* more transparent, she would have been caught almost immediately.

On December 8, 1990, Crundwell used her authority to open a secret bank account with the innocuous name of Reserve Sewer Capital Development Account (RSCDA). It appeared to be a city account, but Crundwell was the only signatory. She deposited revenues into another city account called the Capital Development Fund, created false state invoices, and then wrote checks from the fund payable to "Treasurer," which she would deposit into the RSCDA account. This relatively uncomplicated scheme continued for over two decades, with Crundwell stealing an average of $2.5 million per year from the city.

Crundwell blamed the shortfalls on late transfers from the state. Every year, outside auditors and the city accountant signed off on Crundwell's financial statements—without checking the numbers. She was finally discovered when she went on vacation, and the city clerk who was filling in for her discovered the RSCDA account and the hundreds of checks written against it. Crundwell pleaded guilty to her crimes and was sentenced to nearly 20 years in prison.

Rita Crundwell's scheme had real consequences for the people of Dixon. Budget shortfalls forced city departments to make drastic service cuts, city employees went years without raises, and the police department couldn't get new equipment. The city was forced to lay off three of its nine street repair workers and cut the rate of road maintenance, leading to poor and unsafe roads.

Is there a Rita Crundwell in *your* city or state? Here's the thing—if there is, how would you know? How would you know if $2.5 million a year went unaccounted for, or if government employees were awarding themselves unearned pay raises or overtime paychecks, or if money—YOUR money—were being shuttled from fund to fund to make up for inefficiency and poor planning?

You wouldn't know. This is my point.

90% OF SUCCESS . . .

As a solution for a problem as knotted and intricate as this one, simply "showing up" doesn't seem very awesome. But let me tell you one last story.

Years ago I took a summer job as a videographer in a rural New Hampshire town. I wasn't filming celebrities, capturing meteor showers, or editing memes—this job was a little more . . . prosaic. I was charged with recording—get excited—town hall meetings. I expected it to be the most boring gig in all of creation, kind of like Book TV on C-SPAN only without the thrilling sound of turning pages.

Well, I'm not afraid to admit when I'm wrong. This experience gave me a front row seat to what real change looks like in this country. Town hall meetings are places where people who care about their community, state, and country gather to learn about issues, discuss problems, and make their voices heard. The process isn't always smooth, and usually involves a good deal of unproductive arguing. But even when people disagreed at these meetings, they still agreed on the reason they'd shown up in the first place—they wanted to make their community better.

One night, the town faced a wrenching decision—they needed to let go of a local elementary school teacher. The town's population had declined and the school district no longer had enough kids to justify the number of teachers it had. Of course, no one wanted this kindly teacher who had devoted her young life to children to lose her job, but the town's budget just couldn't sustain the position.

Chaos ensued. The teacher's friends showed up at the meeting and clamored on her behalf—shouting, gesticulating, imploring, crying—you name it. There was weeping and wailing and much gnashing of teeth.

In the end, the teacher kept her job, even though the numbers didn't work without a tax hike. And so, a tax hike is what the town got.

You don't have to be a coldhearted Scrooge to think the town council's decision was bad from a budgetary standpoint. A handful of people at the meeting pointed out that the government is not a jobs program. But in this country, and in our towns and cities, the power belongs to the people who show up and try to understand and handle problems. Outcomes are driven by the expression of interests. Here, multiple outcomes were possible; some made good economic sense while others did not. In the end, the solution that prevailed was the one championed by the people who were most passionate and—more than anything—*present*.

People say 90% of success is just showing up. When you pay your next subway tax on a cable bill, consider asking yourself: Who showed up for the meeting that decided *that* tax?

If you're reading this book, and you aren't hiding out in a moss-covered cabin in the mountains of Alaska, you probably live in some sort of town or city. Your town or city has an elected government, such as a city council or a board of selectmen. There may be a mayor or city manager. These people are accessible, and they're part of your local government—the same local government that levies all sorts of fees on you and your neighbors. You can influence them by:

- Writing to them directly or calling their offices.
- Stopping them on the street and (politely!) expressing your opinion.

- Participating in debates before elections. In most towns, the local newspaper or Chamber of Commerce sponsors debates. Go to them and submit your questions!
- And, of course, voting.

In the long run, barring exceptional situations that garner national attention, it's hard for any one person or small group to grab the federal government's attention and shift the course of major policy decisions. But on the state and local levels, the reality is different. Whether you live in a teeming metropolis like Manhattan or a tiny town like Big Piney, Wyoming, you can be sure that town meetings, town halls, and school board meetings convene far more often than you presently realize. Most of the new regulations and taxes that will affect you are born and decided on in these meetings. These are the forums in which local authorities decide whether to increase transportation fares, impose new charges on utilities, raise pet-licensing fees, or make any number of other decisions that affect your bottom line. The truth is—

We can't get involved in debates to help solve problems we've never heard of.

We can't contribute to conversations we haven't listened to.

We can't participate in meetings we don't attend.

Unless you're closely watching what your local officials are doing to your pocketbook, you won't be around to answer back when they ask on any given day:

How do I tax thee?

Make no mistake about it, America. They are taxing you far more than you know.

ACKNOWLEDGMENTS

Thank you to Ronald Goldfarb, whose unwavering advocacy I hold dear.

Adam Bellow, for affording me the opportunity to write this book and helping to shape its message. I will always be deeply grateful for the confidence you placed in me and in this project.

The world-class editorial team at St. Martin's Press, for excellent contributions during the editing process.

MWA, an assiduous researcher who provided insights while I wrote this book.

My parents, Dawn and Steve, for invaluable encouragement and advice over the years.

Finally, Leonard, for love, laughs, and support—and some hard-nosed input—that helped to see this project through.

NOTES

1. TRANSPORTATION

1. Johnny Knocke, "The MTA Loses Six Billion Dollars a Year and Nobody Cares," *Medium,* July 6, 2016, https://medium.com/@johnnyknocke/the-mta-loses-six-billion-dollars-a-year-and-nobody-cares-d0d23093b2d8.
2. Daniel Roberts, "Riders Outraged by Proposed MTA Fare Hikes," *New York Post,* August 5, 2010, http://nypost.com/2010/08/05/riders-outraged-by-proposed-mta-fare-hikes/.
3. "Paying for Your Ride," *RTAChicago,* http://www.rtachicago.org/index.php/plan-your-trip/travel-tips/paying-for-your-ride.
4. "Metrorail Fares," Washington Metropolitan Area Transit Authority, https://www.wmata.com/fares/rail.cfm.
5. Luke Mullins and Michael J. Gaynor, "The Infuriating History of How Metro Got So Bad," *Washingtonian,* December 9, 2015, https://www.washingtonian.com/2015/12/09/why-does-metro-suck-dangerous-accidents-escalator-outages/.
6. Knocke, "MTA Loses Six Billion."
7. Gus Lubin, "Meet the 8,074 New York Transit Workers Who Earn More Than $100,000," *Business Insider,* June 4, 2010, http://www.businessinsider.com/mta-salaries-2010-6.
8. Alfonso A. Castillo, "Report: 7 LIRR Workers Made over $200,000 in 2016 in OT," *Newsday,* May 1, 2017, http://www.newsday.com/long-island/transportation/report-7-lirr-workers-made-over-200-000-in-2016-in-ot-1.13548078.
9. Dan Rivoli, "MTA Workers Raked in Close to $1B Worth of Overtime in 2016," *New York Daily News,* May 1, 2017, http://www.nydailynews.com/new-york/mta-workers-raked-close-1b-worth-overtime-2016-article-1.3123821.

10. Max Jaeger and Kevin Fasick, "MTA Workers Get Paid 5 Times the Normal Rate on Fourth of July," *New York Post,* July 4, 2017, http://nypost.com/2017/07/04/mta-workers-get-paid-5-times-the-normal-rate-on-fourth-of-july/.

11. Henrick Karoliszyn and Rich Schapiro, "Hop on the Gravy Train: LIRR Engineer Pulls in $250G with OT Pay," *New York Daily News,* May 15, 2011, http://www.nydailynews.com/new-york/hop-gravy-train-lirr-engineer-pulls-250g-ot-pay-article-1.144099.

12. Joshua Sabatini, "Driver Salaries Fueling Deficit," *San Francisco Examiner,* February 22, 2010, https://archives.sfexaminer.com/sanfrancisco/driver-salaries-fueling-deficit/Content?oid=2135249.

13. "MTA Rescue Plan," BALCONY New York, http://www.balconynewyork.com/mtarescue/.

14. Susan Edelman, "$85 'Stealth Tax' Pain," *New York Post,* February 14, 2010, http://nypost.com/2010/02/14/85-stealth-tax-pain/.

15. Edelman, "$85 'Stealth Tax' Pain."

16. Martine Powers, "MassDOT Board Expected to Approve MBTA Fare Hikes," *The Boston Globe,* May 14, 2014, https://www.bostonglobe.com/metro/2014/05/13/massdot-board-expected-mbta-fare-hikes/xWnuhjZ8uLcllEWsjMX7ON/story.html.

17. Lisa DeCanio, "It's Official: The MBTA Votes 4-1 in Approval of a 23% Fare Hike, To Be Implemented July 1," *BOSTINNO,* April 4, 2012, https://www.americaninno.com/boston/mbta-passes-fare-hike/.

18. Shira Schoenberg, "MBTA Payroll Database: Why Are Workers Paid Huge Amounts of Overtime?" *MassLive,* March 3, 2016, http://www.masslive.com/politics/index.ssf/2016/03/mbta_payroll_database_why_are.html.

19. Thomas Peele, "Three BART Janitors Swept Up $365,000 in OT Last Year," *Mercury News,* June 1, 2017, http://www.mercurynews.com/2017/06/01/three-bart-janitors-swept-up-365000-in-ot-last-year/.

20. Council of the City of New York, *Taxi and Limousine Commission: Report on the Fiscal 2017 Preliminary Budget and the Fiscal 2016 Preliminary Mayor's Management Report,* March 2, 2016, https://council.nyc.gov/budget/wp-content/uploads/sites/54/2016/05/156-Taxi-and-Limousine-Commission.pdf.

21. "New York City Taxi and Limousine Commission," *Glassdoor,* updated June 22, 2017, https://www.glassdoor.com/Salary/New-York-City-Taxi-and-Limousine-Commission-Salaries-E136805.htm.

22. "Taxi & Limousine Commission," NYC Green Book, http://a856-gbol.nyc.gov/GBOLWebsite/GreenBook/Details?orgId=2898.

23. Council of the City of New York, *Taxi and Limousine Commission.*

24. "Commercial Motor Vehicle Tax (CMVT)," NYC Department of Finance, http://www1.nyc.gov/site/finance/taxes/business-commercial-motor-ve hicle-tax-cmvt.page.

25. Emma Whitford, "Governor Cuomo: 'The Time Has Come' for Congestion Pricing," *Gothamist,* August 14, 2017, http://gothamist.com/2017/08/14 /cuomo_congestion_pricing.php.

26. Taxi Medallion Owner Driver Association, "Letter to Governor Cuomo on Taxis," April 24, 2017, https://www.scribd.com/document/346690906 /Letter-to-Governor-Cuomo-on-Taxis.

27. "How Much Tax Do We Pay on a Gallon of Gasoline and Diesel Fuel?" U.S. Energy Information Administration, https://www.eia.gov/tools/faqs/faq .php?id=10&t=10.

28. Robert L. Bradley Jr., "Oil Company Earnings: Reality over Rhetoric," *Forbes,* May 10, 2011, https://www.forbes.com/2011/05/10/oil-company -earnings.html.

29. Sophie Quinton, "Reluctant States Raise Gas Taxes to Repair Roads," Pew Charitable Trusts, *Stateline* (blog), July 26, 2017, http://www.pewtrusts .org/en/research-and-analysis/blogs/stateline/2017/07/26/reluctant -states-raise-gas-taxes-to-repair-roads.

30. "Most Americans Live in States with Variable-Rate Gas Taxes," Institute on Taxation and Economic Policy, February 5, 2016, https://itep.org/most -americans-live-in-states-with-variable-rate-gas-taxes-2/.

31. "Gasoline Tax," API, http://www.api.org/oil-and-natural-gas/consumer -information/motor-fuel-taxes/gasoline-tax.

32. cardboardarmor, "Welcome to California, Land of $700 Car Registration," *Oppositelock,* January 8, 2014, http://oppositelock.kinja.com/welcome-to -california-land-of-700-car-registration-1497647393.

2. FOOD

1. Jacob Dayan, "Ancient Taxes from Around the World," Community Tax, *Tax* (blog), July 10, 2017, http://www.communitytax.com/ancient-taxes -around-world/.

2. "Strange & Unusual Taxes throughout History," *efile.com,* https://www.efile .com/tax-rate/federal-income-tax-rates/.

3. Joseph Henchman, Alex Raut, and Kevin Duncan, "Meal Taxes in Major U.S. Cities," *Tax Foundation* (blog), March 1, 2012, https://taxfoundation.org /meals-taxes-major-us-cities-0/.

4. Henchman, Raut, and Duncan, "Meal Taxes."

5. Brad McElhinny, "House's 'Broaden-the-Base' Bill Brings Back Food Tax, Estimates $174 Million in New Revenue," *West Virginia MetroNews,* March 24, 2017, http://wvmetronews.com/2017/03/24/houses-broaden-the-base-bill -brings-back-food-tax-estimates-174-million-in-new-revenue/.

6. Brian Lyman, "The Strange Persistence of Alabama's Grocery Tax," *Mont- gomery Advertiser,* March 23, 2017, http://www.montgomeryadvertiser.com /story/news/politics/southunionstreet/2017/03/23/strange-persistence -alabamas-grocery-tax/99511764/.

7. Tim Carpenter, "Cigarette Tax Hike, Food Sales Tax Cut Fail to Pass Muster in Kansas House," *Topeka Capital-Journal,* April 3, 2017, http://cjonline.com /news/local/state-government/2017-04-02/cigarette-tax-hike-food-sales -tax-cut-fail-pass-muster-kansas.

8. Carpenter, "Cigarette Tax Hike."

9. "The Most Ridiculous Taxes in the World," *Odd Stuff Magazine,* http://odd stuffmagazine.com/ridiculous-taxes-world.html.

10. "Most Ridiculous Taxes."

11. "Most Ridiculous Taxes."

12. Tyler O'Neil, "Here's What Federal Regulations Cost Your Family This Year," *GlennBeck.com,* June 1, 2017, http://www.glennbeck.com/2017/06 /01/heres-what-federal-regulations-cost-your-family-this-year/.

13. Dan Charles, "Congress Just Passed a GMO Labeling Bill. Nobody's Super Happy about It," *The Salt,* NPR, July 14, 2016, http://www.npr.org/sec tions/thesalt/2016/07/14/486060866/congress-just-passed-a-gmo-label ing-bill-nobodys-super-happy-about-it.

14. Michal Addady, "President Obama Signed This GMO Labeling Bill," *Fortune,* July 31, 2016, http://fortune.com/2016/07/31/gmo-labeling-bill/.

15. Charles, "Congress Just Passed."

16. Wilson Ring, "Vermont's GMO Labeling Law Could Cost Grocers up to $10 Million per Day in Fines," *Business Insider,* June 18, 2015, http://www .businessinsider.com/vermonts-gmo-labeling-law-could-cost-grocers-up-to -10-million-per-day-in-fines-2015-6.

17. Annie Gasparro and Jacob Bunge, "GMO Labeling Law Roils Food Com- panies," *Wall Street Journal,* March 20, 2016, https://www.wsj.com/articles /gmo-labeling-law-roils-food-companies-1458510332.

18. Mark Sisson, "7 Foods You Don't Need to Buy Organic," *Mark's Daily Apple,* December 12, 2012, http://www.marksdailyapple.com/7-foods-you-dont -need-to-buy-organic/.

19. "Organic Provisions in the 2014 Farm Act," USDA Economic Research Service, updated April 4, 2017, https://www.ers.usda.gov/topics/natural

-resources-environment/organic-agriculture/organic-provisions-in-the
-2014-farm-act/.

20. Julie Kelly, "The Foodies Are Back to Fight for Counterproductive,
Porky Ag Policies," *The Federalist,* June 27, 2017, http://thefederalist.com
/2017/06/27/foodies-back-fight-counterproductive-porky-ag-policies/.

21. Agnieszka De Sousa, "Billions of Dollars in Farm Aid Hurting Poorest,
OECD Says," *Bloomberg Markets,* June 21, 2017, https://www.bloomberg
.com/news/articles/2017-06-21/billions-of-dollars-in-farm-subsidies-hurt
ing-poorest-oecd-says-j46wjhj3.

22. Allie Howell, "Subsidies Encourage Maine Farmers to Keep Growing Too
Many Blueberries," Reason Foundation, *Hit & Run Blog,* June 16, 2017,
http://reason.com/blog/2017/06/16/governor-of-maine-proposes-state
-sponsor.

3. RENTING

1. New York State Bar Association, *The Use of Tenant Screening Reports and Tenant Blacklisting,* LegalEase Pamphlet Series, July 2017, http://www.nysba.org
/workarea/DownloadAsset.aspx?id=76303.

2. Erin Durkin, "New Bill Would Prevent NYC Landlords from Checking
Credit Scores and Debts of Would-Be Tenants," *New York Daily News,* November 10, 2015, http://www.nydailynews.com/news/politics/bill-prev
ent-nyc-landlords-checking-credit-scores-article-1.2428900.

3. Jessica Silver-Greenberg, "For Tenants Facing Eviction, New York May Guarantee a Lawyer," *New York Times,* September 26, 2016, https://www.nytimes
.com/2016/09/27/nyregion/legal-aid-tenants-in-new-york-housing-court
.html.

4. Josh Barro, "If You Live in New York and You Rent, You're Paying a Huge
Tax You Don't Even Know About," *Business Insider,* June 28, 2013, http://
www.businessinsider.com/if-you-live-in-new-york-and-you-rent-youre-pay
ing-a-huge-tax-you-dont-even-know-about-2013-6.

5. Jessica Dailey, "10 Surprising Facts about NYCHA, New York's 'Shadow
City,'" *Curbed New York,* September 10, 2012, https://ny.curbed.com
/2012/9/10/10330984/10-surprising-facts-about-nycha-new-yorks-shadow
-city.

6. "How the Housing Choice (Section 8) Voucher Program Is Funded," *Eligibi
lity.com,* https://eligibility.com/section-8/how-the-housing-choice-section-8
-voucher-program-is-funded.

7. "New York City Housing Authority," *Wikipedia,* last edited August 7, 2017, https://en.wikipedia.org/wiki/New_York_City_Housing_Authority.

8. Jarrett Murphy, "NYCHA's Budget Crisis: A 'Must Watch' and a 'Must Read,'" *City Limits,* March 13, 2017, https://citylimits.org/2017/03/13/nychas-budget-crisis-a-must-watch-and-a-must-read/.

9. U.S. Department of Housing and Urban Development, "HUD Releases Proposed 2017 Budget," press release HUDNo_16-016, February 9, 2016, https://portal.hud.gov/hudportal/HUD?src=/press/press_releases_media_advisories/2016/HUDNo_16-016.

10. Erin Durkin, "Proposed Bill Takes Aim at New York Landlords Who Try to Force Out Tenants," *New York Daily News,* April 12, 2017, http://www.nydailynews.com/new-york/bill-takes-aim-n-y-landlords-force-tenants-article-1.3048005.

11. "Rent Stabilization in New York City," Furman Center for Real Estate & Urban Policy, New York University, http://furmancenter.org/files/publications/HVS_Rent_Stabilization_fact_sheet_FINAL_4.pdf.

12. U.S. House of Representatives Financial Services Committee, "Subcommittee Examines Waste, Fraud, Abuse in HUD Spending Programs," press release, September 10, 2013, https://financialservices.house.gov/news/documentsingle.aspx?DocumentID=348879.

13. Chris Bragg, "Schoharie State-Funded 72-Unit Project Unfinished by Builder Steven L. Aaron as Contractors Seek Pay," *Albany Times Union,* June 25, 2016, http://www.timesunion.com/local/article/Schoharie-state-funded-72-unit-project-unfinished-8325219.php.

14. Daniel Fitzsimmons, "Lender Looking for Control in Schoharie Housing Project," *The Daily Gazette,* August 20, 2017, https://dailygazette.com/article/2017/08/20/lender-looking-for-control-in-schoharie-housing-project.

15. Anita Hofschneider, "Honolulu May Have to Pay $16M for Misuse of Housing Grants," *Honolulu Civil Beat,* September 20, 2016, http://www.civilbeat.org/2016/09/honolulu-may-have-to-pay-16m-for-misuse-of-housing-grants/.

16. Jenna Pizzi, "Business Administrator Admits He Misused Federal Grant Money, Says Trenton Will Repay Funds," *NJ.com,* November 20, 2013, http://www.nj.com/mercer/index.ssf/2013/11/business_administrator_admits_he_misused_federal_grant_money_says_trenton_will_repay_funds.html.

17. Seth Barron, "The Mayor Who Froze the Rent," *City Journal,* June 30, 2015, https://www.city-journal.org/html/mayor-who-froze-rent-11612.html.

18. Steven Malanga, "The Cost of New York," *City Journal,* Summer 2014, https://www.city-journal.org/html/cost-new-york-13660.html.

19. Teressa Raiford, Tracy Prince, and Jane Cease, "Affordable Housing Bill Was Hijacked (Guest Opinion)," *Oregon Live,* June 27, 2017, http://www.oregon live.com/opinion/index.ssf/2017/06/affordable_housing_bill_was _hi.html.

20. Amanda Fung, "Protest over High-End Building Set for Public-Housing Land," *Crain's New York Business,* May 31, 2017, http://www.crainsnewyork .com/article/20170531/REAL_ESTATE/170539981/protest-over-high -end-building-set-for-new-york-city-housing-authority-land.

4. UTILITIES

1. Bill Sanderson, "6 Things You Don't Know about Your Electric Bill," *Market-Watch,* June 8, 2014, http://www.marketwatch.com/story/6-things-you -dont-know-about-your-electric-bill-2014-05-05.

2. Edelman, "$85 'Stealth Tax' Pain."

3. Sanderson, "6 Things You Don't Know."

4. Edelman, "$85 'Stealth Tax' Pain."

5. Ken Girardin, "Your Coming Electric-Bill Hit, Thanks to Gov. Cuomo," *New York Post,* September 27, 2016, http://nypost.com/2016/09/27/your-com ing-electric-bill-hit-thanks-to-gov-cuomo/.

6. Morgan Lee, "Illegal Tax? Outsized City Fees on Utility Bills Are Challenged," *San Diego Union-Tribune,* March 23, 2015, http://www.sandiegounion tribune.com/news/watchdog/sdut-franchise-fees-or-taxes-2015mar23 -story.html.

7. Jeff Montgomery, "How Electric Bills Subsidize Delaware Budgets," *DelawareOnline: The News Journal,* August 21, 2015, http://www.delawareonline .com/story/news/local/2015/08/21/electric-bills-subsidize-delaware-bud gets/32140773/.

8. Montgomery, "How Electric Bills."

9. Norman Leahy and Paul Goldman, "Richmond Is Ripping Off Its Residents," *Washington Post,* June 13, 2016, https://www.washingtonpost.com /blogs/all-opinions-are-local/wp/2016/06/13/richmond-is-ripping-off-its -residents/?utm_term=.d84801c818a3.

10. Pat Garofalo, "30 Major Corporations Paid No Income Taxes in the Last Three Years, While Making $160 Billion," *ThinkProgress,* November 3, 2011, https://thinkprogress.org/30-major-corporations-paid-no-income-taxes -in-the-last-three-years-while-making-160-billion-ed305efc3fa3.

11. "Pepco Holdings LLC: Executive Salaries & Other Compensation," *Salary .com,* http://www1.salary.com/PEPCO-HOLDINGS-LLC-Executive-Salari es.html.

12. George Avalos, "PG&E Executives Reap Pay Raises despite Scandal, Indictment," *Mercury News,* March 25, 2015, http://www.mercurynews .com/2015/03/25/pge-executives-reap-pay-raises-despite-scandal-indict ment/.

13. Jeff St. John, "Why Are So Many Profitable Utilities Not Paying Income Tax?" *Greentech Media,* November 4, 2011, https://www.greentechmedia .com/articles/read/why-are-so-many-profitable-utilities-not-paying-income -tax.

14. Citizens for Tax Justice Staff, "Utilities Aren't Paying Their Fair Share," *Tax Justice Blog,* July 21, 2016, http://www.taxjusticeblog.org/archive/2016/07 /utilities_arent_paying_their_f.php.

15. Teri Sforza, "'Hidden Tax' on Your Trash Bill?" *Orange County Register,* November 29, 2013, http://www.ocregister.com/2013/11/29/hidden-tax-on -your-trash-bill/.

16. Sforza, "'Hidden Tax.'"

17. Sforza, "'Hidden Tax.'"

5. CABLE

1. Federal Communications Commission, "Proposed Third Quarter 2016 Universal Service Contribution Factor," public notice, June 14, 2016, https:// apps.fcc.gov/edocs_public/attachmatch/DA-16-658A1.pdf.

2. "Corrupt Owner Dipped into $27 Million of FCC Broadband Funds to Support His Lavish Lifestyle," *Wireless Estimator Featured News,* December 22, 2016, http://wirelessestimator.com/articles/2016/corrupt-owner-dipped -into-27-million-of-fcc-broadband-funds-to-support-his-lavish-lifestyle/.

3. Brian M. Riedl, "Congressional Spenders Ignore Deepening Government Waste," Heritage Foundation, November 9, 2009, http://www.heritage .org/budget-and-spending/commentary/congressional-spenders-ignore -deepening-government-waste.

4. Dave Boyer, "FCC Head Sees Waste in School Internet Push," *Augusta Chronicle,* July 17, 2013, http://chronicle.augusta.com/news-washington -times/2013-07-17/fcc-head-sees-waste-school-internet-push.

5. Michael Musto, "10 Public Access Cable Shows That Rocked NYC," *Paper Mag,* January 14, 2015, http://www.papermag.com/10-public-access-cable -shows-that-rocked-nyc-1427495297.html.

6. Bryan Polcyn, "FOX6 Investigation: 911 Fee on Phone Bills Exposed," *FOX6 News,* February 19, 2012, http://fox6now.com/2012/02/19/fox6-investi gation-911-fee-on-phone-bills-exposed/.

7. Fran Spielman, "Chicago Phone Tax Could Rise by 28 Percent to Save Pension Fund," *Chicago Sun-Times,* June 1, 2017, http://chicago.suntimes.com /news/chicago-phone-tax-could-rise-by-28-percent-to-save-pension-fund/.

8. Paul Bond, "Cable TV Cord-Cutting Reaches 'Fastest Rate of Decline on Record,'" *Hollywood Reporter,* August 9, 2017, http://www.hollywood reporter.com/news/cable-tv-cord-cutting-reaches-fastest-rate-decline-record -1027755.

9. Roslyn Layton, "The History of Cable TV Foreshadows What's to Come for the Internet," *AEIdeas,* August 12, 2016, http://www.aei.org/publication /history-cable-tv-foreshadows-whats-come-internet/.

10. Paul Blair, "Florida Legislature Overwhelmingly Passes Tax Cuts in Special Session," Americans for Tax Reform, June 16, 2015, http://www.atr.org /florida-legislature-overwhelmingly-passes-tax-cuts-special-session.

11. Mat Honan, "Why the Government Won't Protect You from Getting Screwed by Your Cable Company," *Gizmodo,* August 15, 2011, http://giz modo.com/5830956/why-the-government-wont-protect-you-from-getting -screwed-by-your-cable-company.

12. Kieren McCarthy, "Sigh. Big Cable Execs Dominate FCC Panel Overseeing Big Cable's Broadband Upgrades," *The Register,* August 14, 2017, https:// www.theregister.co.uk/2017/08/14/fcc_stacks_broadband_group_with _industry_execs/.

13. Alden Abbott, "Microsoft's Plan to Expand Broadband Would Benefit Rural Americans," *Daily Signal,* August 7, 2017, http://dailysignal.com/2017 /08/07/microsofts-plan-to-expand-broadband-would-benefit-rural-ameri cans/.

6. DEBAUCHERY

1. "Budget Documents: Current Reports and Adopted Budgets," City of Berkeley, CA, http://www.ci.berkeley.ca.us/budgetdocuments/.

2. Ed Ring, "California's Government Workers Make TWICE as Much as Private Sector Workers," *California Policy Center,* January 24, 2017, http:// californiapolicycenter.org/californias-government-workers-make-twice-as -much-as-private-sector-workers/.

3. Stanton Peele, "Why Do Low-Income People Smoke More and Drink More Soda, but Drink Less Alcohol?" *HuffPost Blog,* June 29, 2010, http://www

.huffingtonpost.com/stanton-peele/why-do-poor-people-smoke_b_627057
.html.

4. Hayley H. Chouinard, David E. Davis, Jeffrey T. LaFrance, and Jeffrey M.
   Perloff, "Fat Taxes: Big Money for Small Change," *Forum for Health Economics & Policy* 10, no. 2, art. 2 (2007), http://faculty.ses.wsu.edu/LaFrance
   /reprints/CDLP-BEP-2007.pdf.

5. Ed Zwirn, "Philly's Soda Tax Is Crushing the City's Beverage Business," *New
   York Post,* March 5, 2017, http://nypost.com/2017/03/05/phillys-soda-tax
   -is-crushing-the-citys-beverage-business/.

6. Eric Boehm, "Outrage in Philadelphia as New Soda Tax Doubles Drink
   Prices," Reason Foundation, *Hit & Run Blog,* January 5, 2017, http://reason
   .com/blog/2017/01/05/soda-tax-sparks-outrage-in-philadelphia.

7. Zwirn, "Philly's Soda Tax."

8. John Kopp, "Philly's Soda Tax Revenue Dips in April, Looks Like City's Projections off by Millions," *PhillyVoice,* May 31, 2017, http://www.phillyvoice
   .com/phillys-soda-tax-revenue-dips-april/.

9. Joel Mathis, "Report: Philly Public School Graduation Rates Rising," *Philadelphia Magazine,* May 21, 2015, http://www.phillymag.com/news/2015/05
   /21/philadelphia-public-school-graduation-rates/.

10. Scott Drenkard and Morgan Scarboro, "Soda Taxes Have No Pop," *U.S. News
    & World Report,* October 18, 2016, https://www.usnews.com/opinion/econo
    mic-intelligence/articles/2016-10-18/soda-tax-benefits-are-overrated.

11. Jason M. Fletcher, David Frisvold, and Nathan Tefft, "Can Soft Drink Taxes
    Reduce Population Weight?" *Contemporary Economic Policy* 28, no. 1 (Janu-
    ary 2010): 23–35, https://www.ncbi.nlm.nih.gov/pmc/articles/PMC2908
    024/.

12. Drenkard and Scarboro, "Soda Taxes Have No Pop."

13. Zwirn, "Philly's Soda Tax."

14. Bruce Y. Lee, "5 More Locations Pass Soda Taxes: What's Next for Big
    Soda?" *Forbes,* November 14, 2016, https://www.forbes.com/sites/bruce
    lee/2016/11/14/5-more-locations-pass-soda-taxes-whats-next-for-big
    -soda/.

15. Kate Vinton, "Billionaire Mike Bloomberg's $18 Million Helped Soda Tax
    Measures Win in San Francisco, Oakland," *Forbes,* November 9, 2016,
    https://www.forbes.com/sites/katevinton/2016/11/09/michael-bloom
    berg-scores-with-18-million-on-measures-taxing-soda-in-san-francisco-oak
    land-this-election/.

16. Associated Press, "Santa Fe Soda-Tax Effort Gets Boost from Michael Bloom-
    berg," *U.S. News & World Report: Best States,* April 25, 2017, https://www

.usnews.com/news/best-states/new-york/articles/2017-04-25/michael
-bloomberg-boosts-spending-on-santa-fe-tax-initiative.

17. Jazz Shaw, "*Unexpectedly,* Oakland's Soda Tax Money May Be Going . . . Elsewhere," *Hot Air,* May 2, 2017, https://hotair.com/archives/2017/05/02
/unexpectedly-oaklands-soda-tax-money-may-going-elsewhere/.

18. Vann R. Newkirk II, "The Wages of Sin Taxes," *The Atlantic,* March 19, 2016,
https://www.theatlantic.com/international/archive/2016/03/the-wages
-of-sin-taxes/474327/.

19. Richard Williams and Katelyn Christ, "Taxing Sin," *Mercatus Center: Federal
Fiscal Policy,* July 2009, https://www.mercatus.org/publication/taxing-sin.

20. Scott Drenkard, "How High Are Taxes on Distilled Spirits in Your State?
(2016)," *Tax Foundation* (blog), June 2, 2016, https://taxfoundation.org
/how-high-are-taxes-distilled-spirits-your-state-2016/.

21. "Excise Taxes," Citizens for Tobacco Rights, https://tobaccorights.com/issue
/excise-taxes/.

22. Patrick Basham and John Luik, "The Great Cigarette-Tax Lie," *New York Post,*
October 9, 2012, http://nypost.com/2012/10/09/the-great-cigarette-tax
-lie/.

23. "Reporting Gambling Income and Losses to the IRS," US Tax Center,
https://www.irs.com/articles/reporting-gambling-income-and-losses-irs.

24. Ameet Sachdev and Bob Secter, "Defining Candy a Bitter Pill for Illinois
Retailers," *Chicago Tribune,* August 2, 2009, http://articles.chicagotribune
.com/2009-08-02/business/0908010297_1_candy-bar-state-tax-law
-retailers.

25. "Crack Tax," *Wikipedia,* last edited August 13, 2017, https://en.wikipedia
.org/wiki/Crack_tax.

26. William N. Evans and Matthew C. Farrelly, "The Compensating Behavior
of Smokers: Taxes, Tar and Nicotine," *RAND Journal of Economics* 29, no. 3
(Autumn 1998): 578–95, http://www.jstor.org.mutex.gmu.edu/stable/pdf
plus/2556105.pdf/.

7. CELL PHONES

1. "Mobile Fact Sheet," Pew Research Center, January 12, 2017, http://www
.pewinternet.org/fact-sheet/mobile/.

2. Megan Leonhardt, "Wireless Customers Pay over $17 Billion in Taxes & Gov-
ernment Fees Each Year," *Money Magazine,* October 11, 2016, http://time
.com/money/4527164/wireless-taxes-fees-cell-phones/.

3. Marion Brooks, "Illinois' Cell Phone Tax among Highest in Nation," *NBC 5 Chicago,* October 13, 2014, www.nbcchicago.com/news/local/Illinois-Cell-Phone-Tax-Among-Highest-in-Nation-279065641.html.

4. Scott Mackey and Joseph Henchman, "Wireless Taxation in the United States 2014," *Tax Foundation* (blog), October 8, 2014, https://taxfoundation.org/wireless-taxation-united-states-2014/.

5. "New York Has Third Highest Cell Phone Taxes," Reclaim New York, *The Reclaimer* (blog), 2016, http://www.reclaimnewyork.org/2016/10/14/text-from-government-new-york-has-3rd-highest-wireless-tax-burden/.

6. David Lazarus, "Average Taxes on Wireless Bills in California Reach a Record 18%," *Los Angeles Times,* November 24, 2015, http://www.latimes.com/business/la-fi-lazarus-20151124-column.html.

7. *Code of the District of Columbia,* sec. 47–3902, https://beta.code.dccouncil.us/dc/council/code/sections/47-3902.html.

8. "Mississippi Cell Phone Providers Top List of Those Benefiting from 'Bizarre' Telephone Tax," *WDAM-TV 7 Hattiesburg (MS),* http://www.wdam.com/story/6823034/mississippi-cell-phone-providers-top-list-of-those-benefiting-from-bizarre-telephone-tax.

9. Cathy Woodruff, "School Utility Tax Rings Up Cell Bill Cost," *Advocate* (blog), *Albany Times Union,* June 10, 2010, http://blog.timesunion.com/advocate/school-utility-tax-rings-up-cell-bill-cost/2431/.

10. Woodruff, "School Utility Tax."

11. Mackey and Henchman, "Wireless Taxation."

12. Mackey and Henchman, "Wireless Taxation."

13. Austin Berg, "Quinn Passes the Buck on Cell-Phone Tax Hike, Chicago Cashes In," *Illinois Policy,* July 31, 2014, https://www.illinoispolicy.org/quinn-passes-the-buck-on-cell-phone-tax-hike-chicago-cashes-in/.

14. Fran Spielman, "Emanuel Tries to Sell 28.2 Percent Phone Tax Hike," *Chicago Sun-Times,* June 3, 2017, http://chicago.suntimes.com/chicago-politics/emanuel-tries-to-sell-28-2-percent-phone-tax-hike/.

15. Fran Spielman, "Chicago Phone Tax Could Rise by 28 Percent to Save Pension Fund," *Chicago Sun-Times,* June 1, 2017, http://chicago.suntimes.com/news/chicago-phone-tax-could-rise-by-28-percent-to-save-pension-fund/.

16. Marks Paneth LLP, Thomson Reuters, Steven Eliach, and Maria L. Castilla, "U.S. Taxpayers Are Paying More Than They Realize: A Staggering Array of Federal, State and Local Taxes Rarely Enter the Public Debate," *Metropolitan Corporate Counsel,* http://www.metrocorpcounsel.com/articles/34345/us-taxpayers-are-paying-more-they-realize-staggering-array-federal-state-and-local-ta.

17. Michelle Breidenbach, "How the State Abused Your Monthly Cell Phone Tax," *Syracuse Post-Standard,* September 21, 2008, http://www.syracuse .com/news/index.ssf/2008/09/the_cell_phone_bill_says.html.

18. Marc Ferris, "Surcharge on Cellphones, but for What?" *New York Times,* May 4, 2003, http://www.nytimes.com/2003/05/04/nyregion/surcharge-on -cellphones-but-for-what.html.

19. Howard Stephenson, "Taxes Account for up to 16.6% of Phone Bill," *Utah Taxpayers Association* (blog), October 13, 2003, http://www.utahtaxpayers .org/?p=669.

20. Peggy Fikac, "Lawsuit Contends Sprint Is 'Deceptive' to Customers," *Houston Chronicle,* February 6, 2007, http://www.chron.com/news/houston-texas /article/Lawsuit-contends-Sprint-is-deceptive-to-1819029.php.

21. Jim Nelson, "California Class Action Lawsuit Questions Cell Phone State Sales Tax," *Avalara* (blog), April 26, 2016, https://www.avalara.com/blog /2016/04/26/california-class-action-lawsuit-questions-cell-phone-state -sales-tax/.

22. "Place of Primary Use [Mobile Telecommunications] Law and Legal Definition," *USLegal,* https://definitions.uslegal.com/p/place-of-primary-use-mo bile-telecommunications/.

23. Joseph Henchman and Scott Drenkard, "State and Local Governments Impose Hefty Taxes on Cell Phone Consumers," *Tax Foundation* (blog), January 30, 2013, https://taxfoundation.org/state-and-local-governments-impose -hefty-taxes-cell-phone-consumers.

8. LEISURE

1. Troy Johnson, "Why Restaurants Are Adding a Surcharge, and Why Diners Should Gladly Pay It," *San Diego Magazine,* January 18, 2017, http://www .sandiegomagazine.com/Blogs/SD-Food-News/Winter-2017/Why-Res taurants-Are-Adding-a-Surcharge-and-Why-Diners-Should-Gladly-Pay-It/.

2. Nate C. Hindman, "Healthy SF under Fire: San Francisco Restaurants Pocketed Employee Health Care Fees, City Alleges," *Huffington Post,* January 28, 2013, http://www.huffingtonpost.com/2013/01/28/healthy-sf_n _2567446.html.

3. Grant Chen, "Seattle's $15 Minimum Wage Is Driving My Restaurant out of Business," *EcomCrew,* February 22, 2016, https://www.ecomcrew.com /seattles-15-minimum-wage-is-driving-our-restaurant-out-of-business/.

4. Arianna Auber, "Texas Law Alters a Mixed Drinks Tax at Restaurants, Bars," *Austin American-Statesman,* January 26, 2017, http://www.austin360.com

/lifestyles/food—cooking/texas-law-alters-mixed-drinks-tax-restaurants
-bars/CTFwFPBLpEGRuPoWhIp7ZN/.

5. Auber, "Texas Law Alters a Mixed Drinks Tax."

6. Paul Scicchitano, "Miami Beach Wants to Take 'Rampant Shenanigans' off the Menu," *Miami Beach Patch,* February 10, 2017, https://patch.com /florida/miamibeach/miami-beach-wants-take-rampant-shenanigans -menu.

7. "Amusement Tax (7510)," City of Chicago, https://www.cityofchicago.org /city/en/depts/fin/supp_info/revenue/tax_list/amusement_tax.html.

8. "Amusement Tax (7510)."

9. Maryland General Assembly, Department of Legislative Services, *Fiscal and Policy Note for House Bill 1206,* July 1, 2016, http://mgaleg.maryland .gov/2016RS/fnotes/bil_0006/hb1206.pdf.

10. Anthony Didato, "City of Chicago Extends Amusement Tax to Satellite TV Services," *Mondaq,* May 5, 2017, http://www.mondaq.com/unitedstates /x/591746/tax+authorities/City+Of+Chicago+Extends+Amusement +Tax+To+Satellite+TV+Services.

11. Didato, "City of Chicago."

12. Gary Shapiro, "No One's Smiling about Chicago's 'Amusement Tax,'" *Chicago Tribune,* August 24, 2015, http://www.chicagotribune.com/news/opin ion/commentary/ct-amusement-tax-streaming-netflix-hulu-perspec-0825 -20150824-story.html.

13. Michael J. Bologna, "Gamers Challenge Chicago's Amusement Tax," Bloomberg BNA, *Daily Tax Report: State,* June 5, 2017, https://www.bna.com /gamers-challenge-chicagos-n73014451941/.

14. "A Look at Sales Taxation of Cultural Events across the U.S.," Pennsylvania Budget and Policy Center, September 28, 2009, https://www.pennbpc.org /look-sales-taxation-cultural-events-across-us.

15. Liz Malm, "North Carolina Movie Theatres: Ending Our Special Treatment Is 'Crippling Blow,'" *Tax Foundation* (blog), July 24, 2013, https://taxfound ation.org/north-carolina-movie-theatres-ending-our-special-treatment -crippling-blow/.

16. Timothy Guy, "MOVIES: Taxes Change Ticket Prices at AMC Theatres," *Riverside Press-Enterprise,* October 17, 2014, http://www.pe.com/2014/10/17 /movies-taxes-change-ticket-prices-at-amc-theatres/.

17. Ross Ramsey, "Texas Loses Tax Lawsuit, but Not the Way Officials Feared," *Texas Tribune,* January 6, 2017, https://www.texastribune.org/2017/01/06 /state-loses-tax-lawsuit-not-way-officials-feared/.

18. United States Securities and Exchange Commission, "AMC ENTERTAIN-MENT INC Form 10-K Annual Report," May 25, 2012, http://edgar.sec database.com/113/104746912006351/filing-main.htm.

19. Motion Picture Association of America, *Theatrical Market Statistics 2014,* http://www.mpaa.org/wp-content/uploads/2015/03/MPAA-Theatrical -Market-Statistics-2014.pdf.

20. Richard Verrier, "Are Film Tax Credits Cost Effective?" *Los Angeles Times,* August 30, 2014, http://www.latimes.com/entertainment/envelope/cotown /la-et-ct-fi-film-tax-credits-20140831-story.html.

21. Jared Meyer, "If You Watch 'House of Cards,' Thank Maryland Taxpayers," *The Federalist,* March 12, 2015, http://thefederalist.com/2015/03/12/if -you-watch-house-of-cards-thank-maryland-taxpayers/.

22. "Quarterly Earnings," Netflix, https://ir.netflix.com/results.cfm.

23. Frederick Reimers, "Put Your Money Where Your Fun Is," *Outside Magazine,* March 10, 2017, https://www.outsideonline.com/2156701/put-your -money-where-your-fun.

24. Michael Pearce, "Who Would Have Management Control under Hunting-Rights Amendment?" *Wichita Eagle,* October 25, 2016, http://www.kansas .com/news/politics-government/article110480172.html.

25. "Where Does the Money for Conservation Come From?" *Montana Hunter's Ed Course Study Guide,* https://www.hunter-ed.com/montana/studyGuide /Where-Does-the-Money-for-Conservation-Come-From/201027_7000 48372/.

9. SHARING ECONOMY

1. Niam Yaraghi and Shamika Ravi, "The Current and Future State of the Sharing Economy," *Brookings,* December 29, 2016, https://www.brookings.edu /research/the-current-and-future-state-of-the-sharing-economy/.

2. Barry Leigh Weissman and David E. Cannella, "The Shared Economy," *Mondaq,* August 29, 2017, http://www.mondaq.com/unitedstates/x/624158/Pers onal+Injury/The+Shared+Economy.

3. Megan Barber, "Airbnb vs. the City: How Short-Term Rentals Are Changing Urban Neighborhoods," *Curbed Longform,* November 10, 2016, https://www .curbed.com/2016/11/10/13582982/airbnb-laws-us-cities.

4. Steven Hill, "The Unsavory Side of Airbnb," *American Prospect,* October 19, 2015, http://prospect.org/article/evictions-and-conversions-dark-side-airbnb.

5. Hill, "Unsavory Side of Airbnb."

6. Dan Peltier, "Airbnb Faces Big Fines in Portland If Hosts Don't Get City Permits," *Skift,* February 23, 2015, https://skift.com/2015/02/23/airbnb -faces-big-fines-in-portland-if-hosts-dont-get-city-permits/.

7. Hari Sreenivasan, "Why Is New York City Cracking Down on Airbnb?" *PBS Newshour,* August 1, 2015, http://www.pbs.org/newshour/bb/will-new -york-city-shut-airbnb-2/.

8. Heather Kelly, "Why Everyone Is Cracking Down on Airbnb," *CNNMoney,* June 22, 2016, http://money.cnn.com/2016/06/22/technology/airbnb -regulations/index.html.

9. Zaw Thiha Tun, "Top Cities Where Airbnb Is Legal or Illegal," *Investopedia,* August 31, 2015, http://www.investopedia.com/articles/investing /083115/top-cities-where-airbnb-legal-or-illegal.asp.

10. Chabeli Herrera, "How $20,000 Fines Have Made Miami Beach an Airbnb Battleground," *Miami Herald,* November 27, 2016, http://www.miami herald.com/news/business/biz-monday/article117332773.html.

11. City of Austin Code Department, "Austin Code Department Announces Details of New Short-Term Rental Ordinance," press release, March 17, 2016, http://austintexas.gov/article/short-term-rental-news-release-and-faq.

12. Stephen Fishman, "Legal Restrictions to Renting Your Home on Airbnb or Other Rental Services," *Nolo,* https://www.nolo.com/legal-encyclopedia /legal-restrictions-renting-your-home-airbnb-other-rental-services.html.

13. Fishman, "Legal Restrictions."

14. Kip Hill, "Spokane Eyes Tougher Regulations for Uber, Lyft after Outcry from Cab Companies," *Spokane Spokesman-Review,* July 31, 2017, http://www .spokesman.com/stories/2017/jul/31/spokane-eyes-tougher-regulations -for-uber-lyft-aft/#/0.

15. "Taxi Drivers Support WI Senate Bill That Would Regulate Uber and Lyft," *WMTV,* August 24, 2017, http://www.nbc15.com/content/news/Taxi -drivers-support-WI-senate-bill-that-would-regulate-Uber-and-Lyft-44167 9693.html.

16. Ben Poston, "L.A. Apartment Owners Charged with Allegedly Evicting Tenants, Then Renting Their Units via Airbnb," *Los Angeles Times,* June 20, 2016, http://www.latimes.com/local/california/la-me-ln-landlords-illegal -rentals-20160620-snap-story.html.

17. Tomio Geron, "Airbnb Wins New York City Appeal on Short-Term Rentals," *Forbes,* September 27, 2013, https://www.forbes.com/sites/tomiogeron /2013/09/27/airbnb-wins-new-york-city-appeal-on-short-term-rentals/.

18. "Short-Term Rentals," City of Palm Desert, CA, http://www.cityofpalm desert.org/departments/finance-/short-term-rentals.

19. Barber, "Airbnb vs. the City."

20. Barber, "Airbnb vs. the City."

21. Peltier, "Airbnb Faces Big Fines."

22. Jerry Iannelli, "Miami Beach Has Fined Airbnb-Style Landlords $1.6 Million since March," *Miami New Times,* August 24, 2016, http://www.miaminew times.com/news/miami-beach-has-fined-airbnb-style-landlords-16-million -since-march-8712957.

23. Zoe Rosenberg, "Illegal Airbnb Listings in NYC Will Now Incur Hefty Fines," *Curbed New York,* October 21, 2016, https://ny.curbed.com/2016 /10/21/13361942/airbnb-illegal-short-term-rentals-fines-nyc.

24. Julia Marsh, "Landlord Fined after Airbnb-er Rents 9 Rooms to 34 Guests," *New York Post,* August 31, 2017, http://nypost.com/2017/08/31/landlord -fined-after-airbnb-er-rents-9-rooms-to-34-guests/.

25. Rosenberg, "Illegal Airbnb Listings."

26. "Huge Victory in New York for Nigel Warren and Our Host Community," *Airbnb Citizen,* September 27, 2013, https://www.airbnbcitizen.com/huge -victory-in-new-york-for-nigel-warren-and-our-host-community/.

27. Ron Lieber, "A Warning for Hosts of Airbnb Travelers," *New York Times,* November 30, 2012, http://www.nytimes.com/2012/12/01/your-money/a -warning-for-airbnb-hosts-who-may-be-breaking-the-law.html.

28. "Airbnb Tax Collection Program Expands, Has Already Collected $110 Million for Governments," *Airbnb Citizen,* August 1, 2016, https://www .airbnbcitizen.com/airbnb-tax-collection-program-expands-has-already -collected-110-million-for-governments/.

29. "Airbnb Tax Collection Program."

30. Emily Alpert Reyes, "Airbnb Strikes Deal with L.A. to Collect Millions in Lodging Taxes," *Los Angeles Times,* July 18, 2016, http://www.latimes.com /local/lanow/la-me-ln-airbnb-taxes-20160718-snap-story.html.

31. Elijah Chiland, "Nearly Half of All California Airbnb Renters Stay in Los Angeles," *Curbed Los Angeles,* December 16, 2016, https://la.curbed.com /2016/12/16/13973242/airbnb-users-los-angeles-guests-million-renters -housing.

32. Andrew Bender, "New Regulations to Wipe out 80% of Airbnb Rentals in California's Santa Monica," *Forbes,* June 15, 2015, https://www.forbes.com /sites/andrewbender/2015/06/15/new-regulations-to-wipe-out-80-of -airbnb-rentals-in-californias-santa-monica/.

33. Bianca Barragan, "Santa Monica Just Banned Airbnb's Biggest Moneymakers," *Curbed Los Angeles,* May 13, 2015, https://la.curbed.com/2015/5/13 /9961560/santa-monica-just-banned-airbnbs-biggest-moneymakers.

34. Barragan, "Santa Monica."

35. Goldwater Institute, "Gov. Ducey Signs Bill Protecting Right to Rent out Home through Vacation Websites," press release, May 12, 2016, http://gold waterinstitute.org/en/work/topics/constitutional-rights/property-rights /gov-ducey-signs-bill-protecting-right-to-rent-out-/.

36. Jared Meyer, "How to Save Airbnb from Local Governments," *Forbes,* February 1, 2017, https://www.forbes.com/sites/jaredmeyer/2017/02/01/how -to-save-airbnb-from-local-governments/.

37. Ibid.

38. Blake Neff, "Bernie Sanders Bashes Uber, Uses It for All His Taxi Rides," *Daily Caller,* November 3, 2015, http://dailycaller.com/2015/11/03/bernie -sanders-bashes-uber-uses-it-for-all-his-taxi-rides/.

39. Kristin Tate, "Trump Can Reach Millennials through the Sharing Economy," *The Hill,* September 1, 2016, http://thehill.com/blogs/pundits-blog/pres idential-campaign/294044-trump-can-reach-millennials-through-the -sharing.

40. Tate, "Trump Can Reach Millennials."

41. Tate, "Trump Can Reach Millennials."

42. Adrienne LaFrance and Rose Eveleth, "Are Taxis Safer Than Uber?" *The Atlantic,* March 3, 2015, https://www.theatlantic.com/technology/archive /2015/03/are-taxis-safer-than-uber/386207/.

43. Harriet Taylor, "Uber and Lyft Are Getting Pushback from Municipalities All over the US," *CNBC,* September 2, 2016, https://www.cnbc .com/2016/09/02/uber-and-lyft-are-getting-pushback-from-municipalities -all-over-the-us.html.

44. Jeffrey A. Tucker, "New York's Taxi Cartel Is Collapsing. Now They Want a Bailout," Foundation for Economic Education, August 31, 2015, https://fee .org/articles/new-yorks-taxi-cartel-is-collapsing-now-they-want-a-bailout/.

45. Michael DeMasi, "Just in Time: New Regulations Govern Uber, Lyft in Upstate New York," *Albany Business Review,* June 7, 2017, https://www .bizjournals.com/albany/news/2017/06/07/just-in-time-new-regulations -govern-uber-lyft-in.html.

46. Taylor, "Uber and Lyft."

47. Taylor, "Uber and Lyft."

48. Washington Post Editorial Board, "Uber and Lyft's Arguments against Fingerprinting Make Little Sense," *Washington Post,* January 2, 2017, https:// www.washingtonpost.com/opinions/uber-and-lyfts-arguments-against -fingerprinting-make-little-sense/2017/01/02/a0926aae-ce1b-11e6-b8a2 -8c2a61b0436f_story.html.

49. Tess Townsend, "Why Uber Doesn't Want to Fingerprint Drivers," *Inc.com,* August 20, 2015, https://www.inc.com/tess-townsend/uber-rethink-back grounds.html.

50. Alex Samuels, "Uber, Lyft Return to Austin as Texas Gov. Abbott Signs Ride-Hailing Measure into Law," *Texas Tribune,* May 29, 2017, https://www .texastribune.org/2017/05/29/texas-gov-greg-abbott-signs-measure-creat ing-statewide-regulations-rid/.

51. Samuels, "Uber, Lyft Return to Austin."

52. Gino Fanelli, "City Council Eases Taxi Regulations as Uber Sweeps In," *Rochester Business Journal,* August 16, 2017, http://rbj.net/2017/08/16/city -council-eases-taxi-regulations-as-uber-sweeps-in/.

10. CARS

1. Ronald Bailey, "Regular Cars Didn't Need Federal Regulation; Neither Do Driverless Vehicles," Reason Foundation, *Hit & Run Blog,* July 31, 2017, http://reason.com/blog/2017/07/31/new-bill-in-congress-aims-to-jump start-d.

2. "Summary of the Clean Air Act," United States Environmental Protection Agency, https://www.epa.gov/laws-regulations/summary-clean-air-act.

3. Peter Whoriskey, "Regulations an Economic Burden to Manufacturers, Report Says," *Washington Post,* August 21, 2012, https://www.washingtonpost.com /business/economy/regulations-an-economic-burden-to-manufacturers-re port-says/2012/08/20/3aa4501a-eb01-11e1-9ddc-340d5efb1e9c_story.html.

4. James Gattuso and Diane Katz, *Red Tape Rising: Six Years of Escalating Regula- tion under Obama,* Heritage Foundation, May 11, 2015, http://www.heritage .org/government-regulation/report/red-tape-rising-six-years-escalating -regulation-under-obama.

5. Ronald Bailey, "Obama's Fuel Economy Follies," *Reason Magazine,* January 27, 2009, http://reason.com/archives/2009/01/27/obamas-fuel-economy -follies.

6. Ronald Bailey, "Trump Regulatory Rollback: Auto Fuel Efficiency Standards," Reason Foundation, *Hit & Run Blog,* November 11, 2016, http://reason .com/blog/2016/11/11/trump-regulatory-rollback-auto-fuel-eff1.

7. Kelsey Mays, "Everything You Ever Wanted to Know about a Dealer Doc Fee," *Cars.com,* June 10, 2014, https://www.cars.com/articles/2014/06 /everything-you-ever-wanted-to-know-about-a-dealer-doc-fee/.

8. "Driving Citation Statistics," Statistic Brain, http://www.statisticbrain.com /driving-citation-statistics/.

9. Laura Herzog, "We Paid $405M in Tickets Last Year; See Where the Money Went," *NJ.com,* May 10, 2016, http://www.nj.com/news/index.ssf/2016/05/where_your_ticket_payment_money_goes_funds_new_jer.html.

10. Kansas City Star Editorial Board, "Paid a Traffic Ticket in Missouri? The State Could End up Owing You Money," *Springfield News-Leader,* September 19, 2017, http://www.news-leader.com/story/opinion/contributors/2017/09/19/paid-traffic-ticket-missouri-state-could-end-up-owing-you-money/680344001/.

11. Tim Cushing, "Court Orders Small Ohio Speed Trap Town to Refund $3 Million in Unconstitutional Speeding Tickets," *Techdirt,* February 13, 2017, https://www.techdirt.com/articles/20170209/09191536673/court-orders-small-ohio-speed-trap-town-to-refund-3-million-unconstitutional-speeding-tickets.shtml.

12. Cheryl K. Chumley, "Texas Man Busted for Warning Motorists of Police Speed Trap Fights City Hall," *Washington Times,* January 17, 2014, http://www.washingtontimes.com/news/2014/jan/17/texas-man-cited-sign-warns-police-speed-trap-fight/.

13. Jobin Panicker, "Charges Dropped against Texas Speed-Trap Sign Holder," *USA Today,* February 7, 2014, https://www.usatoday.com/story/news/nation/2014/02/07/speed-trap-sign-charges/5280647/.

14. "Federal Judge Rules Drivers Allowed to Flash Headlights to Warn of Speed Traps," *Fox News,* February 5, 2014, http://www.foxnews.com/politics/2014/02/05/federal-judge-rules-drivers-allowed-to-warn-other-motorists-speed-traps.html.

15. Tim Cushing, "Supreme Court Rules That a Traffic Stop Ends When the 'Objective' Is 'Complete,' Rather Than Whenever the Officer Feels It Is," *Techdirt,* April 22, 2015, https://www.techdirt.com/articles/20150422/08105530754/supreme-court-rules-that-traffic-stop-ends-when-objective-is-complete-rather-than-whenever-officer-feels-it-is.shtml.

16. Lawyers' Committee for Civil Rights of the San Francisco Bay Area, *Not Just a Ferguson Problem: How Traffic Courts Drive Inequality in California,* April 20, 2015, http://www.lccr.com/not-just-ferguson-problem-how-traffic-courts-drive-inequality-in-california/.

17. San Diego Union-Tribune Editorial Board, "California's Decision to Stop Suspending Licenses for Traffic Fines Is a Good Start," *San Diego Union-Tribune,* June 30, 2017, http://www.sandiegouniontribune.com/opinion/editorials/sd-driver-license-suspension-traffic-tickets-20170630-story.html.

18. Mimi Elkalla, "Hidden Fees in Traffic Tickets: How Much Does Your Speeding Actually Cost?" *Bakersfield Eyewitness News,* May 12, 2016, http://

bakersfieldnow.com/news/local/hidden-fees-in-traffic-tickets-how-much
-does-your-speeding-actually-cost.

19. Sacramento Bee Editorial Board, "The Way California Collects Fines, Fees
Is Almost Criminal," *Sacramento Bee,* April 8, 2016, http://www.sacbee.com
/opinion/editorials/article70797647.html.

20. Times Editorial Board, "Time to Rein in California's Traffic Ticket Surcharges," *Los Angeles Times,* May 1, 2015, http://www.latimes.com/opinion
/editorials/la-ed-traffic-ticket-assessments-20150501-story.html.

21. "Ticket Fines and Penalties in New York," DMV.org, https://www.dmv.org
/ny-new-york/traffic-ticket-fines-and-penalties.php.

22. Tyler Whitson and Joy Diaz, "Why Your Speeding Ticket Doesn't Pay for
What You Think It Does," *Austin KUT 90.5,* April 22, 2015, http://kut.org
/post/why-your-speeding-ticket-doesn-t-pay-what-you-think-it-does.

23. Sarah Fenske, "St. Louis Parking Ticket Policy Is a Racket, Class-Action
Suit Alleges," *Riverfront Times,* April 17, 2015, https://www.riverfronttimes
.com/newsblog/2015/04/17/st-louis-parking-ticket-policy-is-a-racket
-class-action-suit-alleges.

24. Joshua Rhett Miller, "Speeding, Parking Tickets on Rise as Government
Revenue Source," *Fox News,* February 10, 2009, http://www.foxnews.com
/story/2009/02/10/speeding-parking-tickets-on-rise-as-government-reve
nue-source.html.

11. PETS

1. "Fees & Fines," Seattle Animal Shelter, https://www.seattle.gov/animal
-shelter/animal-control/fees-and-fines.

2. J. D. Tuccille, "The Joys of an Unlicensed Dog," *Reason Magazine,* November 22, 2016, http://reason.com/archives/2016/11/22/the-joys-of-an-unli
censed-dog.

3. Seattle Times Editorial Board, "Pondering Pet Privacy: Big Brother Shouldn't
Peer into Your Groceries," *Seattle Times,* November 3, 2016, https://www
.seattletimes.com/opinion/editorials/pondering-pet-privacy-big-brother
-shouldnt-peer-into-your-groceries/.

4. Jim Hook, "Lawmakers Pose 50 Percent Hike for Dog Licenses," *USA Today,* June 20, 2017, https://www.usatoday.com/story/news/2017/06/20
/lawmakers-pose-50-percent-hike-dog-licenses/412541001/.

5. Melissa Daniels, "State Workers Paying Less Than Most for Health Benefits,"
Pennsylvania TribLIVE, August 23, 2014, http://triblive.com/state/pennsylva
nia/6635751-74/state-health-benefits.

6. *Revised Ordinances of Honolulu,* sec. 7–3.2, https://www.hawaiianhumane
.org/wp-content/uploads/2011/06/Article3.pdf.

7. "Animal Licensing and Regulations Frequently Asked Questions," City of
Des Moines Office of the City Clerk, http://www.dmgov.org/Departments
/CityClerk/PDF/AnimalLicenseFAQ.pdf.

8. Tuccille, "Joys of an Unlicensed Dog."

9. "Compulsory Licensing," The Kennel Club, last updated November 2013,
https://www.thekennelclub.org.uk/our-resources/media-centre/issue
-statements/compulsory-licensing/.

10. "Dangerous Dog License," City of Saint Paul, MN, https://www.stpaul.gov
/departments/safety-inspections/animal-control-information/dog-license
/dangerous-dog-license.

11. "Understanding Denver's Breed Ban for Pit Bulls," Denver Animal Shelter,
https://www.denvergov.org/content/denvergov/en/denver-animal-shel
ter/animal-protection/breed-specific-legislation.html.

12. Jared Jacang Maher, "3,497 Dead Dogs and Other Numbers from Denver's
Pit Bull Ban," *Denver Westword,* September 25, 2009, http://www.westword
.com/news/3-497-dead-dogs-and-other-numbers-from-denvers-pit-bull
-ban-5834767.

13. Jon Bastian, "How Did Pit Bulls Get Such a Bad Rap?" *Cesar's Way,* https://
www.cesarsway.com/about-dogs/pit-bulls/how-did-pit-bulls-get-a-bad-rap.

14. K. R. Olson, J. K. Levy, B. Norby, M. M. Crandall, J. E. Broadhurst, S.
Jacks, R. C. Barton, and M. S. Zimmerman, "Inconsistent Identification of
Pit Bull-Type Dogs by Shelter Staff," *Veterinary Journal* 206, no. 2 (Novem-
ber 2015): 197–202, http://www.sciencedirect.com/science/article/pii
/S109002331500310X.

15. Hannah Smith, "Foxes, Cougars, Skunks: Hoosiers Can Own about Any
Animal," *Indianapolis Star,* August 10, 2014, http://www.indystar.com/story
/life/2014/08/09/exotic-animals-pets/13821383/.

16. Shannon Zimmerman, "10 Stupid Things That Are Illegal in Illinois," *Rockford
(IL) Q98.5,* May 6, 2016, http://q985online.com/10-stupid-things-that-are
-illegal-in-illinois/.

17. Robert W. Wood, "Tax Pet Food? Even Amazon Can't Define It," *Forbes,*
January 2, 2014, https://www.forbes.com/sites/robertwood/2014/01/02
/tax-pet-food-even-amazon-cant-define-it/.

18. Mary Mycio, "The First 1 Percent: Horses May Be the Source of Humans'
Oldest Social Stratifications," *Slate,* July 30, 2012, http://www.slate.com
/articles/health_and_science/science/2012/07/horse_owners_are_the
_one_percent_how_social_inequality_was_born_.html.

19. "Stop the Maryland Pet Food Tax: What This Bill Really Does & Why You Need to Ask People to Sign," Change.org, https://www.change.org/p/stop -the-maryland-pet-food-tax/u/3156580.

20. Shannon Antinori, "More Dog Food Sold in Illinois Recalled for Euthanasia Drug Contamination," *Chicago Patch,* March 6, 2017, https://patch.com/il linois/chicago/more-dog-food-recalled-euthanasia-drug-contamination.

21. Area Development News Desk, "Blue Buffalo Expands Its Heartland Pet Food Complex in Joplin, Missouri," *Area Development,* May 26, 2017, http:// www.areadevelopment.com/newsItems/5-26-2017/blue-buffalo-heartland -manufacturing-campus-joplin-missouri.shtml.

22. "Pet Food," U.S. Food and Drug Administration, https://www.fda.gov /animalveterinary/products/animalfoodfeeds/petfood/default.htm.

23. "Veterinarians & New Jersey Sales Tax," New Jersey Division of Taxation, http://www.state.nj.us/treasury/taxation/pdf/pubs/sales/anj12.pdf.

24. Erin Durkin, "NYC Law that Makes Dog-Sitting Illegal without Kennel License Triggers Rage from Pet Lovers," *New York Daily News,* July 20, 2017, http://www.nydailynews.com/new-york/pet-lovers-rage-law-bans-dog-sit ting-license-article-1.3339994.

25. Aaron Bandler, "WUT: Dog-Sitting Is ILLEGAL in NYC," *Daily Wire,* July 20, 2017, http://www.dailywire.com/news/18833/wut-dog-sitting-now-ill egal-nyc-aaron-bandler.

26. "Animal Care and Handling Course," NYC Business, https://www1.nyc.gov /nycbusiness/description/animal-care-and-handling-course/after_apply.

27. "Small Animal Boarding Establishment Permit," NYC Business, https:// www1.nyc.gov/nycbusiness/description/small-animal-boarding-establish ment-permit/apply.

28. Shoshana Weissman and C. Jarrett Dieterle, "The City's Silly Crackdown on Dog-Sitters," *New York Post,* July 23, 2017, http://nypost.com/2017/07/23 /the-citys-silly-crackdown-on-dog-sitters/.

12. HOUSE

1. Bob Shaw and Tad Vezner, "The Cost of Housing: Fees, Regulations and Lot Prices Drive Up Minn. Prices," *Brainerd Dispatch,* April 16, 2017, http:// www.brainerddispatch.com/news/minnesota/4251576-cost-housing-fees -regulations-and-lot-prices-drive-minn-prices.

2. Shaw and Vezner, "Cost of Housing."

3. "Do I Need a Permit for My Project?" City of Portland, OR, https://www .portlandoregon.gov/bds/article/92685.

4. "Typical Residential Deck Design," Prince William County, VA, Department of Development Services, http://www.pwcgov.org/government/dept /development/bd/Documents/005540.pdf.

5. Alisa Hauser and Tanveer Ali, "As Sign Violations Spike, 'Erratically Enforced' Law Questioned," *Chicago DNAinfo,* September 11, 2017, https:// www.dnainfo.com/chicago/20170911/wicker-park/sign-ordinance-chi cago-business-sign-permits-law-window-signs-chicago.

6. Linda S. Morris, "Property Owner Built Fence Too High Which Landed Him at Zoning Meeting," *Macon Telegraph,* August 28, 2017, http://www.macon .com/news/business/article169836062.html.

7. Jordan Green, "Winston-Salem Imposes Application Fee on Accessory Dwellings," *Triad City Beat,* September 6, 2017, https://triad-city-beat.com /winston-salem-imposes-application-fee-accessory-dwellings/.

8. Jack Shea, "Councilors Propose New Development Parking Fees," *Newburyport Daily News,* September 8, 2017, http://www.newburyportnews.com /news/local_news/councilors-propose-new-development-parking-fees /article_11828b04-76bc-50d3-b873-aa9548a3539c.html.

9. "The Most Costly Federal Rules: Billion Dollar Regulations," U.S. Chamber of Commerce, https://www.uschamber.com/the-most-costly-federal-rules -billion-dollar-regulations.

10. John Daniel Davidson, "EPA to Alaskans in Sub-Zero Temps: Stop Burning Wood to Keep Warm," *The Federalist,* December 30, 2016, http://thefed eralist.com/2016/12/30/epa-alaskans-sub-zero-temps-stop-burning-wood -keep-warm/.

11. U.S. Department of Energy, "New Energy Efficiency Standards for Furnace Fans to Reduce Carbon Pollution, Help Americans Save on Energy Bills," press release, June 25, 2014, https://www.energy.gov/articles/new-energy -efficiency-standards-furnace-fans-reduce-carbon-pollution-help-americans -save.

12. "Residential Furnace Efficiency Standards," American Action Forum, *Regulation Review,* March 11, 2015, https://www.americanactionforum.org/regula tion-review/residential-furnace-efficiency-standards/.

13. "Van Gogh's Mental and Physical Health," Van Gogh Gallery, http://www .vangoghgallery.com/misc/mental.html.

14. Marc Santora, "Planning to Repaint? Read This First," *New York Times,* June 18, 2010, http://www.nytimes.com/2010/06/20/realestate/20epa .html.

15. "Asbestos Laws and Regulations," United States Environmental Protection Agency, https://www.epa.gov/asbestos/asbestos-laws-and-regulations.

16. "New York Recording Fees, Mortgage and Transfer Taxes," Chicago Title Insurance Company, New York National Commercial Services, http://newyorkncs.ctic.com/Assets/NewYork-NCS-CTIC/pdfs/NY_Recording_Fees_Taxes.pdf.

17. Polyana da Costa, "FHA Smacks Buyers with Fee Hike," *Bankrate* (blog), January 31, 2013, http://www.bankrate.com/financing/mortgages/fha-smacks-buyers-with-fee-hike/.

18. Kathryn Vasel, "Trump Administration Suspends Mortgage Premium Rate Cut," *CNNMoney,* January 21, 2017, http://money.cnn.com/2017/01/20/real_estate/trump-suspends-fha-premium-rate-cut/index.html.

13. VACATION TAXES

1. "Airport and Airway Trust Fund (AATF) Fact Sheet," Federal Aviation Administration, https://www.faa.gov/about/budget/aatf/media/AATF_Fact_Sheet.pdf.

2. Drew Johnson, "At FAA, Bigger Budgets for Less Work Lead to Waste," Golden Hammer, *Washington Times,* November 20, 2014, http://www.washingtontimes.com/news/2014/nov/20/golden-hammer-at-faa-bigger-budgets-for-less-work-/.

3. "FAA Receives Golden Fleece Award for Fleecing Taxpayers at Tampa International Airport," Taxpayers for Common Sense, November 2, 2000, http://www.taxpayer.net/library/article/faa-receives-golden-fleece-award-for-fleecing-taxpayers-at-tampa-internatio.

4. "Air Traffic Control Modernization: Progress and Challenges in Implementing NextGen," U.S. Government Accountability Office, August 31, 2017, https://www.gao.gov/products/GAO-17-450.

5. Citizens Against Government Waste (CAGW) Staff, "Because They Could," Citizens Against Government Waste, *The Swine Line* (blog), May 7, 2013, https://www.cagw.org/swineline/because-they-could.

6. J. D. Tuccille, "The TSA Turns Harassing Travelers into a Fine—and Pointless—Art," *Reason Magazine,* June 6, 2017, https://reason.com/archives/2017/06/06/the-tsa-turns-harassing-travelers-into-a.

7. Brandon Morse, "Another Example of How the TSA Is an Awful, Useless, Waste of Taxpayer Money," *RedState,* July 1, 2016, https://www.redstate.com/brandon_morse/2016/07/01/another-example-tsa-awful-useless-waste-taxpayer-money/.

8. "Rental Car Taxes," National Conference of State Legislatures, March 18, 2015, http://www.ncsl.org/research/fiscal-policy/rental-car-taxes.aspx.

9. "Columnist Bashes Rental Car Fees and Taxes," *Auto Rental News,* October 26, 2011, http://www.autorentalnews.com/channel/rental-operations/news/story/2011/10/columnist-bashes-rental-car-fees-and-taxes.aspx.

10. Andrew Chamberlain, "The Case against Special Rental Car Excise Taxes," *Tax Foundation* (blog), April 18, 2006, https://taxfoundation.org/case-against-special-rental-car-excise-taxes/.

11. Jordan Golson, "What Are All Those Weird Fees on Your Rental Car Receipt?" *WIRED,* December 23, 2014, https://www.wired.com/2014/12/silly-fees-rental-car-blame-local-politicians/.

12. City and County of Denver, Office of the Auditor, *Audit Report: Denver International Airport: Rental Car Agreements,* February 2017, https://www.denvergov.org/content/dam/denvergov/Portals/741/documents/Audits_2017/DenverInternationalAirportRentalCarAgreements_February2017.pdf.

13. Erik Engquist, "Hotel Tax Surchage to Expire—or Will It?" *Crain's New York Business,* October 11, 2013, http://www.crainsnewyork.com/article/20131011/hospitality_tourism/131019970/hotel-tax-surchage-to-expire-or-will-it.

14. Josh Margolin, "State $463M Face Lift on Javits Ctr. Corpse," *New York Post,* January 16, 2012, http://nypost.com/2012/01/16/state-463m-face-lift-on-javits-ctr-corpse/.

15. "State Lodging Taxes," National Conference of State Legislatures, July 21, 2017, http://www.ncsl.org/research/fiscal-policy/state-lodging-taxes.aspx.

16. Catharine Hamm, "Those Hotel Taxes and Fees Are Enough to Give You and Your Pocketbook Nightmares. Can You Do Anything about Them?" *Los Angeles Times,* January 23, 2017, http://www.latimes.com/travel/la-tr-spot-20170122-story.html.

17. United States Department of State, *The Budget in Brief: Fiscal Year 2010,* 2009, https://www.state.gov/documents/organization/122511.pdf.

18. David Martosko, "US State Department Spends $1 MILLION on a Single Granite Sculpture to Decorate New Embassy in London," *Daily Mail,* December 3, 2013, http://www.dailymail.co.uk/news/article-2517666/US-State-Department-spends-1-MILLION-single-granite-sculpture-decorate-new-embassy-London.html.

19. Jason Devaney, "RNC: Hillary's State Department Spent $5.4 Million on Stemware," *Newsmax,* October 27, 2016, https://www.newsmax.com/Politics/RNC-state-department-spending/2016/10/27/id/755702/.

20. "Tax and Fee Rates," U.S. Department of the Treasury, Alcohol and Tobacco Tax and Trade Bureau (TTB), last updated March 4, 2016, https://www.ttb.gov/tax_audit/atftaxes.shtml.

14. EDUCATION

1. "Tuition and Fees and Room and Board over Time, 1976–77 to 2016–17, Selected Years," CollegeBoard Trends in Higher Education, https://trends .collegeboard.org/college-pricing/figures-tables/tuition-and-fees-and -room-and-board-over-time-1976-77_2016-17-selected-years.

2. Patty Lamberti, "Millennials Just Aren't That into Starting Families; Is That Such a Bad Thing?" *Money Under 30,* January 23, 2015, https://www.money under30.com/millenials-waiting-to-start-a-family.

3. David Jesse, "Government Books $41.3 Billion in Student Loan Profits," *USA Today,* November 25, 2013, https://www.usatoday.com/story/news/nation /2013/11/25/federal-student-loan-profit/3696009/.

4. Brianna McGurran, "6 Must-Know Facts about Income-Based Repayment," *NerdWallet,* September 29, 2016, https://www.nerdwallet.com/blog/loans /student-loans/what-is-income-based-repayment/.

5. Lukas Mikelionis, "Bernie Sanders' Wife's Land Deal Still under FBI Probe; Witness Recently Questioned," *Fox News,* December 8, 2017, http://www .foxnews.com/politics/2017/12/08/bernie-sanders-wifes-land-deal-still -under-fbi-probe-witness-recently-questioned.html.

6. John Bat, "Bernie and Jane Sanders, under FBI Investigation for Bank Fraud, Hire Lawyers," *CBS News,* June 24, 2017, https://www.cbsnews.com/news /bernie-and-jane-sanders-under-fbi-investigation-for-bank-fraud-hire-law yers/.

7. Dave Huber, "Report: Women's and Gender Studies Degrees Have Increased 300% since 1990," *College Fix,* March 6, 2017, https://www.thecollegefix .com/post/31521/.

8. Jenna Robinson, "Why You Should Think Twice about Majoring in Women's Studies and Theatre Arts," James G. Martin Center for Academic Renewal, October 8, 2014, https://www.jamesgmartin.center/2014/10/why -you-should-think-twice-about-majoring-in-womens-studies-and-theatre -arts/.

9. University at Albany, "UAlbany Launches Fountain and Water Tower Renovation Plans," press release, December 8, 2011, http://www.albany.edu /news/19694.php.

10. "The Lower Sproul Redevelopment Project," University of California, Berkeley, http://lowersproul.berkeley.edu/.

11. Dean Dalvit, "Cost per Square Foot of Commercial Construction by Region," *EVstudio* (blog), August 6, 2009, http://evstudio.com/cost-per-square-foot -of-commercial-construction-by-region/.

12. Kellie Woodhouse, "Lazy Rivers and Student Debt," *Inside Higher Ed,* June 15, 2015, https://www.insidehighered.com/news/2015/06/15/are-lazy-rivers-and-climbing-walls-driving-cost-college.

13. Woodhouse, "Lazy Rivers and Student Debt."

14. Will Hobson and Steven Rich, "Colleges Spend Fortunes on Lavish Athletic Facilities," *Chicago Tribune,* December 23, 2015, http://www.chicagotribune.com/sports/college/ct-athletic-facilities-expenses-20151222-story.html.

15. Amy Scott, "Climbing Walls and College Costs," *Marketplace,* July 26, 2012, https://www.marketplace.org/2012/07/26/education/climbing-walls-and-college-costs.

16. David Harris, "$450 Million Renovation Will Make Kyle Field Largest College Stadium in Texas," *Bryan (TX) Eagle,* May 2, 2013, http://www.theeagle.com/news/local/million-renovation-will-make-kyle-field-largest-college-stadium-in/article_fd2c681e-a632-56f2-9861-4d8df398a2f0.html.

17. Michael Stratford, "Clery Fines: Proposed vs. Actual," *Inside Higher Ed,* July 17, 2014, https://www.insidehighered.com/news/2014/07/17/colleges-often-win-reduction-fines-federal-campus-safety-violations.

18. Katie Thomas, "Long Fights for Sports Equity, Even with a Law," *New York Times,* July 28, 2011, http://www.nytimes.com/2011/07/29/sports/review-shows-title-ix-is-not-significantly-enforced.html.

19. Lyndsey Layton, "Civil Rights Complaints to U.S. Department of Education Reach a Record High," *Washington Post,* March 18, 2015, https://www.washingtonpost.com/news/local/wp/2015/03/18/civil-rights-complaints-to-u-s-department-of-education-reach-a-record-high/.

20. Patrick deHahn, "Study: 89% of Colleges Reported Zero Campus Rapes in 2015," *USA Today College,* May 11, 2017, http://college.usatoday.com/2017/05/11/study-89-of-colleges-reported-zero-campus-rapes-in-2015/.

21. "Federal Coordination and Compliance Section," United States Department of Justice, updated August 6, 2015, https://www.justice.gov/crt/federal-coordination-and-compliance-section-152.

22. Anemona Hartocollis, "Professors' Group Says Efforts to Halt Sexual Harassment Have Stifled Speech," *New York Times,* March 24, 2016, https://www.nytimes.com/2016/03/24/us/professors-group-says-efforts-to-halt-sexual-harassment-have-stifled-speech.html.

23. Tyler Kingkade, "University of Maryland Passes Title IX Costs on to Students," *BuzzFeed News,* October 11, 2016, https://www.buzzfeed.com/tylerkingkade/university-of-maryland-title-ix-fee.

24. Adam Zielonka, "Four of the Bills UMD's SGA Passed This Semester While You Weren't Paying Attention," *The Diamondback,* November 27, 2016, http://www.dbknews.com/2016/11/28/university-of-maryland-sga-bills/.

25. Joseph P. Williams, "College of Tomorrow: The Changing Demographics of the Student Body," *U.S. News & World Report,* September 22, 2014, https://www.usnews.com/news/college-of-tomorrow/articles/2014/09/22/college-of-tomorrow-the-changing-demographics-of-the-student-body.

26. Anthony Gockowski, "EXCLUSIVE: Diversity Chiefs Drowning in Dough," *Campus Reform,* July 12, 2017, https://www.campusreform.org/?ID=9428.

27. San Diego Union-Tribune Editorial Board, "UC Tuition Hikes? First Justify Your Administrative Bloat," *San Diego Union-Tribune,* January 6, 2017, http://www.sandiegouniontribune.com/opinion/editorials/sd-uc-tuition-hikes-administrative-bloat-20170105-story.html.

28. Patrick McGreevy, "University of California Administration Is Paying Excessive Salaries and Mishandling Funds, State Audit Says," *Los Angeles Times,* April 25, 2017, http://www.latimes.com/politics/essential/la-pol-ca-essential-politics-updates-university-of-california-administration-1493137774-html story.html.

29. Jon Marcus, "New Analysis Shows Problematic Boom in Higher Ed Administrators," *HuffPost College,* February 6, 2014, http://www.huffingtonpost.com/2014/02/06/higher-ed-administrators-growth_n_4738584.html.

30. "Median Salaries of Senior College Administrators, 2015–16," *Chronicle of Higher Education,* March 14, 2016, http://www.chronicle.com/article/Median-Salaries-of-Senior/235668.

31. "Organization Urges Teachers, Students to Skip School & Protest Trump," *Fox News Insider,* January 19, 2017, http://insider.foxnews.com/2017/01/19/nea-urges-teachers-students-protest-trump-schools.

32. New York State United Teachers, "NYSUT Blasts Charter School Industry's Attempt to Bypass Teaching Standards," press release, July 5, 2017, https://www.nysut.org/news/2017/july/nysut-blasts-charter-school-industrys-attempt-to-bypass-teaching-standards.

33. James C. Wetherbe, "It's Time for Tenure to Lose Tenure," *Harvard Business Review,* March 13, 2013, https://hbr.org/2013/03/its-time-for-tenure-to-lose-te.

34. Wetherbe, "It's Time for Tenure to Lose Tenure."

35. Philip G. Altbach and Brendan Rapple, "Anarchy and Commercialism," *Inside Higher Ed,* March 8, 2012, https://www.insidehighered.com/views/2012/03/08/essay-problems-state-journal-publishing.

36. Chris Enloe, "Fake Academic Paper Published in Liberal Journal Hilariously Exposes the Absurdity of Gender Studies," *TheBlaze,* May 21, 2017, http://www.theblaze.com/news/2017/05/21/fake-academic-paper-published-in-liberal-journal-hilariously-exposes-the-absurdity-of-gender-studies/.

37. "Fast Facts from Our Fact Sheet," American Association of Community Colleges, http://www.aacc.nche.edu/AboutCC/Pages/fastfactsfactsheet.aspx.

15. MEDICAL

1. Adam Liptak, "Supreme Court Upholds Health Care Law, 5–4, in Victory for Obama," *New York Times,* June 28, 2012, http://www.nytimes.com/2012/06/29/us/supreme-court-lets-health-law-largely-stand.html.
2. Larry Levitt and Gary Claxton, "What Is a Mini-Med Plan?" Kaiser Family Foundation, July 5, 2011, http://www.kff.org/health-reform/perspective/what-is-a-mini-med-plan/.
3. Bram Sable-Smith, "Would You Like Some Insurance with Your Insurance?" *Shots,* NPR, September 13, 2016, http://www.npr.org/sections/health-shots/2016/09/13/493695824/would-you-like-some-insurance-with-your-insurance.
4. "Health Insurance: Premiums and Increases," National Conference of State Legislatures, September 20, 2017, http://www.ncsl.org/research/health/health-insurance-premiums.aspx.
5. "Average Annual Workplace Family Health Premiums Rise Modest 3% to $18,142 in 2016; More Workers Enroll in High-Deductible Plans with Savings Option Over Past Two Years," Kaiser Family Foundation, September 14, 2016, http://www.kff.org/health-costs/press-release/average-annual-workplace-family-health-premiums-rise-modest-3-to-18142-in-2016-more-workers-enroll-in-high-deductible-plans-with-savings-option-over-past-two-years/.
6. "Average Individual Health Insurance Premiums Increased 99% since 2013, the Year before Obamacare, & Family Premiums Increased 140%, According to eHealth.com Shopping Data," eHealth, January 23, 2017, http://news.ehealthinsurance.com/news/average-individual-health-insurance-premiums-increased-99-since-2013-the-year-before-obamacare-family-premiums-increased-140-according-to-ehealth-com-shopping-data.
7. Josh Levs, "What the Supreme Court Ruled on Health Care 'Tax,'" *CNNPolitics,* July 5, 2012, http://www.cnn.com/2012/07/05/politics/scotus-health-care-tax/index.html.
8. Reed Abelson and Margot Sanger-Katz, "Obamacare Options? In Many Parts of Country, Only One Insurer Will Remain," The Upshot, *New York Times,* August 19, 2016, https://www.nytimes.com/2016/08/20/upshot/obamacare-options-in-many-parts-of-country-only-one-insurer-will-remain.html.
9. Haeyoun Park and Audrey Carlsen, "For the First Time, 45 Counties Could Have No Insurer in the Obamacare Marketplaces," *New York Times,* June 9,

2017, https://www.nytimes.com/interactive/2017/06/09/us/counties-wi
th-one-or-no-obamacare-insurer.html.

10. Alex Smith, "Health Care Uncertainty Leaves Many Missouri Counties
without ACA Marketplace Coverage," *Kansas City KCUR 89.3,* June 29, 2017,
http://kcur.org/post/health-care-uncertainty-leaves-many-missouri-coun
ties-without-aca-marketplace-coverage#stream/0.

11. Chris Jacobs, *How Obamacare Undermines American Values: Penalizing Work,
Marriage, Citizenship, and the Disabled,* Heritage Foundation, November 21,
2013, http://www.heritage.org/health-care-reform/report/how-obamaca
re-undermines-american-values-penalizing-work-marriage.

12. "2015 Employer Health Benefits Survey," Kaiser Family Foundation, September 22, 2015, http://www.kff.org/report-section/ehbs-2015-section-one
-cost-of-health-insurance/.

13. Don Lee, "Why American Workers Aren't Changing Jobs, and What It
Means for the Economy," *Los Angeles Times,* April 1, 2016, http://www.la
times.com/business/la-fi-job-mobility-declines-20160401-story.html.

14. Brian Blase, "New Gruber Study Raises Major Questions about Obamacare's
Medicaid Expansion," *Forbes,* November 27, 2016, https://www.forbes
.com/sites/theapothecary/2016/11/27/new-gruber-study-raises-major
-questions-about-obamacares-medicaid-expansion/.

15. Kevin Dayaratna, *Studies Show: Medicaid Patients Have Worse Access and Outcomes
than the Privately Insured,* Heritage Foundation, November 7, 2012, http://
www.heritage.org/health-care-reform/report/studies-show-medicaid-pa
tients-have-worse-access-and-outcomes-the.

16. Stephen Zuckerman, Laura Skopec, and Kristen McCormack, *Reversing the
Medicaid Fee Bump: How Much Could Medicaid Physician Fees for Primary Care Fall
in 2015?* Urban Institute, December 10, 2014, https://www.urban.org/re
search/publication/reversing-medicaid-fee-bump-how-much-could-medic
aid-physician-fees-primary-care-fall-2015.

17. "U.S. Health Plans Have History of Cost Overruns," *Washington Times,* November 18, 2009, http://www.washingtontimes.com/news/2009/nov/18
/health-programs-have-history-of-cost-overruns/.

18. "HHS FY 2017 Budget in Brief—CMS—Medicaid," U.S. Department of
Health & Human Services, last reviewed January 26, 2017, https://www
.hhs.gov/about/budget/fy2017/budget-in-brief/cms/medicaid/index
.html.

19. "HHS FY 2018 Budget in Brief—CMS—Medicaid," U.S. Department of
Health & Human Services, last reviewed May 23, 2017, https://www.hhs
.gov/about/budget/fy2018/budget-in-brief/cms/medicaid/index.html.

20. "Drug Price Competition and Patent Term Restoration Act," *Wikipedia,* last edited August 2, 2017, https://en.wikipedia.org/wiki/Drug_Price_Com petition_and_Patent_Term_Restoration_Act.

21. Garth Boehm, Lixin Yao, Liang Han, and Qiang Zheng, "Development of the Generic Drug Industry in the US after the Hatch-Waxman Act of 1984," *Acta Pharmaceutica Sinica B* 3, no. 5 (September 2013): 297–311, http://www .sciencedirect.com/science/article/pii/S2211383513000762.

22. Charles Seife, "Are Your Medications Safe?" *Slate,* February 9, 2015, http:// www.slate.com/articles/health_and_science/science/2015/02/fda_insp ections_fraud_fabrication_and_scientific_misconduct_are_hidden_from .html.

23. Dennis Thompson, "Fewer Medical Malpractice Lawsuits Succeed, but Pay- outs Are Up," *CBS News,* March 28, 2017, https://www.cbsnews.com/news /medical-malpractice-lawsuits-fewer-claims-succeed-payouts-rise/.

24. Thompson, "Fewer Medical Malpractice Lawsuits."

25. John Kartch, "Full List of Obamacare Tax Hikes: Listed by Size of Tax Hike," Americans for Tax Reform, June 29, 2012, https://www.atr.org/conserva tive-groups-urge-passage-budget-resolution-2017.

26. Stephanie Scurlock, "St. Jude Says It Is Safe from Obamacare Fines," *Memphis News Channel 3 TV WREG,* October 18, 2013, http://wreg.com/2013/10/18 /st-jude-says-safe-from-obamacare-fines/.

27. Paul Alexander, "How to Fund Obamacare? Gimmicks Like a Tanning Tax Are Not the Answer," *HuffPost Blog,* July 10, 2015, http://www.huffington post.com/paul-alexander/how-to-fund-obamacare-gim_b_7767568.html.

28. Associated Press, "Tanning Industry Blames 10,000 Salon Closings on Tax in Affordable Care Act," *Denver Post,* August 20, 2016, http://www.denver post.com/2016/08/20/tanning-industry-blames-10000-salon-closings-on -obamacare/.

29. Treasury Inspector General for Tax Administration, *Affordable Care Act: The Number of Taxpayers Filing Tanning Excise Tax Returns Is Lower Than Expected,* September 22, 2011, https://www.treasury.gov/tigta/auditreports/2011re ports/201140115fr.html.

16. DEATH

1. Eddie Metrejean and Cheryl Metrejean, "Death Taxes in the United States: A Brief History," *Journal of Business & Economics Research* 7, no. 1 (January 2009): 33–40, https://www.researchgate.net/publication/242604629_Death_Tax es_In_The_United_States_A_Brief_History.

2. Gary Robbins, *Estate Taxes: An Historical Perspective,* Heritage Foundation, January 16, 2004, http://www.heritage.org/taxes/report/estate-taxes-his torical-perspective.

3. Ashlea Ebeling, "Final Tax Bill Includes Huge Estate Tax Win for the Rich: The $22.4 Million Exemption," *Forbes,* December 21, 2017, https://www. forbes.com/sites/ashleaebeling/2017/12/21/final-tax-bill-includes-huge-estate-tax-win-for-the-rich-the-22-4-million-exemption/#47885e661d54.

4. Alan Cole, "The Estate Tax Is a Poor Source for Federal Revenue," *Tax Foundation* (blog), September 10, 2014, https://taxfoundation.org/estate-tax -poor-source-federal-revenue/.

5. Darla Mercado, "Thanks, Congress. Wealthy Investors Hold off on Estate Tax Planning," *CNBC,* July 11, 2017, https://www.cnbc.com/2017/07/11 /thanks-congress-wealthy-investors-hold-off-on-estate-tax-planning.html.

17. NOT A SINGLE PENNY

1. Zachariah Hughes, "PDF Amount Announced: $1,100," *Alaska Public Media,* September 15, 2017, https://www.alaskapublic.org/2017/09/15/pfd -amount-announced-1100/.

18. PURSUING ALTERNATIVES

1. James Salzer, "Ga. Diverts Taxpayer Fees to General Fund," *Politically Georgia,* October 31, 2015, http://www.myajc.com/news/state—regional-govt—politics/diverts-taxpayer-fees-general-fund/pF9s2wPbcqZYQKBfZQW I1O/.

2. Michael J. Riley, "Stop Diverting Highway Funds," *Hartford Courant,* March 14, 2014, http://www.courant.com/opinion/op-ed/hc-op-riley-connecti cut-highway-funds-must-be-dedi-20140314-story.html.

3. Matt Weiser and Kevin Yamamura, "Hidden California State Parks Funds Spark Outrage," *The Sacramento Bee,* October 8, 2014, http://www.sacbee .com/news/investigations/state-parks-funding/article2575188.html.

4. Howard Fischer Capitol Media Services, "Balanced Arizona Budget Relies on Diverting School Funds," *Tuscon.com,* March 16, 2015, http://tucson.com /news/local/education/balanced-arizona-budget-relies-on-diverting-school -funds/article_c951e7b5-0fbf-5beb-97c0-b6498e3fc646.html.

5. Mark Magyar, "Raids on Dedicated Funds Climb under Christie," *NJ Spotlight,* July 8, 2013, http://www.njspotlight.com/stories/13/07/08/raids -on-dedicated-funds-climb-under-christie/.

6. James Sherk, *Inflated Federal Pay: How Americans Are Overtaxed to Pay the Civil Service,* Heritage Foundation, July 7, 2010, http://www.heritage.org/jobs-and-labor/report/inflated-federal-pay-how-americans-are-overtaxed-over pay-the-civil-service.

7. James Sherk, *Comparing Pay in the Federal Government and the Private Sector,* Heritage Foundation, July 16, 2010, http://www.heritage.org/jobs-and-labor/report/comparing-pay-the-federal-government-and-the-private-sector.

8. Olivera Perkins, "Public Sector Workers Make More in Salary and Benefits Than Those in the Private Sector, Labor Department Says," *Cleavland .com,* September 12, 2013, http://www.cleveland.com/business/index.ssf /2013/09/public_sector_workers_make_mor.html.

9. Matt Pearce, "How One of the Biggest Swindlers in American History Built a Horse-Breeding Empire," *The Los Angeles Times,* November 1, 2015, http:// www.latimes.com/nation/la-na-horse-swindler-crundwell-20151030-story .html.